D1470687

# V FOR VENDETTA

# ALAN MOORE
# DAVID LLOYD

# V FOR

## COLLECTED BOOKS

**KC Carlson**
Editor, collected edition

**KAREN BERGER**
Editor, original series

**DALE CRAIN**
Publication design

**DAVID LLOYD**
Cover painting

**DAVID LLOYD**
**STEVE WHITAKER**
**SIOBHAN DODDS**
Interior coloring

**JENNY O'CONNOR**
**STEVE CRADDOCK**
**ELITTA FELL**
Lettering

**TONY WEARE**
Art for "Vincent."
Additional art for
"Valerie" and "The Vacation."

## DC COMICS

**KAREN BERGER**
VP-Executive Editor, VERTIGO

**ROBBIN BROSTERMAN**
Senior Art Director

**PAUL LEVITZ**
President & Publisher

**GEORG BREWER**
VP-Design & DC Direct Creative

**RICHARD BRUNING**
Senior VP-Creative Director

**PATRICK CALDON**
Senior VP-Finance & Operations

**CHRIS CARAMALIS**
VP-Finance

**TERRI CUNNINGHAM**
VP-Managing Editor

**STEPHANIE FIERMAN**
Senior VP-Sales & Marketing

**ALISON GILL**
VP-Manufacturing

**RICH JOHNSON**
VP-Book Trade Sales

**HANK KANALZ**
VP-General Manager, WildStorm

**LILLIAN LASERSON**
Senior VP & General Counsel

**PAULA LOWITT**
Senior VP-Business & Legal Affairs

**JIM LEE**
Editorial Director-WildStorm

**DAVID McKILLIPS**
VP-Advertising & Custom Publishing

**JOHN NEE**
VP-Business Development

**GREGORY NOVECK**
Senior VP-Creative Affairs

**CHERYL RUBIN**
Senior VP-Brand Management

**JEFF TROJAN**
VP-Business Development, DC Direct

**BOB WAYNE**
VP-Sales

## V FOR VENDETTA

COPYRIGHT © 1988, 1989 DC COMICS
COVER AND COMPILATION COPYRIGHT © 1990 DC COMICS. ALL RIGHTS RESERVED.
INTRODUCTIONS COPYRIGHT © 1988, 1990 DC COMICS. ALL RIGHT RESERVED.
BOOKS 1 AND 2, "VERTIGO" AND "VINCENT" FIRST PUBLISHED 1982-83 IN THE UNITED KINGDOM
BY QUALITY COMMUNICATIONS LIMITED.
ORIGINALLY PUBLISHED IN MAGAZINE FORM IN THE UNITED STATES AS V FOR VENDETTA #1-10.

THE STORIES, CHARACTERS AND INCIDENTS FEATURED IN THIS PUBLICATION ARE ENTIRELY FICTIONAL.
VERTIGO, ALL CHARACTERS FEATURED IN THIS PUBLICATION, THE DISTINCTIVE LIKENESSES THEREOF,
AND ALL RELATED ELEMENTS ARE TRADEMARKS OF DC COMICS. DC COMICS DOES NOT READ OR
ACCEPT UNSOLICITED SUBMISSIONS OF IDEAS, STORIES OR ARTWORK.

DC COMICS
1700 BROADWAY
NEW YORK, NY 10019

A WARNER BROS. ENTERTAINMENT COMPANY
PRINTED IN CANADA. NINTH PRINTING.
ISBN: 0-930289-52-8

**A** few nights ago, I walked into a pub on my way home and ordered a Guinness.

I didn't look at my watch, but I knew it was before 8 o'clock. It was Tuesday and I could hear the television in the background still running the latest episode of "EastEnders"—a soap about the day-to-day life of cheeky, cheery working-class people in a decaying, mythical part of London.

I sat in a booth and picked up a copy of a free newspaper someone had left on the seat beside me. I'd read it before. There wasn't much news in it. I put down the paper and decided to sit at the bar.

It wasn't a busy night. I could hear the murmuring of the distant TV above the chatter of the people at the bar and the clack-clack of colliding snooker balls.

After "EastEnders" came "Porridge"—a re-run of a situation comedy series about a cheeky, cheery prisoner in a comfortably unoppressive, decaying, Victorian prison.

Almost imperceptibly, spirits leaked from the optics of upturned bottles behind the bar. Droplets of whisky and vodka formed and fell soundlessly as I watched.

I finished my drink. I looked up and the barman caught my eye. "Guinness?" he asked, already reaching for a fresh glass. I nodded.

The barman's wife arrived and began to help with the trickle of customers' orders.

At 8:30, following "Porridge," came "A Question Of Sport"—a simple panel quiz game featuring cheeky, cheery sports celebrities answering questions about other sports celebrities, many of whom were as cheeky and cheery as themselves.

Jocularity reigned.

"I'll tell the barman about the leaking optics," I thought.

"The Nine o'Clock News" followed "A Question Of Sport." Or, at least for 30 seconds it did, before the television was switched off and cheeky, cheery pop music took its place.

I looked over at the barman. "Just half this time," I said.

As he filled the glass, I solemnly asked him why he'd switched off the News. "Don't ask me—that was the wife," he replied, in a cheeky, cheery manner, as the subject of his playful targeting bustled in a corner of the bar.

The leaking optics had ceased to have any importance for me.

I finished my drink and left, almost certain the TV would be silent for the rest of the evening. For after "The Nine o'Clock News" would have come "The Boys From Brazil," a film with few cheeky, cheery characters in it, which is all about a bunch of Nazis creating 94 clones of Adolf Hitler.

There aren't many cheeky, cheery characters in V FOR VENDETTA either; and it's for people who don't switch off the News.

**David Lloyd**
14 January 90

**I** began V FOR VENDETTA in the summer of 1981, during a working holiday upon the Isle of Wight. My youngest daughter, Amber, was a few months old. I finished it in the late winter of 1988, after a gap in publishing of nearly five years from the discontinuation of England's *Warrior* magazine, its initial home. Amber is now seven. I don't know why I mentioned that. It's just one of those unremarkable facts that strike you suddenly, with unexpected force, so that you have to go and sit down.

Along with Marvelman (now Miracleman), V FOR VENDETTA represents my first attempt at a continuing series, begun at the outset of my career. For this reason, amongst others, there are things that ring oddly in earlier episodes when judged in the light of the strip's later development. I trust you'll bear with us during any initial clumsiness, and share our opinion that it was for the best to show the early episodes unrevised, warts and all, rather than go back and eradicate all trace of youthful creative inexperience.

There is also a certain amount of political inexperience upon my part evident in these early episodes. Back in 1981 the term "nuclear winter" had not passed into common currency, and although my guess about climatic upheaval came pretty close to the eventual truth of the situation, the fact remains that the story to hand suggests that a nuclear war, even a limited one, might be survivable. To the best of my current knowledge, this is not the case.

Naiveté can also be detected in my supposition that it would take something as melodramatic as a near-miss nuclear conflict to nudge England towards fascism. Although in fairness to myself and David, there were no better or more accurate predictions of our country's future available in comic form at that time. The simple fact that much of the historical background of the story proceeds from a predicted Conservative defeat in the 1982 General Election should tell you how reliable we were in our role as Cassandras.

It's 1988 now. Margaret Thatcher is entering her third term of office and talking confidently of an unbroken Conservative leadership well into the next century. My youngest daughter is seven and the tabloid press are circulating the idea of concentration camps for persons with AIDS. The new riot police wear black visors, as do their horses, and their vans have rotating video cameras mounted on top. The government has expressed a desire to eradicate homosexuality, even as an abstract concept, and one can only speculate as to which minority will be the next legislated against. I'm thinking of taking my family and getting out of this country soon, sometime over the next couple of years. It's cold and it's mean spirited and I don't like it here anymore.

Goodnight England. Goodnight Home Service and V for Victory.

Hello the Voice of Fate and V FOR VENDETTA.

**Alan Moore**
Northampton, March 1988

This was Alan Moore's introduction from the original DC Comics run of V FOR VENDETTA and is reprinted from the first DC issue.

BOOK **1**

EUROPE AFTER THE REIGN

# V FOR VENDETTA

GOOD EVENING, LONDON. IT'S NINE O'CLOCK AND THIS IS *THE VOICE OF FATE* BROADCASTING ON *275* AND *285* IN THE MEDIUM WAVE... IT IS THE FIFTH OF THE ELEVENTH, NINETEEN-NINETY-SEVEN...

THE WEATHER WILL BE FINE UNTIL *12:07 A.M.* WHEN A *SHOWER* WILL COMMENCE, LASTING UNTIL 1:30 A.M...

THE TEMPERATURE WILL VARY BETWEEN 13 AND 14 DEGREES CENTIGRADE THROUGHOUT THE NIGHT.

FOR YOUR PROTECTION

THE PEOPLE OF LONDON ARE ADVISED THAT THE BRIXTON AND STREATHAM AREAS ARE *QUARANTINE ZONES* AS OF TODAY. IT IS SUGGESTED THAT THESE AREAS BE AVOIDED FOR REASONS OF HEALTH AND SAFETY.

PRODUCTIVITY REPORTS FROM HEREFORDSHIRE INDICATE A POSSIBLE END TO *MEAT RATIONING* STARTING FROM MID-FEBRUARY, 1998...

THIS GOOD NEWS FOLLOWS SIMILAR ANNOUNCEMENTS CONCERNING THE IN-CREASED PRODUC-TION OF BOTH *EGGS* AND *POTATOES,*

POLICE RAIDED SEVENTEEN HOMES IN THE BIRMINGHAM AREA EARLY THIS MORNING, UNCOVERING WHAT IS BELIEVED TO BE A MAJOR *TERRORIST RING.*

TWENTY PEOPLE, EIGHT OF THEM WOMEN, ARE CURRENTLY IN DETENTION AWAITING TRIAL.

QUEEN ZARA TODAY APPEAR-ED AT THE OPENING OF A NEW WASTE-RECLAMA-TION PLANT IN PLAISTOW. THIS WAS THE QUEEN'S FIRST PUBLIC APPEARANCE SINCE HER SIXTEENTH BIRTH-DAY IN JUNE.

THE QUEEN WAS WEARING A SUIT OF PEACH SILK CREATED SPECIALLY FOR THE OCCASION BY THE ROYAL COUTURIER.

IN A SPEECH TODAY MR. ADRIAN KAREL, PARTY MINISTER FOR INDUSTRY, STATED THAT BRITAIN'S INDUSTRIAL PROSPECTS ARE BRIGHTER THAN AT ANY TIME SINCE THE LAST WAR.

MR. KAREL WENT ON TO SAY THAT IT IS THE DUTY OF EVERY MAN IN THIS COUNTRY TO SEIZE THE INITIATIVE AND MAKE BRITAIN GREAT AGAIN.

...AND THAT IS THE FACE OF LONDON TONIGHT. WE REMIND YOU THAT TOMORROW IS THE FINAL DATE FOR THE COM-PLETION OF YOUR CENSUS FORMS...

...AND THE TARGET DATE FOR THE CONCLUSION OF THE DEPTFORD MARSH-CLEARANCE PROJECT. THIS IS THE VOICE OF FATE SIGNING OFF.

HAVE A PLEASANT EVENING.

Jimmy his New Hit from

WARNER BROS

Chapter One

# THE VILLAIN

PARLIAMENT'S COLD SHADOW FALLS ON WEST-MINSTER BRIDGE, AND SHE SHIVERS. THERE WAS POWER HERE ONCE, POWER THAT DECIDED THE DESTINY OF MILLIONS.

HER TRANSACTIONS, HER DECISIONS, ARE INSIGNIFICANT. THEY AFFECT NO ONE...

MISTER?

...EXCEPT HER.

...UH... WOULD... WOULD YOU LIKE TO... UH... SLEEP WITH ME OR ANYTHING?

...I MEAN ...UH...FOR MONEY?

THAT'S THE CLUMSIEST PIECE OF PROPOSITIONING I'VE EVER HEARD. YOU'VE NOT BEEN DOING THIS VERY LONG, HAVE YOU?

OH GOD. I MUST BE REALLY TERRIBLE.

YEAH, YOU'RE RIGHT. IT'S MY FIRST NIGHT. YOU'RE MY FIRST...

... CUSTOMER?

CUSTOMER. YEAH.

I...I'VE GOT A JOB IN MUNITIONS, BUT THE MONEY IS, YOU KNOW, IT ISN'T ENOUGH...LOOK MISTER, I REALLY NEED THAT MONEY. I'D BE OK I MEAN, I'M SIXTEEN. I KNOW WHAT I'M DOING...

NO. YOU DON'T KNOW WHAT YOU'RE DOING.

...BECAUSE IF YOU DID YOU WOULDN'T HAVE PICKED A VICE DETAIL ON STAKE-OUT.

OH CHRIST. YOU'RE A FINGERMAN.

THAT'S RIGHT. AND THESE ARE MY COLLEAGUES.

YOU KNOW THE LAWS ON PROSTITUTION. THAT'S A CLASS-H OFFENCE. THAT MEANS WE GET TO DECIDE WHAT HAPPENS TO YOU. THAT'S OUR PREROGATIVE.

PLEASE DON'T KILL ME.

OH NO. LOOK, PLEASE, MISTER, IT WAS MY FIRST TIME. I'LL DO ANY-THING YOU WANT.

STRENGTH THROUGH PURITY PURITY THROUGH FAITH

YOU'VE GOT IT WRONG, MISS. YOU'LL DO ANYTHING WE WANT AND THEN WE'LL KILL YOU.

THAT'S OUR PREROGATIVE.

OH PLEASE DON'T OH JESUS NO PLEASE.

"THE MULTIPLYING VILLAINIES OF NATURE DO SWARM UPON HIM..."

WHO THE HELL ..

"AND FORTUNE, ON HIS DAMNED QUARREL, SMILING, SHOWED LIKE A REBEL'S WHORE."

WHO'S HE?

I DUNNO. MUST BE SOME KINDA *RETARD* GOT OUT OF A *HOSPITAL...* HEY *YOU!*

"BUT ALL'S TOO WEAK; FOR BRAVE MACBETH... WELL HE DESERVES THAT NAME..."

WHAT ARE YOU DOING?

YOU'RE IN *TROUBLE,* CHUM. *BIG* TROUBLE. THIS WOMAN IS A *CRIMINAL.* WE'RE *POLICE OFFICERS.*

SHE'S WANTED FOR *INTERROGATION,* SO KEEP YOUR...

...HANDS OFF?

"DISDAINING FORTUNE, WITH HIS BRANDISHED STEEL,

"WHICH SMOKED WITH BLOODY EXECUTION.

"LIKE VALOUR'S MINION, CARVED OUT HIS PASSAGE...

"...TILL HE FACED THE SLAVE;

OH.

"WHICH NE'ER SHOOK HANDS,

"NOR BADE FAREWELL TO HIM,"

TEAR GAS! +COUGH+ HOLY CHRIST, IT'S *TEAR GAS!*

I GOT HIS *HAND*, WHAT SHALL I DO WITH HIS—

OH JESUS...

WHAT THE HELL *HAPPENED??* HE JUST CAME OUT OF *NOWHERE* AND... JUST WHAT THE HELL *HAPPENED??*

FRANK'S DEAD. THEY'RE *ALL* DEAD. OH CHRIST, WHAT ARE WE GOING TO *DO??*

FIND HIM. WE'VE GOT TO FIND HIM OR THE *HEAD* WILL HAVE OUR GUTS...

HOW DID HE *DO* IT? I NEVER SEEN ANYBODY MOVE SO FAST. HE KILLED *FRANK*...

THAT BASTARD. WE'VE GOT TO *FIND* HIM...

YOU... YOU *RESCUED* ME! LIKE IN A *STORY!!* I DON'T BELIEVE IT.

WH-WHO ARE YOU?

ME? I'M THE KING OF THE TWENTIETH CENTURY. I'M THE BOGEYMAN. THE VILLAIN.

...THE BLACK SHEEP OF THE FAMILY.

UH... YEAH. BUT WHAT WERE YOU *DOING* AROUND HERE? I DIDN'T THINK *ANYBODY* CAME TO *WESTMINSTER* AT NIGHT EXCEPT. YOU KNOW...

...WOMEN.

AHH, BUT TONIGHT IS *SPECIAL*. TONIGHT IS A *CELEBRATION.* A *GRAND OPENING.* WERE YOU NEVER TAUGHT *THE RHYME?*

"REMEMBER, REMEMBER THE FIFTH OF NOVEMBER, THE GUNPOWDER TREASON AND PLOT. I KNOW OF NO REASON WHY THE GUNPOWDER TREASON...

...SHOULD EVER BE FORGOT."

OH. OH. THE HOUSES OF PARLIAMENT! THEY'VE... THEY'VE BEEN... DID YOU DO THAT?

I DID THAT.

BUT THAT... THAT'S AGAINST THE LAW! THEY'LL KILL YOU... THEY'LL...

DID YOU REALLY DO THAT?

I REALLY DID THAT. NOW HUSH. THERE'S MORE...

THE RUMBLE OF THE EXPLOSION HAS NOT YET DIED AWAY AS FROM FAR BELOW COMES THE RATTLE OF SMALLER REPORTS...

AND SUDDENLY THE SKY IS ALIGHT WITH...

FIREWORKS! REAL FIREWORKS!

OH GOD, THEY'RE SO BEAUTIFUL!

...AND ALL OVER LONDON WINDOWS ARE THROWN OPEN AND FACES LIT WITH AWE AND WONDER GAZE AT THE OMEN SCRAWLED IN FIRE ON THE NIGHT.

THERE. THE OVERTURE IS FINISHED.

COME. WE MUST PREPARE FOR THE FIRST ACT...

ME?? B-BUT...

...OH OKAY.

IT IS PRECISELY 12.07 A.M. IT BEGINS TO RAIN...

NOVEMBER THE SIXTH, 1997. IT IS SIX-THIRTY IN THE MORNING...

I WILL HEAR YOUR REPORTS NOW, GENTLEMEN.

MR. HEYER WILL SPEAK FOR THE EYE.

WE HAVE JUST UNDER THREE MINUTES OF USEABLE FOOTAGE, LEADER. THE LARGE MAJORITY OF OUR VI-RECORDERS WERE DAMAGED IN THE EXPLOSION.

TO MY LEFT IS AN ENLARGEMENT OF THE SUSPECT'S FACE. I'M AFRAID THE MASK MAKES RET-INAL IDENTIFICA-TION IM-POSSIBLE.

CLOSE-UP IF YOU PLEASE, MR. HEYER...

AH.

THANK YOU MR. HEYER. MR. ETHERIDGE WILL NOW SPEAK FOR THE EARS.

UH... PHONE SURVEILLANCE INDICATES THAT A LARGE PROPORTION OF THE, UH, PEOPLE ARE TALKING ABOUT THE, UH, EXPLOSION, THAT'S INSIDE LONDON.

ALL SUSPECT OR SIGNIFICANT TRANSCRIPTS ARE BEING FORWARDED TO MR., UH, ALMOND AT THE FINGER.

MR. ALMOND IS WITH ME AT PRESENT. I SHALL IN-FORM HIM. MR. FINCH WILL SPEAK FOR THE NOSE...

WE'VE FOUND THE DEVICE PRO-BABLY USED TO LAUNCH THE FIREWORKS AND SOME SPENT CASINGS. INDIVIDUALLY WEIGHTED FLARES AT A GUESS.

DESPITE ITS SOPHISTI-CATION I SHOULD SAY THAT THE DEVICE WAS ALMOST CER-TAINLY HOME-MADE, AND THUS UNTRACEABLE. SORRY, LEADER. NOTHING ELSE YET.

THANK YOU, MR. FINCH. THE THREE OF YOU WILL INFORM ME OF ANY FURTHER DEVELOP-MENTS AND AWAIT MY DIRECTIVE. ENGLAND PREVAILS, GENTLEMEN.

WELL, WE HAVE HEARD FROM THE REST OF THE HEAD, THAT LEAVES YOU, MR. ALMOND. THREE FINGERMEN WERE KILLED LAST NIGHT BY ONE SOLITARY LUNATIC.

IT IS ALSO HIGHLY PROBABLE THAT THIS SAME PERSON HAD EARLIER PLANTED AN EX-PLOSIVE DEVICE OF STARTLING CAPABILITY WITHIN THE HOUSES OF PAR-LIAMENT.

LEADER, I...

YOUR *INCOMPETENCE* HAS COST US OUR OLDEST SYMBOL OF AUTHORITY AND A JARRING *PROPAGANDA* DEFEAT. DO YOU UNDERSTAND WHAT *HAPPENED* LAST NIGHT?

YOU WILL BE *SILENT,* MR. ALMOND!

SOME-ONE DID THE UN-THINKABLE. SOME-ONE *HURT* US.

...AND YOU ALLOWED THEM TO DO IT. I WANT THIS CREATURE AND HIS ASSOCIATES *FOUND,* MR. ALMOND. I WANT HIS *HEAD.*

...OR BY GOD I'LL HAVE YOURS INSTEAD.

YOU WILL CONSULT MR. DASCOMBE AT JORDAN TOWER BEFORE MAKING ANY OFFICIAL PRO-NOUNCEMENTS.

THAT WILL BE ALL, MR. ALMOND. ENGLAND PREVAILS.

ENGLAND PREVAILS, LEADER.

*JORDAN TOWER, SEVEN O'CLOCK:*

PUT YOUR TRUST IN FATE

OF *COURSE* YOU DID, LEWIS! WE ALL GOT UP EARLY THIS MORNING, DIDN'T WE? NOW IF WE CAN *JUST* RUN THROUGH IT *ONCE MORE* BEFORE WE PUT IT IN THE CAN, THEN...

AH. EXCUSE ME FOR A MOMENT, LEWIS...

*DEREK!!* WE DON'T SEE YOU DOWN HERE IN THE *MOUTH* VERY OFTEN...

O-OH! *"DOWN IN THE MOUTH"!* I COULD HAVE MADE A JOKE OUT OF THAT, COULDN'T I?

YOU *HAVE* DONE, DASCOMBE. SEVERAL TIMES. WHAT'S *FATE* PUTTING OUT ON THE *PARLIAMENT BOMB-ING?*

WE-E-LL, *FATE* WANTS US TO SAY IT WAS A *SCHEDULED DEMO-LITION* UNDERTAKEN AT NIGHT TO AVOID *TRAFFIC CON-GESTION.*

IT'S GOING OUT ON THE *EIGHT O'CLOCK* BROADCAST... I WAS JUST RUNNING THROUGH IT WITH *LEWIS* WHEN YOU CAME IN.

*LEWIS?*

*LEWIS PROTHERO.* HE DOES THE *VOICE.* THE VOICE OF FATE.

GOOD MORNING, LONDON. THIS IS *THE VOICE OF FATE* BROADCASTING ON 275 AND 285 METRES IN THE MEDIUM WAVE...

HMM. WHAT ARE YOU SAYING ABOUT THE *FIREWORKS?*

*FATE* DOESN'T THINK WE SHOULD MENTION THE FIREWORKS. IF ANYONE ASKS LATER WE'LL SAY IT WAS A FREAK EFFECT OF THE BLAST.

## Chapter Two
## THE VOICE

LISTEN TO LEWIS...ISN'T HE *MARVELLOUS?* IF FATE *REALLY* HAD A VOICE IT WOULD SOUND *JUST* LIKE THAT. IF ONLY PEOPLE *KNEW* WHAT A GOOD JOB HE'S DOING...

DON'T BE *STUPID*, DASCOMBE. THE WHOLE *IDEA* IS THAT PEOPLE THINK IT'S *FATE* TALKING. IT MAKES FATE APPEAR MORE HUMAN. GIVES PEOPLE CONFIDENCE.

*HMMM....*

HE COLLECTS *DOLLS*, YOU KNOW. WOULDN'T *THINK* IT, WOULD YOU? BIG MAN LIKE THAT, COLLECTING DOLLS. HE'S *SENSITIVE*, YOU SEE. YOU CAN TELL BY HIS *VOICE.*

YES, A *LOT OF YOU MEDIA* PEOPLE ARE "*SENSITIVE*," AREN'T YOU? I DON'T KNOW WHY THE *LEADER TOLERATES* YOU.

*MY DEAR DEREK...* THE LEADER IS THE *MOST SENSITIVE* OF US ALL.

...IN FACT, WHEN YOU'D FINISHED EXPLAINING HOW A LONE LUNATIC COULD KILL *THREE* FINGERMEN AND BLOW UP *PARLIAMENT*, I SHOULD IMAGINE HE WAS *VERY* SENSITIVE.

YOU'RE A *DEGENERATE*, DASCOMBE.

YOU'RE BITTER, ALMOND.

"*BITTER ALMOND*"! OH *DEAR* ME! HA HA HA HA HA HA!

PLEASE YOUR-SELF.

ALRIGHT, LEWIS... FROM THE TOP.

"BITTER ALMOND"! OH DEAR ME! HA HA HA HA HA!

THE SHADOW GALLERY.

LOOK, I DON'T WANT TO SOUND UNGRATEFUL, I MEAN, AFTER YOU RESCUED ME? BUT I DON'T UNDERSTAND ANY OF THIS. WHO YOU ARE, OR WHAT YOU WANT OR ANYTHING.

I MEAN, I KNOW YOU MUST HAVE HAD A REASON FOR BLINDFOLDING ME WHEN YOU BROUGHT ME HERE, BUT COULDN'T YOU JUST TELL ME WHERE WE ARE? ARE WE STILL IN LONDON?

WE ARE IN THE SHADOW GALLERY. THIS IS MY HOME.

DO YOU LIKE IT? I BUILT IT MY-SELF, YOU KNOW.

IT...IT'S UN-BELIEVABLE! ALL OF THESE PAINTINGS AND BOOKS... I DIDN'T EVEN KNOW THERE WERE THINGS LIKE THIS.

YOU COULDN'T BE EXPECTED TO KNOW. THEY HAVE ERADICATED CULTURE... TOSSED IT AWAY LIKE A FISTFUL OF DEAD ROSES...

ALL THE BOOKS, ALL THE FILMS... ALL THE MUSIC...

THE MUSIC IS BEAUTIFUL! YOU MUST THINK I'M REALLY STUPID... ALL I'VE EVER HEARD IS THE MILITARY STUFF THEY PLAY ON THE RADIO.

BUT ALL THIS STUFF ON YOUR DUKE-BOX SOUNDS SO... I DUNNO... ALIVE! WHAT'S THIS PLAYING NOW? THE WOMAN'S VOICE DOESN'T EVEN SOUND ENGLISH.

IT'S NOT. AND THE WORD IS "JUKE-BOX" WITH A "J"!

THE SONG IS CALLED "DANCING IN THE STREETS." IT'S BEING SUNG BY MARTHA AND THE VANDELLAS, PERHAPS THE TERM "TAMLA MOTOWN" IS FAMILIAR TO YOU?

OBVIOUSLY NOT. HARDLY SURPRISING, I SUPPOSE. AFTER ALL...

...THEY ERADICATED *SOME* CULTURES MORE *THOROUGHLY* THAN THEY DID OTHERS.

*NO TAMLA* AND NO *TROJAN.* NO *BILLIE HOLIDAY* OR *BLACK UHURU*...

JUST *HIS MASTER'S VOICE.* EVERY HOUR. ON THE HOUR.

WE'LL HAVE TO *SEE* WHAT WE CAN DO ABOUT THAT...

SORRY. THIS COMPARTMENT IS *FULL.*

*FULL??* DON'T BE *RIDICULOUS,* MAN! IT'S *EMPTY* APART FROM YOU THREE! THERE'S PLENTY OF...

I SAID IT'S *FULL,* CRAPHEAD.

OH MY GOD. I'M *SORRY*... I DIDN'T REALISE.

*FULL.* YES. OF COURSE. *FULL.*

WELL BLOCKED, TED! CAN'T HAVE THE CARRIAGE FULL OF CIVILIANS. CIVILIANS DON'T *APPRECIATE* TRAINS. TAKES A *MILITARY* MAN TO APPRECIATE TRAINS...

LIKE *DOLLS,* YOUR AVERAGE CITIZEN DOES NOT GIVE A *MONKEY'S* ABOUT DOLLS. NO APPRECIATION, YOU SEE? DID I TELL YOU I COLLECTED DOLLS, GEORGE?

ER...YES, MR. PRO-THERO. I THINK YOU *MAY* HAVE MEN-TIONED IT ONCE OR TWICE. VERY INTERESTING.

*INTERESTING!* THAT'S EXACTLY *RIGHT!* MIND YOU, YOU'RE A MILITARY MAN. ASK YOUR AVERAGE CITIZEN, HE'D SAY DOLLS WERE FOR *POOFTAHS.* IGNORANT, YOU SEE.

MYSELF, I'VE ALWAYS BEEN A *LADIES'* MAN. TALES I COULD TELL YOU ABOUT WHEN I WAS IN *ADEN.* I REMEMBER ONCE, PORKY APPLEBY AND MYSELF MET THESE TWO *NATIVE* GELS...

JESUS CHRIST! WHAT THE HELL'S *THAT??*

WHAT WAS *WHAT?*

JUST BEFORE WE WENT INTO THE TUNNEL I THOUGHT I SAW SOMETHING UP ON THE BRIDGE.

I DUNNO... IT COULD HAVE BEEN *RAGS* CAUGHT ON A FENCE OR SOMETHING, I SUPPOSE.

HMMM.

...SO ANYWAY, WE'D BOTH HAD A FEW *TINCTURES* BY THAT TIME, AND PORKY SAYS TO ONE OF THESE LOCAL BINTS...THE ELDEST GEL, I THINK IT WAS... HE SAYS...

...EXCUSE ME, MR. PROTHERO...

TED...*DID* YOU JUST *HEAR* SOMETHING? A BANG ON THE ROOF OF THE TRAIN?

I *SAY!* WE'RE STOPPING! IS EVERYTHING *ALL RIGHT,* D'YOU THINK?

I DON'T... AY!! WHAT'S HAPPENED TO THE *LIGHTS?*

...OH BLOODY HELL...

0730

HMMPH. SHOULDN'T WORRY IF I WERE YOU, LADS. BRITISH RAIL ACTING UP AGAIN. LIGHTS'LL BE BACK ON IN A MINUTE, YOU'LL SEE.

NOW, AS I WAS SAYING, THERE WAS PORKY WITH ONE HAND...

JUST A MINUTE, MR. PROTHERO! SHOOTERS OUT, TED. JUST IN CASE.

I'M SORRY, MR. PROTHERO... PLEASE GO ON....

AND SO THE ELDEST GEL SAYS "WITH A MONKEY?? I SHOULD BLOODY COCOA!!" HA HA HA HA! GOOD ONE, EH?

HMM. THEY DO SEEM TO BE TAKING THEIR TIME, DON'T THEY? PERHAPS YOU SHOULD GO AND HAVE A WORD WITH THE DRIVER, GEORGE.

GEORGE?

... GEORGE?

DON'T TAKE OFFENCE, GEORGE. IT WAS JUST A NAUGHTY YARN. WE'RE ALL MEN OF THE WORLD, EH, GEORGE?

...GEORGE?

OH MY GOD! TED, IT'S GEORGE! HE'S...

...TED?

OH LORD. WHAT'S THE MATTER WITH THE PAIR OF YOU?? FOR CHRIST'S SAKE, SOMEBODY SAY SOMETHING!!

HELLO.

NOVEMBER 6TH 1997...

...SO LET'S JUST HEAR IT ONCE MORE IN YOUR OWN WORDS. THE TRAIN ENTERED THE TUNNEL... AND *THEN* WHAT?

W-WELL, I MEAN, IT'S DIFFICULT TO SAY. IT ALL HAPPENED SO *QUICK*, DIDN'T IT?

I DIDN'T ACTUALLY *HEAR* ANYTHING... JUST SORT OF CAUGHT SOMETHING MOVING OUT THE CORNER OF ME EYE. AND BY THEN IT WAS ALL OVER, WANNIT?

COULD YOU GIVE US A *DESCRIPTION* OF YOUR ATTACKER? HEIGHT, DRESS, ANYTHING LIKE THAT?

WELL, IT WAS JUST SORT OF *BLACK*, KNOW WHAT I MEAN? JUST THIS *BIG*, *BLACK SHAPE* COMIN' AT ME FROM THE SIDE-WINDOW OF THE CAB...

AND IT HAD A *FACE*, ONLY NOT A *PROPER* FACE, SEE? AN' IT WAS *SMILING*.

I SEE. AND *THEN* WHAT HAPPENED? DID IT *HIT* YOU, *STRIKE* YOU IN ANY WAY?

NO. I MEAN, THAT WAS THE FUNNY BIT. IT JUST SORT OF *TOUCHED* ME, UP HERE ON ME NECK.

I FELT THIS... IT WAS LIKE AN *ELECTRIC SHOCK*, SORT OF. AN' THEN I JUST PASSED OUT.

...AND CAME TO AN HOUR LATER WHEN THE SECURITY FORCE ARRIVED ON THE SCENE. I SEE.

WELL, I THINK THAT'S ABOUT *IT*, MR. BISHOP. THE OFFICER WILL TAKE YOUR ADDRESS IN CASE WE NEED TO CONTACT YOU. THANK YOU FOR YOUR TROUBLE.

WELL, MR. FINCH, WHAT DO YOU THINK? IS IT THE SAME BLOKE WHO DID THE PARLIAMENT BOMBING, OR WHAT?

I *HOPE* SO, DOMINIC. BECAUSE IF IT'S *NOT*, THEN THERE MUST BE *TWO* OF 'EM...

...AND *THAT'S* A POSSIBILITY I'D RATHER NOT CONSIDER WITHOUT A STIFF DRINK TO HAND.

ME NEITHER. MR. FINCH, WHAT EXACTLY ARE WE *UP AGAINST* HERE? WHO *IS* THIS CHARACTER?

I MEAN, ALL THIS BUSINESS ABOUT BOARDING MOVING TRAINS IS LIKE SOMETHING OUT OF THE *PICTURES*. *NORMAL* PEOPLE CAN'T *DO* THINGS LIKE THAT.

YOU'RE RIGHT, DOMINIC. *OR* KNOCK OUT A THIRTEEN STONE TRAIN DRIVER BY TOUCHING HIM LIGHTLY ON THE NECK. *NORMAL* PEOPLE CAN'T *DO* THINGS LIKE THAT.

...IN FACT, I DON'T THINK IT'S GOING TOO FAR TO SAY THAT *MOST* NORMAL PEOPLE HAVE NEVER EVEN *CONSIDERED* BLOWING UP THE HOUSES OF PARLIAMENT.

SO WHAT WE'RE UP AGAINST IS SOMEONE WHO *ISN'T* NORMAL PEOPLE... EITHER PHYSICALLY OR MENTALLY. IT'S THE "MENTALLY" BIT THAT BOTHERS ME.

BECAUSE IF I'M GOING TO *CRACK* THIS CASE... AND I *AM*... I'M GOING TO HAVE TO GET RIGHT INSIDE HIS HEAD, TO THINK THE WAY *HE* THINKS. AND THAT SCARES ME.

AHH. HERE WE ARE.

ANYTHING BEEN TOUCHED IN HERE?

NO, SIR. EVERYTHING'S AS WE FOUND IT WHEN WE GOT THE TRAIN OUT OF THE TUNNEL.

Chapter Three

# VICTIMS

HMM... I'LL NEED SOME PHOTOGRAPHS OF THIS *CHEST WOUND*. IT WASN'T A *KNIFE* OR *BULLET* THAT DID THIS...

IN FACT, I'VE GOT A NASTY SUSPICION THAT WHO- EVER DID THAT DID IT WITH THEIR *FINGERS*.

WHAT DO YOU MAKE OF *THIS*, MR. FINCH?

DAMNED IF I KNOW. GET A PHOTOGRAPH OF IT. AND LET ME HAVE SOME *PAINT SCRAPINGS* FOR *ANALYSIS*...

PERHAPS THE *FORENSIC* PEOPLE BACK AT *THE NOSE* WILL BE ABLE TO TELL US SOMETHING. ALTHOUGH FRANKLY I *DOUBT* IT.

...OTHER THAN THAT, JUST THE USUAL STUFF. DUST THE CARRIAGE FOR *DABS*. GET A *PATH* REPORT ON THE BODIES.

*FATE* WILL WANT A COPY, REMEMBER...

HELLO. WHAT'S THIS?

A ROSE. A "VIOLET CARSON" ROSE. FUNNY... I THOUGHT THEY'D BEEN EXTINCT SINCE THE WAR...

OUR FRIEND IN THE MASK HAS GOT QUITE A THING ABOUT THE LETTER "V." WOULDN'T YOU SAY?

AND UNLESS WE FIND A BODY IN THE NEXT COUPLE OF HOURS, IT LOOKS LIKE HE'S GOT LEWIS PROTHERO AS WELL.

BLOWING UP THE HOUSES OF PARLIAMENT, KIDNAPPING OUR TOP BROADCASTER...

DO YOU THINK HE'S TRYING TO TELL US SOMETHING?

I DON'T KNOW, SIR. JESUS CHRIST, WHAT HE'D DONE TO THOSE MEN...

I'VE SEEN WORSE, DOMINIC, PHYSICALLY SPEAKING. LIKE I SAY, IT'S THE MENTAL SIDE THAT BOTHERS ME...HIS ATTITUDE TO KILLING.

THINK ABOUT IT. HE KILLED THEM RUTHLESSLY, EFFICIENTLY, AND WITH A MINIMUM OF FUSS. WHATEVER THEIR FAULTS, THOSE WERE TWO HUMAN BEINGS...

...AND HE SLAUGHTERED THEM LIKE CATTLE!

THE SHADOW GALLERY...

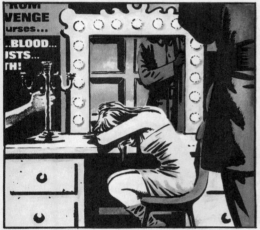

OH.

I-I'M SORRY. YOU *STARTLED* ME. I DIDN'T HEAR YOU COME IN...

NOBODY EVER *DOES*. YOU'VE BEEN *CRYING*.

YES. DON'T TAKE ANY NOTICE OF ME. I'M A BABY.

I-IT WAS WHEN YOU WENT OUT EARLIER ON AND DIDN'T SAY WHERE YOU WERE GOING... I THOUGHT ... I DIDN'T THINK... THAT IS, I MEAN...

I WAS SCARED YOU WOULDN'T COME BACK.

I KNOW I'M STUPID, BUT MY LIFE'S SUDDENLY BE-COME VERY STRANGE. I DON'T KNOW WHAT'S *HAPPENING* ANYMORE.

LAST NIGHT... THOSE MEN, THEY WERE GOING TO... THEY SAID THEY'D *KILL* ME. AND YOU *RESCUED* ME.

YOU RESCUED ME AND BROUGHT ME TO THIS FAN-TASTIC PLACE, AND IT'S SO *BEAUTIFUL* AND IT MAKES ME FEEL SO *SAFE* AND...AND...

I DON'T *HAVE* A NAME. YOU CAN CALL ME *"V."*

WHAT SHALL I CALL *YOU?*

...AND I DON'T EVEN KNOW WHAT YOUR *NAME* IS.

MY NAME IS EVEY... EVEY HAMMOND.

I'M *NOBODY.* NOBODY *SPECIAL,* NOT LIKE YOU.

EVERYBODY IS SPECIAL. *EVERYBODY.* EVERYBODY IS A *HERO,* A *LOVER,* A *FOOL,* A *VILLAIN,* EVERYBODY.

EVERYBODY HAS THEIR *STORY* TO TELL. EVEN EVEY HAMMOND. I SHOULD VERY MUCH LIKE TO HEAR EVEY HAMMOND'S STORY.

B-BUT THERE'S NOTHING TO *TELL.* I'M ONLY SIX-TEEN. I HAVEN'T *DONE* ANYTHING.

SIXTEEN, THEN YOU WERE BORN IN *1981* ?

Y-YES. IN SEPTEMBER. WE USED TO LIVE ON SHOOTERS HILL IN SOUTH LONDON. IT WAS NICE THERE. I- I'VE GOT A PHOTO-GRAPH IF YOU WANT TO SEE...

JUST ME AND MUM AND DAD. I DIDN'T HAVE ANY BROTHERS OR SISTERS... DAD SAID HE COULDN'T AFFORD ANY MORE KIDS...

THIS WAS DURING THE *RECESSION* OF THE EIGHTIES?

YEAH... I DON'T REMEMBER MUCH ABOUT THAT... I KNOW DAD SAID THINGS DIDN'T GET MUCH BETTER WHEN *LABOUR* GOT INTO POWER...

HE SAID THAT THE ONLY ELECTION PROMISE THAT THEY KEPT WAS GETTING RID OF THE *AMERICAN MISSILES* THAT WERE STATIONED OVER HERE.

AND THE *WAR,* EVEY. DO YOU REMEMBER THE *WAR?*

"OF COURSE I DO. I WAS ONLY SEVEN BUT I REMEMBER WHEN THE NEWS CAME OVER THE RADIO. DAD KEPT TELLING MUM NOT TO WORRY. HE WAS SCARED TO DEATH... IT WAS ABOUT *POLAND* AND THE *RUSSIANS,* WASN'T IT? AND PRESIDENT KENNEDY SAID HE'D USE THE BOMB IF THEY DIDN'T GET OUT. THAT'S WHAT DAD TOLD ME.

"IT WAS HORRIBLE. NOBODY KNEW IF BRITAIN WOULD GET BOMBED OR NOT. I REMEMBER MUM SAYING *'AFRICA'S NOT THERE ANYMORE.'* THAT'S ALL SHE SAID.

"I THOUGHT ABOUT ALL THE LIONS AND ELEPHANTS BEING DEAD. IT MADE ME CRY. I WAS ONLY SEVEN.

"BUT BRITAIN *DIDN'T* GET BOMBED. NOT THAT IT MADE MUCH *DIFFERENCE.* ALL THE BOMBS AND THINGS HAD DONE SOMETHING TO THE *WEATHER.* SOMETHING *BAD.*

"I REMEMBER ONE DAY DAD CALLED MUM AND ME INTO THE BACK BEDROOM. HE SAID HE WANTED TO SHOW US SOMETHING...

"WE COULD SEE RIGHT ACROSS LONDON FROM THE BEDROOM WINDOW. IT WAS NEARLY ALL UNDER WATER. THE *THAMES BARRIER* HAD BURST.

"THE SKY WAS ALL YELLOW AND BLACK. I'VE NEVER SEEN A SKY LIKE IT. DAD SAID LONDON WAS FINISHED. HE WANTED TO TAKE MUM AND ME TO THE COUNTRY.

"MUM WOULDN'T GO. JUST AS WELL, I SUPPOSE. IT TURNED OUT THAT THE COUNTRYSIDE WAS WORSE THAN THE TOWNS.

"THE WEATHER HAD DESTROYED ALL THE CROPS, SEE? AND THERE WAS NO FOOD COMING FROM EUROPE, BECAUSE EUROPE HAD GONE. LIKE AFRICA.

"I-I DIDN'T LIKE TO THINK ABOUT THE NEXT FOUR YEARS. WE'D GOT TOGETHER WITH SOME NEIGHBOURS IN A PROTECTION COMMITTEE. IT DIDN'T HELP MUCH...

"THERE WAS NO FOOD. AND THE SEWERS WERE FLOODED AND EVERYBODY GOT SICK. MUM DIED IN 1991. DAD WOULDN'T LET ME SEE HER.

"THERE WERE *RIOTS*, AND PEOPLE WITH *GUNS*. NOBODY KNEW WHAT WAS GOING ON. EVERYONE WAS WAITING FOR THE GOVERNMENT TO *DO* SOMETHING...

"BUT THERE *WASN'T* ANY GOVERNMENT ANYMORE, JUST LOTS OF LITTLE GANGS, ALL TRYING TO *TAKE OVER*. AND THEN IN 1992, SOMEBODY FINALLY *DID*...

"IT WAS ALL THE FASCIST GROUPS, THE RIGHT-WINGERS. THEY'D ALL GOT TOGETHER WITH SOME OF THE BIG CORPORATIONS THAT HAD SURVIVED. *'NORSEFIRE'* THEY CALLED THEMSELVES.

"I REMEMBER WHEN THEY MARCHED INTO LONDON. THEY HAD A FLAG WITH THEIR SYMBOL ON. EVERYONE WAS CHEERING. *I* THOUGHT THEY WERE *SCARY*.

"THEY SOON GOT THINGS UNDER CONTROL. BUT THEN THEY STARTED TAKING PEOPLE AWAY... ALL THE *BLACK PEOPLE* AND THE *PAKISTANIS*...

"WHITE PEOPLE, TOO. ALL THE *RADICALS* AND THE MEN WHO, YOU KNOW, LIKED OTHER MEN. THE HOMOSEXUALS. I DON'T KNOW WHAT THEY DID WITH THEM ALL.

"DAD HAD BEEN IN A SOCIALIST GROUP WHEN HE WAS YOUNGER. THEY CAME FOR HIM ONE SEPTEMBER MORNING IN 1993...

"IT WAS MY BIRTHDAY. I WAS TWELVE. I NEVER SAW HIM AGAIN.

"THEY MADE ME GO AND WORK IN A FACTORY WITH A LOT OF OTHER KIDS. WE WERE PUTTING MATCHES INTO BOXES.

"I LIVED IN A HOSTEL. IT WAS COLD AND DIRTY AND I JUST USED TO CRY ALL THE TIME. I WANTED MY DAD."

...THAT'S HOW IT WAS FOR FOUR YEARS... NOT ENOUGH FOOD, NOT ENOUGH MONEY. SOME OF THE OLDER GIRLS MADE MONEY GOING WITH MEN.

THAT'S WHAT I WAS GOING TO DO, LAST NIGHT. BUT THEY WERE FINGERMEN. THEY WERE GOING... THEY WERE G-GOING TO...

THEY WERE GOING TO RUH... RUH... RUH...

HUSH, CHILD, HUSH. IT'S OVER NOW. YOU'RE SAFE. THE PAST CAN'T HURT YOU ANYMORE. NOT UNLESS YOU LET IT.

THEY MADE YOU INTO A *VICTIM*, EVEY. THEY MADE YOU INTO A STATISTIC. BUT THAT'S NOT THE *REAL* YOU. THAT'S NOT WHO YOU ARE *INSIDE*.

JUST *TRUST* ME, EVEY, AND WE CAN WIPE IT *ALL AWAY*. ALL THE *PAIN*, ALL THE *CRUELTY*, ALL THE *BEREAVEMENT*. WE CAN START AGAIN.

THERE, YOU SEE?

ALL GONE.

...AND EVEY HAMMOND *SOBS* LIKE THE CHILD SHE IS. SOBS BECAUSE AT LONG LAST, HER *NIGHTMARE IS OVER*...

NOW, LEWIS PROTHERO, ON THE OTHER HAND...

≡ MNNUH ≡ WHERE *AM I*? WHAT *HAPPENED*?

...AND WHAT AM I DOING WEARING THIS *UNIFORM*?

HIS NIGHTMARE IS ONLY JUST BEGINNING!

OH MY GOD.

LARKHILL RESETTLEMENT CAMP

NOVEMBER THE SEVENTH, 1997.
THE LEADER AND MR. FINCH.

I THINK HE'S A PSYCHOPATH, LEADER.

I USE THE WORD IN ITS MOST PRECISE SENSE.

I SEE. THEN WE CAN'T ASSUME THAT "CODE-NAME 'V'" WILL BE-HAVE LIKE A CONVEN-TIONAL TERRORIST.

WE CAN'T ASSUME THAT HE WILL EVENTUALLY ISSUE A SET OF DEMANDS OR ASK FOR THE USUAL CONCESSIONS.

I DON'T THINK HE'S OUT FOR CONCESSIONS, LEADER.

I THINK HE'S OUT FOR BLOOD.

THEN HE'S CERTAINLY GETTING IT, ISN'T HE, MR. FINCH? HE'S BLOWN UP THE HOUSES OF PARLIAMENT, DISPATCHED FIVE OF MR. ALMOND'S FINGER-MEN...

...AND NOW HE'S ABDUCT-ED OUR TOP BROADCASTER. IF PROTHERO IS UNABLE TO MAKE HIS "VOICE OF FATE" BROADCASTS AS SCHED-ULED, OUR CRED-IBILITY WILL SUFFER.

TWO DAYS, MR. FINCH. THAT'S ALL IT'S TAKEN HIM.

COULDN'T MR. DASCOMBE ARRANGE A STAND-IN FOR PROTHERO, LEADER?

OH YES. BUT THE PROBLEM IS THAT MR. DASCOMBE IS TOO GOOD AT HIS WORK. THE PEOPLE ACTUALLY BE-LIEVE THAT THE VOICE OF LEWIS PROTHERO IS THAT OF THE FATE COMPUTER.

BRITAIN'S BELIEF IN THE IN-TEGRITY OF FATE IS THE CORNERSTONE OF OUR NEW ORDER. ANY CHANGE IN THE VOICE AND... IT JUST WON'T BE THE SAME.

I SEE. FROM A PROPA-GANDA ANGLE WE'VE BEEN PUT IN A BIT OF A SPOT, HAVEN'T WE?

ALTHOUGH PERSONALLY I DON'T GO MUCH FOR THIS "NEW ORDER" BUSINESS. IT'S JUST MY JOB, TO HELP BRITAIN OUT OF THIS MESS. YOU ALREADY KNOW THAT, LEADER.

INDEED I DO, MR. FINCH. YOU HAVE EX-PRESSED SUCH SENTIMENTS BEFORE. THAT YOU ARE STILL ALIVE IS A MARK OF MY RESPECT FOR YOU AND YOUR CRAFT.

LEAVE ME NOW. THERE ARE MANY PROBLEMS TO CONSIDER. I WISH TO SPEAK WITH FATE.

ENGLAND PREVAILS, MR. FINCH.

ENGLAND PREVAILS, LEADER.

THE SHADOW GALLERY.
EVEY HAMMOND:

Y...

HMM?

OH... UH... NOTHING. I WAS JUST TRYING TO GET USED TO SAYING IT OUT LOUD. Y... IT'S A FUNNY THING TO CALL YOURSELF.

I'M A FUNNY PERSON, EVEY. YOU'LL FIND THAT OUT WHEN YOU'VE KNOWN ME LONGER. A VERY FUNNY PERSON INDEED.

YOU'RE A KIND PERSON. LISTENING TO ME TELLING YOU MY SOB STORY, ALL ABOUT THE WAR, AND MUM AND DAD. ALL ABOUT MY STUPID LIFE.

WHAT ARE YOU GOING TO DO, V? THE WORLD IS SO BIG AND HORRIBLE AND THERE'S JUST YOU... AND ME, I SUPPOSE.

YOU AND ME, EVEY. YOU AND ME AGAINST THE WORLD! HA HA HA HA! MELODRAMA, EVEY! ISN'T IT STRANGE HOW LIFE TURNS INTO MELODRAMA?

THAT'S VERY IMPORTANT TO YOU, ISN'T IT? ALL THAT THEATRICAL STUFF.

IT'S EVERYTHING, EVEY. THE PERFECT ENTRANCE, THE GRAND ILLUSION.

IT'S EVERYTHING.

...AND I'M GOING TO BRING THE HOUSE DOWN.

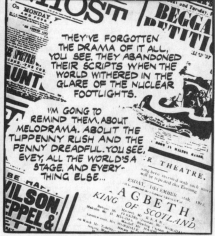

THEY'VE FORGOTTEN THE DRAMA OF IT ALL, YOU SEE. THEY ABANDONED THEIR SCRIPTS WHEN THE WORLD WITHERED IN THE GLARE OF THE NUCLEAR FOOTLIGHTS.

I'M GOING TO REMIND THEM. ABOUT MELODRAMA. ABOUT THE TUPPENNY RUSH AND THE PENNY DREADFUL. YOU SEE, EVEY, ALL THE WORLD'S A STAGE, AND EVERYTHING ELSE...

...IS VAUDEVILLE.

THE SHADOW GALLERY.
LEWIS PROTHERO:

HELLO? I SAY, IS THERE ANYBODY THERE?

Chapter Four
VAUDEVILLE

I SUPPOSE YOU THINK ALL THIS IS BLOODY FUNNY, ALL THIS RESETTLEMENT CAMP MALARKEY, ALL THIS PUTTING ME IN UNIFORM.

WELL, ALL I CAN SAY IS THAT YOU'VE GOT A DAMN QUEER SENSE OF HUMOUR.

LARKHILL RESETTLEMENT CAMP

DAMN QUEER.

YOU'VE GOT THE WRONG MAN, CHUMMY. THE RE-SETTLEMENT CAMPS MEAN BUGGER ALL TO ME. BUGGER ALL. YOU'VE GOT THE WRONG MAN!!

OH GOD. IS THERE ANYBODY THERE?

GOOD MORNING, CAMPERS.

UNIFORM ALL BRUSHED, PRESSED AND READY FOR DUTY, I SEE. GOOD MAN, COMMANDER PROTHERO. GOOD MAN.

I....

LET'S GET TO WORK, SHALL WE? THESE CONCENTRATION CAMPS... SORRY... THESE RESETTLEMENT CAMPS DON'T RUN THEM-SELVES, DO THEY?

LOOK. I DON'T KNOW WHO YOU ARE OR HOW YOU GOT THIS BLOODY SILLY IDEA INTO YOUR BONNET, BUT YOU'VE GOT THE WRONG MAN!

...I, UH...

I'M A BROADCASTER. I DIDN'T HAVE ANY-THING TO DO WITH THE CON... WITH THE RESETTLEMENT CAMPS. I...

LARKHILL. 1993.

I WAS THERE, COM-MANDER PROTHERO.

YOU WERE TH...

OH GOD.

LOOK SMART, COMMANDER. WE'VE GOT TO MAKE THE TOUR OF INSPECTION NOW. YOU REMEMBER...

THE WAY YOU USED TO MAKE IT EVERY EVEN-ING. BACK IN THE GOOD OLD DAYS.

OH GOD.

ALL COMING BACK TO YOU, EH? THE MAIN BODY OF THE PRISONERS WOULD BE GATHERED IN THE YARD AWAITING YOUR INSPECTION...

YOU SIMPLY HAD TO WALK FROM YOUR OFFICE DOWN PAST THE NISSEN HUTS, TURN THE CORNER...

AND THERE THEY WERE...

MY DOLLS. THAT'S PART OF MY DOLL COLLECTION. HOW DID YOU... THEY WERE ALL SAFELY LOCKED AWAY WHEN I LEFT FOR WORK YESTERDAY...

WHAT ARE YOU DOING WITH MY DOLLS?

MY GOD, IF YOU'VE DAMAGED ANY OF THEM...THEY'RE PRICELESS! HARDLY ANY OF THE BIG COLLECTIONS SURVIVED THE WAR. IF YOU'VE DAMAGED THEM...

ADMIRABLE CONCERN, COMMANDER. YET IT'S DEUCED ODD, ISN'T IT? HOW YOU CAN SHOW SO MUCH CONCERN FOR PORCELAIN AND PLASTIC...

...AND SHOW SO LITTLE FOR FLESH AND BLOOD.

DO YOU REMEMBER, COMMANDER? DO YOU REMEMBER WHEN IT WAS PEOPLE GATHERED IN THIS SORDID LITTLE ENCLOSURE? PEOPLE HALF DEAD WITH STARVATION AND DYSENTERY?

LOOK, YOU KNOW AS WELL AS I DO... WE HAD TO DO WHAT WE DID. ALL THE DARKIES, THE NANCY BOYS AND THE BEATNIKS...IT WAS US OR THEM.

US OR THEM. DON'T YOU UNDERSTAND?

PERFECTLY.

COME ALONG, COMMANDER, YOUR TOUR ISN'T OVER YET. THERE ARE STILL THE SPECIAL PRISONERS TO SEE. THE ONES IN THE MEDICAL COMPOUND.

JUST ALONG HERE. THIS IS WHERE YOU KEPT THE ONES WHO'D TAKEN PART IN YOUR SCIENTISTS'... EXPERIMENTS, I BELIEVE THEY USED TO CALL THEM.

YOU HAD TO WALK PAST THIS ROW OF DOORS EVERY NIGHT. ROOM ONE, ROOM TWO, ROOM THREE...

...ROOM FOUR...

ROOM FIVE

ROOM FIVE? BUT THAT WAS WHERE THEY KEPT... WHERE THEY KEPT...

OH, NO. THAT WAS YOU, WASN'T IT? YOU'RE... YOU'RE THE MAN...

YOU'RE THE MAN FROM ROOM FIVE.

THAT'S RIGHT.

I REMEMBER YOU USED TO CALL OUT TO US SOMETIMES. LITTLE JOKES. YOU HAD A SPECIAL NAME FOR THE MEDICAL BLOCK. YOU USED TO CALL IT THE FUNNY FARM.

I REMEMBER WHAT A GOOD VOICE YOU HAD. I IMAGINE THAT'S WHY THEY PICKED YOU TO DO THE FATE BROADCASTS.

A MAN OF MANY TALENTS, EH, COMMANDER?

AND THEN, OF COURSE, THERE WAS THAT OTHER LITTLE JOB YOU USED TO DO.

THE OVENS, COMMANDER. YOU USED TO WORK THE OVENS.

OH, NO. MY DOLLS. PLEASE ...YOU CAN'T...

PLEASE. I'M BEGGING YOU. PLEASE.

MA··MA·· MA··MA·· MA··MA··

NOT MY DOLLS!

IGNITE

MA··MA... MA··MA... MA··MA...

MA'MAAA—

NOOOOOOOOOO

NEW SCOTLAND YARD. LATER:

UHH?

OH, HELLO, SARGE. IT'S NOT THE END OF MY SHIFT AL-READY, IS IT? I WAS JUST...

OH GOD. BUT WHO..?

WHO..?

HELLO, SERGEANT? YES, THIS IS GODDARD, AT THE FRONT. COULD YOU GET OUT HERE, QUICKLY, PLEASE?

YES, I THINK IT'S AN EMERGENCY. YES, I'VE GOT SOME-THING OUT HERE...

NO, I'M NOT SURE WHAT...

JORDAN TOWER, ROGER DASCOMBE!

WHO...? HAVEN'T I TOLD YOU THAT I MUSTN'T BE DISTURBED WHILE...

OH. IT'S YOU.

GOOD OLD BITTER ALMOND. DO COME IN.

IF YOU'VE COME TO TELL ME WHAT A THOROUGHLY MISERABLE JOB YOU'VE MADE OF FINDING POOR LEWIS, THEN SPARE ME THE AGONY. I EXPECTED AS MUCH.

OH, ON THE CONTRARY, ROGER, OLD BOY. WE'VE FOUND HIM.

YOU'VE...?

I DON'T BELIEVE IT.

WHEEL HIM IN, BOYS. OH, WE'VE FOUND HIM ALL RIGHT. OR, AT LEAST...

...WE FOUND WHAT'S LEFT OF HIM.

MA-MA...

L-LEWIS?

THAT'S ALL HE'S SAID FOR THE PAST THREE HOURS. GOOD LUCK WITH TONIGHT'S BROADCAST, ROGER, OLD BOY.

MA-MA... MA-MA...

...MA-MA...

THE VOICE OF FATE IS RECORDED FORTY-EIGHT HOURS IN ADVANCE. THE PRE-RECORDINGS RAN OUT AT TEN O'CLOCK. IT IS NOW ELEVEN.

GOOD EVENING, LONDON. THIS IS THE VOICE OF FATE BROADCASTING ON.. UH... 275 AND 285 IN THE MEDIUM WAVE...

AND THE CAPITAL LISTENS. THERE IS SOMETHING WRONG. THERE IS SOMETHING WRONG WITH THE VOICE OF FATE.

SUCH A SMALL THING TO CAST SUCH A LONG AND UNEASY SHADOW OVER THE FUTURE. FOR WHATEVER THE FUTURE HOLDS, ONE THING IS CERTAIN...

IT JUST WON'T BE THE SAME.

DECEMBER 12TH, 1997. FIRST VERSION:

**Chapter Five**

**VERSIONS**

MY NAME IS ADAM SUSAN. I AM THE LEADER.

LEADER OF THE LOST, RULER OF THE RUINS.

I AM A MAN, LIKE ANY OTHER MAN.

I LEAD THE COUNTRY THAT I LOVE OUT OF THE WILDERNESS OF THE TWENTIETH CENTURY. I BELIEVE IN SURVIVAL, IN THE DESTINY OF THE NORDIC RACE. I BELIEVE IN FASCISM.

OH YES, I AM A FASCIST. WHAT OF IT? FASCISM... A WORD. A WORD WHOSE MEANING HAS BEEN LOST IN THE BLEATINGS OF THE WEAK AND THE TREACHEROUS.

THE ROMANS INVENTED FASCISM. A BUNDLE OF BOUND TWIGS WAS ITS SYMBOL.

ONE TWIG COULD BE BROKEN. A BUNDLE WOULD PREVAIL. FASCISM... STRENGTH IN UNITY.

I BELIEVE IN STRENGTH. I BELIEVE IN UNITY.

AND IF THAT STRENGTH, THAT UNITY OF PURPOSE, DEMANDS A UNIFORMITY OF THOUGHT, WORD AND DEED THEN SO BE IT.

I WILL NOT HEAR TALK OF FREEDOM. I WILL NOT HEAR TALK OF INDIVIDUAL LIBERTY. THEY ARE LUXURIES. I DO NOT BELIEVE IN LUXURIES.

THE WAR PUT PAID TO LUXURY.

THE WAR PUT PAID TO FREEDOM.

THE ONLY FREEDOM LEFT TO MY PEOPLE IS THE FREEDOM TO STARVE. THE FREEDOM TO DIE, THE FREEDOM TO LIVE IN A WORLD OF CHAOS.

SHOULD I ALLOW THEM THAT FREEDOM?

I THINK NOT. I THINK NOT.

DO I RESERVE FOR MYSELF THE FREEDOM I DENY TO OTHERS? I DO NOT. I SIT HERE WITHIN MY CAGE AND I AM BUT A SERVANT. I, WHO AM MASTER OF ALL THAT I SEE.

I SEE DESOLATION. I SEE ASHES. I HAVE SO VERY MUCH. I HAVE SO VERY LITTLE.

I AM NOT LOVED, I KNOW THAT. NOT IN SOUL OR BODY. I HAVE NEVER KNOWN THE SOFT WHISPER OF ENDEARMENT. NEVER KNOWN THE PEACE THAT LIES BETWEEN THE THIGHS OF WOMAN.

BUT I AM RESPECTED. I AM FEARED. AND THAT WILL SUFFICE.

BECAUSE I LOVE. I, WHO AM NOT LOVED IN RETURN. I HAVE A LOVE THAT IS FAR DEEPER THAN THE EMPTY GASPS AND CONVULSIONS OF BRITISH COUPLING.

SHALL I SPEAK OF HER? SHALL I SPEAK OF MY BRIDE?

SHE HAS NO EYES TO FLIRT OR PROMISE. BUT SHE SEES ALL. SEES AND UNDERSTANDS WITH A WISDOM THAT IS GOD-LIKE IN ITS SCALE.

I STAND AT THE GATES OF HER INTELLECT AND I AM BLINDED BY THE LIGHT WITHIN. HOW STUPID I MUST SEEM TO HER. HOW CHILD-LIKE AND UNCOMPREHENDING.

HER SOUL IS CLEAN, UNTAINTED BY THE SNARES AND AMBIGUITIES OF EMOTION. SHE DOES NOT HATE. SHE DOES NOT YEARN. SHE IS UNTOUCHED BY JOY OR SORROW.

I WORSHIP HER THOUGH I AM NOT WORTHY.

I CHERISH THE PURITY OF HER DISDAIN. SHE DOES NOT RESPECT ME. SHE DOES NOT FEAR ME.

SHE DOES NOT LOVE ME.

THEY THINK SHE IS HARD AND COLD, THOSE WHO DO NOT KNOW HER. THEY THINK SHE IS LIFELESS AND WITHOUT PASSION.

THEY DO NOT KNOW HER. SHE HAS NOT TOUCHED THEM.

SHE TOUCHES ME, AND I AM TOUCHED BY GOD, BY DESTINY. THE WHOLE OF EXISTENCE COURSES THROUGH HER. I WORSHIP HER. I AM HER SLAVE.

NO FREEDOM EVER WAS SO SWEET.

MY LOVE, I WOULD STAY WITH YOU FOREVER, WOULD SPEND MY LIFE WITHIN YOU.

I WOULD WAIT UPON YOUR EVERY UTTERANCE AND NEVER ASK THE MEREST SPLINTER OF AFFECTION.

FATE...

FATE...

I LOVE YOU.

THE OLD BAILEY. SECOND VERSION:

HELLO, DEAR LADY. A LOVELY EVENING, IS IT NOT?

FORGIVE ME FOR INTRUDING. PERHAPS YOU WERE INTENDING TO TAKE A STROLL. PERHAPS YOU WERE MERELY ENJOYING THE VIEW.

NO MATTER. I THOUGHT THAT IT WAS TIME WE HAD A LITTLE CHAT, YOU AND I.

AHH... I WAS FORGETTING THAT WE ARE NOT PROPERLY INTRODUCED.

DO I HAVE A NAME. YOU CAN CALL ME V.

MADAM JUSTICE... THIS IS V.

V. THIS IS MADAM JUSTICE.

HELLO, MADAM JUSTICE.

"GOOD EVENING, V."

THERE. NOW WE KNOW EACH OTHER. ACTUALLY, I'VE BEEN A FAN OF YOURS FOR QUITE SOME TIME. OH, I KNOW WHAT YOU'RE THINKING...

"THE POOR BOY HAS A CRUSH ON ME... AN ADOLESCENT INFATUATION."

I BEG YOUR PARDON, MADAM. IT ISN'T LIKE THAT AT ALL.

I'VE LONG ADMIRED YOU... ALBEIT ONLY FROM A DISTANCE. I USED TO STARE AT YOU FROM THE STREETS BELOW WHEN I WAS A CHILD.

I'D SAY, TO MY FATHER, "WHO IS THAT LADY?" AND HE'D SAY, "THAT'S MADAM JUSTICE." AND I'D SAY, "ISN'T SHE PRETTY."

PLEASE DON'T THINK IT WAS MERELY PHYSICAL. I KNOW YOU'RE NOT THAT SORT OF GIRL. NO, I LOVED YOU AS A PERSON. AS AN IDEAL.

THAT WAS A LONG TIME AGO. I'M AFRAID THERE'S SOMEONE ELSE NOW...

"WHAT? V! FOR SHAME! YOU HAVE BETRAYED ME FOR SOME HARLOT, SOME VAIN AND POUTING HUSSY WITH PAINTED LIPS AND A KNOWING SMILE!"

I, MADAM? I BEG TO DIFFER! IT WAS YOUR INFIDELITY THAT DROVE ME TO HER ARMS!

AH-HA! THAT SURPRISED YOU, DIDN'T IT? YOU THOUGHT I DIDN'T KNOW ABOUT YOUR LITTLE FLING. BUT I DO. I KNOW EVERYTHING!

FRANKLY, I WASN'T SURPRISED WHEN I FOUND OUT. YOU ALWAYS DID HAVE AN EYE FOR A MAN IN UNIFORM.

"UNIFORM? WHY, I'M SURE I DON'T KNOW WHAT YOU'RE TALKING ABOUT. IT WAS ALWAYS YOU, V. YOU WERE THE ONLY ONE..."

LIAR! SLUT! WHORE! DENY THAT YOU LET HIM HAVE HIS WAY WITH YOU, HIM WITH HIS ARMBANDS AND JACKBOOTS!

WELL! CAT GOT YOUR TONGUE?

I THOUGHT AS MUCH.

VERY WELL. SO YOU STAND REVEALED AT LAST. YOU ARE NO LONGER *MY* JUSTICE. YOU ARE HIS JUSTICE NOW. YOU HAVE BEDDED ANOTHER.

WELL, *TWO* CAN PLAY AT *THAT* GAME!

"*SOB! CHOKE!* WH-WHO IS SHE, V? WHAT IS HER *NAME?*"

HER NAME IS *ANARCHY*, AND SHE HAS TAUGHT ME MORE AS A MISTRESS THAN YOU *EVER* DID!

*SHE* HAS TAUGHT ME THAT JUSTICE IS MEANINGLESS WITHOUT FREEDOM. SHE IS HONEST. SHE MAKES NO PROMISES AND BREAKS NONE. UNLIKE *YOU*, JEZEBEL.

I USED TO WONDER WHY YOU COULD NEVER LOOK ME IN THE EYE. NOW I KNOW.

SO GOODBYE, DEAR LADY. I WOULD BE SADDENED BY OUR PARTING EVEN NOW, SAVE THAT YOU ARE NO LONGER THE WOMAN THAT I ONCE LOVED.

HERE IS A FINAL GIFT. I LEAVE IT AT YOUR FEET.

THE FLAMES OF FREEDOM. HOW LOVELY. HOW JUST. AHH, MY PRECIOUS ANARCHY...

" O BEAUTY, 'TIL NOW I NEVER KNEW THEE."

EPILOGUE: MR. PROTHERO... LEWIS... IT'S ME. MR. FINCH. I'M YOUR *FRIEND* LEWIS. YOUR *FRIEND*.

CAN YOU HEAR ME, LEWIS?

I WANT TO KNOW WHAT *HAPPENED* TO YOU, LEWIS. I WANT TO KNOW WHAT HE *DID* TO YOU...

YOU KNOW WHO I'M TALKING ABOUT, DON'T YOU, LEWIS?

I'M TALKING ABOUT THE MAN IN THE CLOAK, LEWIS.

I'M TALKING ABOUT THE SMILING MAN.

MAMA...

OH CHRIST. I THOUGHT WE'D GOT HIM AWAY FROM HIS MAMA.

ALL RIGHT, LEWIS. YOU'RE SAFE. WE'RE YOUR FRIENDS. HE CAN'T HURT YOU NOW. HE CAN'T FIND YOU HERE.

LEWIS?

OH, WHAT'S THE USE. WHATEVER THAT BEGGAR DID TO HIM, IT WAS FOR KEEPS.

COME ON, DOMINIC. WE'LL HAVE ANOTHER CRACK AT HIM AFTER A CUP OF TEA AND A HAND OF BRAG. LET'S TAKE FIVE.

FIVE...

FIVE, FIVE...

ROOM FIVE.

FIVE...

THE SHADOW GALLERY.
DECEMBER 15TH, 1997...

"V. V. V. V. V."

EVEY
EVEY EVEY
EVEY EVEY.

SOMETIMES I COULD JUST PUNCH YOU IN YOUR STUPID SMILEY FACE! "V.V.V.V.V." IT'S THE INSCRIPTION ON THAT ARCH IN THE BIG HALL. YOU KNOW IT IS.

I JUST WONDERED WHAT IT MEANT, THAT'S ALL.

IT'S A QUOTATION. A MOTTO... "VI VERI VENIVERSUM VIVUS VICI."

"BY THE POWER OF TRUTH, I, WHILE LIVING, HAVE CONQUERED THE UNIVERSE." LATIN.

HMMM. I SUPPOSE YOU HAVE, SORT OF. YOU CAN DO WHATEVER YOU WANT, CAN'T YOU? I SUPPOSE THAT'S CONQUERING THE UNIVERSE. DOING WHAT YOU WANT.

THIS PLACE IS THE ONLY UNIVERSE I'VE GOT AT THE MOMENT.

DOES THAT BOTHER YOU?

NO. YES. OH, I DUNNO.

IT'S JUST THAT I KEEP THINKING I SHOULD TRY TO HELP YOU, THE WAY YOU'RE HELPING ME. I MEAN, THAT'S THE DEAL, ISN'T IT?

NO DEALS, EVEY. NOT UNLESS YOU WANT THEM.

I.. I THINK I DO. I MEAN, PART OF ME JUST WANTS TO STAY IN HERE FOREVER AND NEVER HAVE TO GO OUTSIDE AND FACE WHAT'S GOING ON...

BUT THAT'S NOT RIGHT, IS IT? THAT'S NOT TAKING RESPONSIBILITY FOR MYSELF, LIKE WHAT YOU SAID. I WANT TO HELP YOU, V. I WANT TO DO SOMETHING.

I WON'T GET IN THE WAY, I PROMISE. CAN I, V? CAN WE MAKE A DEAL?

"IF YOU LIKE, I THINK I KNOW A WAY THAT YOU COULD HELP ME. VERY SOON. VERY SOON INDEED."

"YES, I THINK THAT WE CAN MAKE A DEAL."

"GOOD. THAT'S THAT, THEN, RIGHT."

"V, YOU SAID THAT "V.V.V.V." THING WAS A QUOTE. WHO SAID IT IN THE FIRST PLACE?"

"NOBODY YOU'D HAVE HEARD OF. A GERMAN GENTLE-MAN NAMED DR. JOHN FAUST."

"HE MADE A DEAL, TOO."

WESTMINSTER ABBEY, DECEMBER 20TH:

"WHOSE GLORIOUS FEET IN IRON ARE SHOD·WHOSE HEART IS TEMPERED STEEL·HIM WHO HATH GRANTED US THIS DAY·AND AT WHOSE THRONE WE KNEEL."

"WHO SENT THE FIRE, THE SCOURGING RAIN·OF THAT MOST DREADFUL NIGHT· WHO PURGED THE WICKED WITH HIS SWORD·YET GRANTED US RESPITE."

"ONE RACE, ONE CREED, ONE HOPE IN THEE·WHO LOVED US IN OUR PAIN,· WHO LET US FALL NOT VERY FAR·THAT WE SHOULD RISE AGAIN!"

"LET US PRAY."

"DEAR GOD, THOU WHO HAS GRANTED US REPRIEVE FROM THY FINAL JUDGMENT, THOU WHO HAS PROVIDED US WITH THAT MOST TERRIBLE WARNING..."

"HELP US TO BE WORTHY OF YOUR MERCY, AS WE WERE WHEN THOU DIDST TURN ASIDE THY WRATH, THAT WRATH WHICH DID RAIN FIRE FROM THE HEAVENS."

"HELP US TO RESIST THE TEMPTATIONS OF THE EVIL ONE, WHO IS SURELY COME AMONGST US IN THIS HOUR OF OUR GREATEST TRIAL."

FOR I HAVE SEEN A VISION... A VISION OF DARK AND SATANIC EVIL THAT COMETH FORTH FROM THE NIGHT TO ENSNARE THE WEAK AND THE SINFUL ...

AN AVATAR OF DAMNATION, WHO WILL SEEK TO SULLY THY TRUTH WITH HIS VENOMOUS LIES AND SHALLOW SOPHISTICATIONS.

OH, GOD, THOU WHO KNOWEST ALL THAT WE DO, THOU WHO ART OUR FATE AND FINAL DESTINY, HELP US TO CLEARLY PERCEIVE THY HOLY WILL.

HELP US TO RESIST THE WILES OF THE EVIL ONE AND STAND FIRM IN THEE. ONE RACE, ONE NATION, UNITED IN THY LOVE.

THIS WE ASK IN THE NAME OF THE FATHER, AND OF THE SON, AND OF THE HOLY GHOST.

THROUGH JESUS CHRIST, OUR LORD

AMEN

Chapter Six
THE VISION

HELLO, DEREK. ROSEMARY. DIDN'T GET A CHANCE TO SPEAK TO YOU BEFORE WE WENT IN. HOW'S THINGS?

HELLO, CONRAD. HELLO, HELEN. NOT SO BAD. THE OLD MAN'S BEEN RIDING ME A BIT ABOUT THIS TERRORIST CASE, BUT WHO CARES? HOW ARE THINGS IN THE EYE?

WELL, WE'VE HAD A FEW TECHNICAL PROBLEMS WITH THE MARK IX VI-CORDERS, BUT...

OH, CONRAD, DON'T BE SUCH A BLOODY BORE. TELL US ABOUT THE TERRORIST, DEREK. IS IT TRUE HE BLEW UP THE OLD BAILEY?

WELL, YES, I'M AFRAID IT IS, ACTUALLY. BUT WE'LL CATCH HIM, SOONER OR LATER HE'LL MAKE A MISTAKE AND WHEN HE DOES...

OOH, IT SOUNDS DREADFULLY EXCITING. AREN'T YOU GLAD YOU'VE GOT SUCH A RUTHLESS, IMPLACABLE BRUTE FOR A HUSBAND, ROSEMARY?

HA, HA. WELL, I...

BELIEVE ME, YOU'RE LUCKY. YOU COULD BE STUCK WITH A PROFESSIONAL PEEPING TOM LIKE CONRAD HERE. ENGLAND'S HIGHEST-PAID VOYEUR, AREN'T YOU, DARLING?

HELEN, I THINK WE'D BETTER...

OH, YES. I KNOW. YOU WANT TO GET HOME SO THAT YOU CAN WATCH WHAT THE NEIGHBOURS DO AFTER SUNDAY LUNCH. RATHER THAN DO ANYTHING OURSELVES, OF COURSE.

CIAO!

HA, HA. HA! 'BYE, HELEN. 'BYE, CONRAD.

'BYE.

SHE'S A BIT HARD ON HIM, ISN'T SHE?

LISTEN, WHEN YOU'RE HALF AS LIVELY AND SOPHISTICATED AS HELEN HEYER, PERHAPS YOU CAN AFFORD TO TALK ABOUT HER. UNTIL THEN I SHOULD JUST SHUT UP IF I WERE YOU.

JUST SHUT UP. THAT'S ALL.

AHH, THERE THEY GO, MY HAPPY AND CONTENTED FLOCK...

SPIRITUALLY REFRESHED AND READY TO FACE THE WORLD AGAIN. DID YOU ENJOY THE SERMON TODAY, DENNIS?

VERY INSPIRING, YOUR GRACE. DIDN'T QUITE SEE THE POINT OF THAT BIT ABOUT THE FORCES OF SATAN AMONGST US, THOUGH.

HMM. YES. A TRIFLE PURPLE, I THOUGHT. STILL, FATE WANTED IT INCLUDED AND WHO ARE WE TO ARGUE WITH THE ALMIGHTY, MISERABLE SINNERS THAT WE ARE?

...AND SPEAKING OF SIN, I WONDER WHICH OF THE SEVEN DEADLIES THE GOOD LORD WILL SEE FIT TO TEMPT ME WITH TODAY?

PERHAPS PRIDE, YOUR GRACE?

HA, HA, HA, I WAS THINKING OF SOMETHING A LITTLE LESS ETHEREAL, MYSELF.

HAS THE YOUNG LADY ARRIVED YET, DENNIS?

SHE HAS, YOUR GRACE. SHE'S WAITING OUTSIDE AT THE MOMENT.

IT SEEMS THERE WAS SOME SORT OF MIX-UP AT THE AGENCY. IT'S NOT ONE OF THE USUAL GIRLS. SHE'S A LITTLE OLDER...

OH, DEAR, DENNIS. OH, DEAR. NOT TOO OLD, I TRUST?

SHE SAYS SHE'S FIFTEEN, YOUR GRACE. A VERY NICELY SPOKEN YOUNG LADY IF YOU DON'T MIND ME SAYING SO...

FIFTEEN. HMMM.

AH, WELL, IF JOB COULD BEAR HIS DISAPPOINTMENTS, I SUPPOSE I MUST HAVE THE GOOD GRACE TO LIKEWISE BEAR MINE. SHOW HER IN, DENNIS, THERE'S A GOOD CHAP.

AT ONCE, YOUR GRACE.

THE YOUNG LADY, YOUR GRACE.

OH MY WORD! AND TO THINK THAT I DOUBTED FOR EVEN AN INSTANT YOUR DAZZLING LOVELINESS. MEA CULPA, MY CHILD. MEA CULPA.

YOU ARE A VISION. A PERFECT... ANGELIC... VISION..!

UHHH... HEH.

THANKS.

PLEASE DON'T THANK ME, MY CHILD. BELIEVE ME...

THE PLEASURE IS ALL MINE.

THE SHADOW GALLERY.

"BRING ME MY BOW OF BURNING GOLD, BRING ME MY ARROWS OF DESIRE, BRING ME MY SPEAR, O CLOUDS UNFOLD, BRING ME MY CHARIOT OF FIRE...

"I WILL NOT CEASE FROM MENTAL FIGHT...

"NOR SHALL MY SWORD SLEEP IN MY HAND...

"TILL WE HAVE BUILT JERUSALEM...

"IN ENGLAND'S GREEN AND PLEASANT LAND."

DEAN'S YARD, WESTMINSTER ABBEY. DECEMBER 20TH 1997.

HERE YOU ARE, GENTS. SOMETHING TO WARM THE INNARDS ON A BLUSTERY NIGHT.

NICE ONE, DENNIS. SHOULDN'T YOU BE TENDING TO HIS GRACE?

OH, I'M SURE HIS GRACE WON'T MIND ME EXPENDING A BIT OF CHRISTIAN CHARITY ON HIS GUARDIAN ANGELS.

BEATS ME WHY YOU PEOPLE HAVE TO STAND OUT HERE AT ALL, THOUGH. LOOKING AFTER HIS GRACE IS MY JOB. NO OFFENCE, MIND YOU.

NO, WELL, IT'S ORDERS, ENNIT? FROM PRETTY BOY ALMOND. THIS TERRORIST THING'S PUT THE WIND UP THE PARTY A BIT.

ALL THE V.I.P.'S HAVE GOT DOUBLE SECURITY RATINGS NOW. WASTE O' TIME IN MY OPINION.

COR, THAT'S SMASHIN' THAT IS, DENNIS. GUZ DOWN A TREAT. DROP OUT O' THE BISHOP'S PRIVATE STOCK, IZZIT?

THAT'S RIGHT. HE WON'T MISS IT THOUGH. NOT TONIGHT. HIS GRACE IS DINING UPON FINEST VEAL THIS EVENING.

VEAL? WHAT... OH, OH YEAH. THAT LITTLE CHICK WITH THE PIGTAILS. VER-EE NICE.

EZA LAD, ENEE, THE BISHOP? DUNNO WHERE HE GETS THE ENERGY FROM.

OH, THE LORD PROVIDES, THERE MAY BE NO PEACE FOR THE WICKED...

...BUT THE RIGHTEOUS CAN GET A PIECE WHENEVER THEY FEEL LIKE IT.

Chapter Seven
VIRTUE VICTORIOUS

INSIDE:

OF COURSE, "HATE THE SIN, LOVE THE SINNER" I ALWAYS SAY. HA HA HA HA!

HA.

NOW, IF WE TAKE THAT DOCTRINE ONE STAGE FURTHER, WE...

UH, LOOK, DO YOU MIND IF I OPEN A WINDOW?

A WINDOW?

UH... IT'S JUST SUCH A NICE NIGHT WITH THE WIND AND EVERYTHING...

I LIKE TO HEAR THE WIND. I THINK IT'S... UH... EXCITING. KNOW WHAT I MEAN?

EXCITING. BUT OF COURSE. EXCITING.

I LIKE THAT. A WILD AND PRIMAL IMPULSE. WE SHOULD NEVER IGNORE OUR PRIMAL IMPULSES...

"DON'T YOU AGREE?"

"THOSE RICH AND MYSTERIOUS FORCES THAT STIR IN THE SHADOWY DEPTHS OF THE HUMAN SOUL...

"THOSE INEXPRESSIBLE LONGINGS...

"WHEN THEIR MOMENT IS COME THEY SHALL NOT BE DENIED."

"DEAR GOD...

"THOU WHO HAS GRANTED US REPRIEVE FROM THY FINAL JUDGMENT, THOU WHO HAS PROVIDED US WITH THAT MOST TERRIBLE WARNING...

"HELP US TO BE WORTHY OF THY MERCY, AS WE WERE WHEN THOU DIDST TURN ASIDE THY WRATH...

"THAT WRATH WHICH DID RAIN FIRE FROM THE HEAVENS.

"HELP US TO RESIST THE TEMPTATIONS OF THE EVIL ONE...

"WHO IS SURELY COME AMONGST US IN THIS, THE HOUR OF OUR GREATEST TRIAL.

"FOR I HAVE SEEN A VISION...

"A VISION OF DARK AND SATANIC EVIL THAT COMETH FORTH FROM THE NIGHT TO ENSNARE THE WEAK AND THE SINFUL...

"AN AVATAR OF DAMNATION, WHO WILL SEEK TO SULLY THY TRUTH WITH HIS VAIN LIES AND SHALLOW SOPHISTICATIONS.

"OH GOD, THOU WHO KNOWEST ALL THAT WE DO...

"THOU WHO ART OUR FATE AND OUR FINAL DESTINY...

HELP US TO CLEARLY PERCEIVE THY WILL.

"HELP US TO PERCEIVE THE WILES OF THE EVIL ONE AND STAND FIRM IN THEE. ONE RACE, ONE NATION, UNITED IN THY LOVE.

"THIS WE ASK IN THE NAME OF THE FATHER...

"AND OF THE SON...

"AND OF THE HOLY GHOST."

AMEN.

TAKE YOUR DRESS OFF, PLEASE.

WHAT??

BUT, LOOK, UH, I WAS...

OH NEVER MIND. ALLOW ME TO...

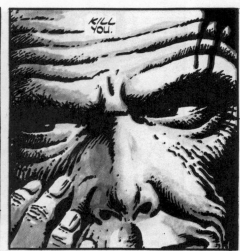

THE EAR. DECEMBER 20TH, 1997.

WELL?

WELL WHAT?

WHAT DO YOU MEAN, "WELL WHAT"?

OH, BLOODY STROLL ON...

SWITCH IT OFF, NORM, FOR CHRIST'S SAKE. IT'S DOIN' MY HEAD IN.

WHAT?

SLOW? IT'S ROLLED OVER AND DIED, MATE. WHAT IS IT, EH? IS THE ART OF CONVERSATION ON THE WAY OUT OR SOMETHING?

SLOW NIGHT.

"WHAT?" "WHAT WHAT?" GIMME A BREAK.

I MEAN, WHAT IS IT WITH PEOPLE? WHY DON'T PEOPLE HAVE IT OFF ON A SUNDAY NIGHT ANYMORE?

WELL, IN MY CASE IT'S BECAUSE I WORK NIGHT-SHIFTS WITH PILLOCKS LIKE YOU.

SHALL I TRY AND GET THE BISHOP?

OH YEAH. IT'S SUNDAY, ISN'T IT? "CHILDREN'S HOUR." I'D FORGOTTEN IN ALL THE EXCITEMENT.

YEAH. TUNE HER IN AND LET'S SEE WHAT THE FILTHY OLD DEVIANT'S UP TO THIS WEEK.

HANG ON...

...WAS LIKE HELL. MEN BURNING... CHOKING IN THE YELLOW FOG...

THAT'S HIS GRACE. GOT A LOT OF MUSIC ON IN THE BACKGROUND.

...AND I SAW A BLACK SHAPE AGAINST THE FLAMES, A MAN, OH GOD, WHO ARE YOU? WHO ARE YOU REALLY?

I AM THE DEVIL, AND I COME TO DO THE DEVIL'S WORK.

THAT'S A MAN'S VOICE.

YOU'VE GOT TOO MUCH ECHO ON IT.

NO... NO, IT'S TUNED IN EXACT.

I DO NOT HAVE A NAME.

LISTEN.

YOU CAN CALL ME V.

THE LORD IS MY SHEPHERD: THEREFORE I CAN LACK NOTHING: HE SHALL FEED ME IN GREEN PASTURE AND LEAD ME FORTH BESIDE THE WATERS OF COMFORT.

PHONE BUNNY ETHERIDGE. GET HIM OUT OF BED AND WHATSIZNAME AT THE FINGER. ALMOND.

AND ERIC FINCH.

HE SHALL CONVERT MY SOUL AND BRING ME FORTH IN THE PATHS OF RIGHTEOUS-NESS, FOR HIS NAME'S SAKE.

YEA, THOUGH I WALK THROUGH THE VALLEY OF THE SHADOW OF DEATH, I WILL FEAR NO EVIL.

BLOODY HELL.

OH BLOODY HELL.

Chapter Eight
**THE VALLEY**

WESTMINSTER ABBEY. LATER.

WHO IS IT, DOMINIC?

WHO IS IT, OUT THERE?

THE EAR. DECEMBER 21ST, 1997.

HOW'S IT GOING, BRIAN? ANY LUCK?

WELL, UH, ERIC ... WE'VE GOT A PROBLEM. BACK-GROUND MUSIC.

WE CAN ELIMINATE IT FROM THE, UH, MIX IN MOST PLACES, BUT NOT EVERY-WHERE. SO BITS OF THE, UH, CONVERSATION WILL BE LOST...

I THINK THAT, UH, CODENAME V MUST HAVE INTENDED THAT TO BE THE CASE...

THAT'S BEETHOVEN'S FIFTH...

DA DA DA DUM!

HEH. HEH. THAT'S MORSE CODE, Y'KNOW.

UH, MORSE CODE?

HMM. IT'S MORSE CODE FOR THE LETTER "V".

HEH.

WESTMINSTER ABBEY. THAT AFTERNOON.

SO HE SURPRISED THE BISHOP ABOUT HERE... THE BISHOP CAME THROUGH THE DOOR AND RAN SMACK INTO HIM.

WE DON'T HEAR THE GIRL WHO THE BISHOP WAS WITH AFTER THAT POINT SO I THINK IT'S SAFE TO ASSUME SHE WAS AN ACCOMPLICE AND SHE SCARPERED...

LITTLE GIRLS. HONESTLY, THAT'S... WE FOUND THESE MAGAZINES...

YEAH. JUST LET ME THINK A MINUTE, DOMINIC... NOW, BEFORE THE GIRL VANISHED SHE MUST HAVE REMOVED ONE OF THE LIGHT FUSES, PLUNGING THE APARTMENT INTO DARKNESS.

WE KNOW THAT BECAUSE THE CLOCK-RADIO WAS ON THE SAME CIRCUIT AND IT STOPPED AT THIRTEEN MINUTES PAST FIVE.

HE PUSHES THE BISHOP THROUGH INTO THIS ROOM.

THEN HE PUTS A RECORD ON.

THE STEREO IS ON A DIFFERENT CIRCUIT TO THE LIGHTS.

IT'S DARK. HE PUTS THE RECORD ON IN THE DARK.

AND THEN HE SAYS SOMETHING TO THE BISHOP... SOMETHING WE CAN'T HEAR BECAUSE OF THE MUSIC.

NEXT TIME WE HEAR THE BISHOP, IT'S THIS BIT:

"...FIVE, OF COURSE. IT WAS YOU ON THAT NIGHT. MY GOD, I STILL DREAM ABOUT IT. I HAVEN'T STOPPED DREAMING ABOUT IT IN FOUR YEARS.

" IT WAS LIKE HELL. MEN BURNING... CHOKING IN THE YELLOW FOG. AND A BLACK SHAPE AGAINST THE FLAMES. A MAN.

" OH GOD, WHO ARE YOU? WHO ARE YOU REALLY?"

"I AM THE DEVIL, AND I COME TO DO THE DEVIL'S WORK.

" I DO NOT HAVE A NAME. YOU CAN C– "

THAT'S A QUOTE. THAT BIT ABOUT THE DEVIL'S WORK.

FAMOUS MURDER CASE. NEARLY TWENTY YEARS AGO NOW. BEFORE YOUR TIME, I EXPECT.

THEN CODENAME V READS OUT THE TWENTY-THIRD PSALM.

I'LL FAST FORWARD UNTIL WE GET TO THAT BIT WHERE...

RIGHT. SHOULD BE ABOUT THERE...

... OF THE SHADOW OF DEATH, I WILL FEAR NO EVIL .

ALRIGHT, CHUMMY. ALRIGHT. HOLD IT RIGHT THERE...

THIS IS THE BIT WHERE THE VALET, DENNIS, COMES IN. LISTEN. THE STEREO SUDDENLY SHUTS OFF.

"YOUR GRACE? ARE YOU ALRIGHT?"

"HE HASN'T HURT ME. BE CAREFUL, DENNIS. HE'S..."

REMEMBER, DOMINIC. DENNIS HAS GOT A GUN. THIS IS IN THE DARK, BY THE DOOR.

"ALRIGHT, ALRIGHT. I'M GOING TO COUNT TO FIVE. I WANT YOU TO STEP OVER BY THE WINDOW WITH YOUR HANDS ON YOUR HEAD."

"ONE... TWO..."

HE NEVER GOT PAST TWO.

ALL IN DEAD SILENCE : IN THE DARK.

AND THEN THE MUSIC COMES BACK ON. WE DON'T HEAR ANY MORE FROM DENNIS.

THEY'RE TALKING ON THIS BIT, BUT THE MUSIC NEAR ENOUGH WIPES IT OUT. TALKING ABOUT RELIGION.

THERE'S SOMETHING THAT SOUNDS LIKE "KILL ME SENTIMENT"... JUST GIBBERISH... AND THEN THEY TALK ABOUT COMMUNION AND THE COMMUNION WAFER...

THERE'S THE WORD "TRANSUB-STANTIATION": THAT'S THE MIRACLE OF TRANSUBSTAN-TIATION WHEN THE WAFER TRANSFORMS INTO THE BODY OF CHRIST. CATHOLIC CONCEPT ORIGINALLY.

THERE. NOW LISTEN TO THIS...

"... AND AT THE MOMENT THIS ENTERS YOUR MOUTH IT BECOMES THE FLESH OF THE SAVIOUR?"

"YES. YES. LOOK, PLEASE..."

"AND WHATEVER IT IS MADE OF NOW IT WILL BECOME THE BODY OF CHRIST?"

"YES. WHATEVER IT IS NOW. WHATEVER."

I WANT YOU TO SWALLOW IT.

AND THEN THERE'S A FUNNY LITTLE NOISE. HUMAN NOISE.

AND THEN THERE'S JUST BEETHOVEN'S FIFTH.

END OF TAPE.

WE'VE JUST HAD THE PATH REPORTS THROUGH. THE BISHOP WAS POISONED. THE HOST WAS FULL OF CYANIDE.

AND DO YOU KNOW WHAT?

WHEN IT REACHED HIS ABDOMEN IT WAS STILL CYANIDE.

THE NOSE, NEW SCOTLAND YARD. DECEMBER 23RD, 1997.

THERE...

THE WOUND'S BEEN CLEANED UP A LITTLE, ERIC, BUT YOU CAN SEE THAT IT HAS A FAIRLY RAGGED EDGE.

SO YOU'RE RIGHT, IT ISN'T A KNIFE WOUND. IT LOOKS LIKE SOMETHING'S BEEN PUNCHED THROUGH THE SKIN WITH INCREDIBLE FORCE.

HMM.

AHH, WELL. THANKS FOR THE HELP, DELIA. ME AND THE LAD ARE SITTING UP WITH THIS CASE TONIGHT. YOU'VE GIVEN US SOMETHING ELSE TO CHEW OVER.

SOUNDS LIKE YOU'VE ALREADY BITTEN OFF ENOUGH TO RUIN YOUR CHRISTMAS. DIDN'T DOMINIC TELL ME THAT YOU WERE GOING TO CONSULT FATE?

MM. THE LEADER'S AUTHORIZED AN EXTENSION LINK FOR ME. THINGS MUST BE DESPERATE. HE'S USUALLY FUNNY ABOUT OTHER PEOPLE USING FATE...

OOH, DELIA... BEFORE I FORGET...

CAN YOU TELL US ANYTHING ABOUT THIS? WE FOUND TWO OF THEM... ONE IN THE CARRIAGE WHEN HE GRABBED LEWIS PROTHERO...

THE OTHER IN THE BISHOP'S ROOM...

WHY... YES, YES OF COURSE. I'M KNOCKING OFF IN A FEW MINUTES, BUT...

PERHAPS I COULD TAKE IT HOME...

IT'S A VIOLET CARSON. I'D HEARD THAT STRAIN HAD DIED SINCE THE WAR. THOUGHT A BOTANIST MIGHT BE ABLE TO SHED SOME LIGHT ON IT...

'BYE.

MAGIC. SEE YOU TOMORROW THEN, DELIA. 'BYE.

THE SHADOW GALLERY.

IT'S WRONG, V.

# Chapter Nine
## VIOLENCE

V, IT'S ME AS WELL! I'M IN-VOLVED. YOU INVOLVED ME.

V
I DIDN'T KNOW YOU WERE GOING TO KILL HIM!

KILLING'S WRONG.

ISN'T IT?

WHY ARE YOU ASKING ME?

AND AS FOR ME INVOLVING YOU, I SEEM TO RE-MEMBER THAT YOU WERE THE ONE ANXIOUS TO MAKE A DEAL.

I DIDN'T KNOW THAT YOU WERE GOING TO...

YOU WERE THE ONE WHO...

OH CHRIST, V...

"THERE IS MORE BEHIND AND INSIDE V THAN ANY OF US HAD SUSPECTED. NOT WHO, BUT WHAT: WHAT IS SHE."

YOU'LL LEARN, EVEY...

YOU'LL LEARN.

KNIGHTSBRIDGE. MR. AND MRS. ALMOND.

DEREK?

I DON'T WANT TO TALK ABOUT IT, ROSEMARY...

DEREK...

LEAVE IT.

DEREK, I WON'T!

DEREK, WE CAN'T JUST CARRY ON AND NOT TALK ABOUT IT...

YOU DON'T TALK TO ME, YOU DON'T EAT WITH ME, YOU DON'T HAVE SEX WITH...

NOW YOU LISTEN! I DON'T HAVE TO TAKE ANY OF THIS CRAP FROM YOU! NOT ANY OF IT!

I HAVE THAT FAT BASTARD RIDING ME ALL DAY ABOUT THIS TERRORIST CASE, I HAVE...

AH UH

AH UH

ROSEMARY, WILL YOU SHUT UP!

IF WE DON'T SLEEP TOGETHER LIKE WE USED TO IT'S NOTHING TO DO WITH ME.

MAYBE IF YOU TOOK THE TIME TO MAKE YOUR-SELF MORE ATTRACTIVE...

OH, GET OUT OF MY SIGHT.

I'LL BE UP LATER.

I'M CLEANING MY GUN.

THE SHADOW GALLERY.

V...

I'M SORRY. I WAS TRYING TO GET OUT OF TAKING THE BLAME.

I'M SORRY ABOUT THAT. BUT I WON'T DO ANY MORE KILLING, V...

NOT EVEN FOR YOU.

NOT EVER AGAIN.

PLAISTOW. 9.17 P.M.

THE SHADOW GALLERY.

"LET'S DIG AN *ENORMOUS CASTLE!*" CRIED MOON-FACE. "THEN WE CAN ALL SIT ON THE TOP OF IT WHEN THE SEA COMES IN."

"WE CAN'T," SAID SILKY, SUDDENLY LOOKING SAD. "WHY NOT? WHY NOT?" CRIED JO IN SURPRISE. "ISN'T THIS *THE LAND OF DO-AS-YOU-PLEASE?*"

"YES," SAID SILKY. "BUT IT'S TIME WE WENT BACK TO THE FARAWAY TREE. THIS LAND WILL SOON BE MOVING ON-- AND NICE AS IT IS, WE DON'T WANT TO LIVE HERE FOREVER."

"GRACIOUS NO," SAID JO. "OUR MOTHER AND FATHER COULDN'T POSSIBLY DO WITHOUT US..."

THE NOSE.

...SO SAY THAT AGAIN, DOMINIC. YOU RAN A CHECK ON ALLOCATIONS OF ROOM NUMBERS AND...

...AND IT WAS THE RESETTLEMENT CAMPS. THEY WERE THE ONLY PLACES THAT NUMBERED ROOMS WITH ROMAN NUMERALS.

YOU SEE, YOU SAID THAT IT WAS THE "V" THING THAT WAS THE KEY TO IT ALL, AND LEWIS PROTHERO KEPT TALKING ABOUT "ROOM FIVE" AND IN ROMAN NUMERALS FIVE IS V, AND...

ER.. WELL, I MEAN, IT'S ONLY A SORT OF THEORY. I DON'T SUPPOSE IT MEANS ANYTHING...

IT'S BRILLIANT, DOMINIC. BRILLIANT...

NOW, LET'S FOLLOW THIS THROUGH ...LET'S SEE IF ANY OF THE TEN VICTIMS WERE AT ANY OF THE CAMPS... JUST A SEC. ... THERE!

REC/BLK SIZE 80/720

RESTRICTED DATA
ACCESS CODE A

CODE <382/99>

LILLIMAN, REV. ANTHONY JAMES

LARKHILL RESETTLEMENT CAMP
1992-1993.

LARKHILL R2

CI CODE <382/116>

PROTHERO, LEWIS

LILLIMAN?

THE BISHOP, BY CHRIST, LAD. I THINK YOU'VE CRACKED IT. I SUPPOSE IT COULD BE COINCIDENCE BUT IT'S THE BEST LEAD WE'VE HAD UP TO YET.

AND PROTHERO WAS AT LARKHILL TOO.

THERE MUST HAVE BEEN DOZENS OF MEN WORKING AT THAT CAMP. WE CAN INTERVIEW THEM AND SEE WHAT ELSE COMES UP. FATE CAN GIVE US A LIST OF NAMES. HANG ON...

PACK/FATE 2 ON DSK      REC/BLK SIZE 5   80 / 720

RESTRICTED DATA

ACCESS CODES <1.5>

FILE  CODE <382/006>
BLAND, ADRIAN STEVEN
COWLEY, PAUL PETER
CROSS, DUNCAN
GREAVES, JOHN ANTHONY
GOSLING, JOHN LIONEL
IRONS, RICHARD

DECEASED 8.11.94  FILE CLOSED
DECEASED 24.3.94  FILE CLOSED
DECEASED 18.5.95  FILE CLOSED
DECEASED 23.12.93 FILE CLOSED
DECEASED 14.7.96  FILE CLOSED
DECEASED 23.12.96 FILE CLOSED

K/FATE 3 ON DSK        REC/BLK  SIZE 5  80/ 720

DECEASED 15.2.95  FILE CLOSED
DECEASED 23.12.93 FILE CLOSED
INNES, RAYMOND PAUL
JONES, MICHAEL OLIVER           DECEASED 20.12.97 FILE CURRENTLY
LILLIMAN, REV. ANTHONY JAMES    DECEASED 14.9/FILE CLOSED
MALPAS, KENNETH DAVID

OH HELL...

DECEASED...DECEASED... DECEASED. THEY'RE DEAD, DOMINIC, ALL DEAD.

PLAISTOW.

ROSES

IT'S YOU, ISN'T IT? YOU'VE COME...

YOU'VE COME TO KILL ME.

YES.

OH THANK GOD.

THANK GOD.

DECEMBER 23rd, 1997. KNIGHTSBRIDGE. MR. AND MRS. ALMOND...

DEREK? WHAT...

DEREK?

DEREK, DON'T...

BANG.

DON'T WORRY, ROSE.

I DIDN'T LOAD IT.

NOT TONIGHT.

## Chapter Ten
### VENOM

THE NOSE. NEW SCOTLAND YARD. MR FINCH AND DOMINIC...

QUINN, ANDREW EAMON. DECEASED 23.12.93. FILE CLOSED. ROUSE, WILLIAM. DECEASED 18.7.97. FILE CLOSED. RAPPITT, PETER KEVIN. DECEASED 5.11.94...

...FILE CLOSED. HE'S KILLED THEM, DOMINIC, EVERYONE WHO EVER WORKED AT LARKHILL CAMP ONE BY ONE, OVER THE PAST FOUR YEARS...

HE'S KILLED THE BLOODY LOT OF 'EM.

BUT YOU DON'T KNOW THAT, SIR. SOME OF THEM COULD BE ACCIDENTAL DEATHS... NATURAL DEATHS...

OR SOMETHING THAT LOOKS VERY MUCH *LIKE* NATURAL DEATH. FOR CHRIST'S SAKE, DOMINIC, *LOOK* AT IT! WE HAD IT ALL WRONG.

WE THOUGHT HE APPEARED OUT OF THE BLUE TWO MONTHS AGO.

...AND ALL THIS TIME... OH GOD, ALL THOSE PEOPLE. THAT'S MONSTROUS. THAT'S PURE BLOODY EVIL.

THIS IS A LIST OF ALL THE MEN AT LARKHILL. WERE THERE ANY WOMEN?

I DON'T KNOW. CHECK IT WITH FATE.

HE WAS AT LARKHILL. HE MUST HAVE BEEN. AND NOW EVERYBODY WHO COULD HAVE TOLD US ANY— THING...

OH CHRIST, MR. FINCH. LOOK AT THIS...

DELIA, I WAS TALKING TO HER A COUPLE OF HOURS AGO. I GAVE HER THAT ROSE TO LOOK AT...

REC/BLK SIZE S 80/ 120

PACK/V1 ON DSK

BEGIN:

✳✳✳✳✳✳✳✳✳✳✳✳✳✳✳✳✳✳
✳✳✳ RESTRICTED ACCESS : CODE 002
✳✳✳✳✳✳✳✳✳✳✳✳✳✳✳✳✳✳

C666: SURRIDGE, DR. DELIA ANNE...LARKHILL RESETTLEMENT CAMP (1992-1993)

667: CURRENT EMPLOYMENT........PATHOLOGIST

668: (SEE DEPT. OF INVESTIGATIONS AA/1855/9272)

END

PHONE HER, DOMINIC. AND THEN PHONE ALMOND.

I'M TRYING. THE DOCTOR'S LINE'S ENGAGED...

ALL RIGHT. PHONE ALMOND ANYWAY. CODENAME Y'S MADE HIS FIRST AND LAST COCK UP. HE COULDN'T KNOW THAT YOU'D CRACK THE LARKHILL CONNEC- TION BEFORE HE GOT TO DELIA...

THIS TIME WE'LL BE WAITING FOR HIM.

PLAISTOW, DR. DELIA SURRIDGE...

ARE YOU AFRAID?

NO. NO. I THOUGHT I WOULD BE. BUT I'M NOT. I'M... RELIEVED. OH GOD, ALL THESE YEARS, ALL THIS WAITING...

YOU SEE, I ALWAYS KNEW YOU'D COME BACK...

WHEN I SAW YOU THAT NIGHT... THE NIGHT YOU ESCAPED. YOU WERE STANDING AGAINST THE FLAMES. YOU TURNED AND YOU LOOKED STRAIGHT AT ME.

I KNEW THEN THAT ONE DAY YOU'D COME LOOKING FOR ME, THAT YOU'D FIND ME.

WHAT... WHAT WE DID, WHAT I DID AT LARKHILL... THAT TERRIBLE KNOWLEDGE. IT'S BEEN WITH ME FOR SO LONG, THAT I COULD DO THINGS LIKE THAT.

I HEARD OF AN EXPERIMENT ONCE, ONE THE AMERICANS DID. THEY HAD VOLUNTEERS WORKING A SHOCK GENERATOR. THE VOLUNTEERS WERE TOLD THAT IT WAS WIRED TO A PATIENT IN AN ADJOINING ROOM...

IT WASN'T THERE WAS ONLY AN ACTOR, WHOSE VOICE COULD BE HEARD THROUGH THE INTERCOM. THE VOLUNTEERS WERE INSTRUCTED BY A DOCTOR TO START ADMINISTERING ELECTRIC SHOCKS.

THEY WERE TOLD TO GRADUALLY INCREASE THE VOLTAGE. THE "VICTIM" BEGAN BEGGING THEM TO STOP. THEY WERE TOLD TO INCREASE IT AGAIN. THIS TIME THE VICTIM STARTED SCREAMING.

AFTER A WHILE THE SCREAMS WERE CHOKED OFF TO BE REPLACED BY SILENCE. THE VOLUNTEERS WERE TOLD TO INCREASE THE VOLTAGE ONCE MORE...

NEARLY 80% OF THOSE TESTED CARRIED ON ADMINISTERING SHOCKS AFTER THE "VICTIM" BEGGED THEM TO STOP. NEARLY 60% CONTINUED EVEN AFTER THEY BELIEVED THAT THEY'D KILLED HIM.

THEY WERE ORDINARY PEOPLE, AND THEY WERE PREPARED TO TORTURE A STRANGER TO DEATH, JUST BECAUSE THEY WERE TOLD TO BY SOMEONE IN AUTHORITY.

SOME OF THEM SAID THEY'D EVEN ENJOYED IT. I THINK I ENJOYED WHAT I DID AT THE TIME. PEOPLE ARE STUPID AND EVIL. THERE'S SOMETHING WRONG WITH US...

WE DESERVE TO BE CULLED.

WE DESERVE IT...

SOME HIDEOUS FLAW...

KNIGHTSBRIDGE. HELLO? YES, ALMOND SPEAKING.

YEAH.

YOU HAVE? HOW DID YOU?

WAIT A MINUTE. YOU'RE TALKING ABOUT DELIA SURRIDGE? THE DOCTOR?

BUT WHAT'S SHE GOT TO DO WITH ...NO.

NO, ALL RIGHT. LATER. YEAH.

YEAH, I KNOW THE ADDRESS. IN PLAISTOW.

YEAH, PHONE THROUGH DOWNSTAIRS AND ASK THEM TO SEND A SQUAD OVER CHOP-CHOP.

YEAH, I'M ALREADY ON MY WAY. YEAH. 'BYE.

IT'S FUNNY.

I WAS GIVEN ONE OF YOUR ROSES TODAY. ERIC FINCH GAVE IT TO ME. HE'S WITH THE NOSE, THE INVESTIGATION DEPARTMENT. HE'S AFTER YOU.

I WASN'T SURE THAT YOU WERE THE TERRORIST, NOT UNTIL I SAW THE ROSE. WHAT A STRANGE COINCIDENCE, THAT I SHOULD BE GIVEN IT TODAY...

THERE IS NO COINCIDENCE, DELIA. ONLY THE ILLUSION OF COINCIDENCE.

I HAVE ANOTHER ROSE...

THEN... YOU ARE GOING TO KILL ME.

IT'S FOR YOU.

THEN... YOU ARE GOING TO KILL ME.

I KILLED YOU TEN MINUTES AGO, WHILE YOU WERE ASLEEP.

IS THERE ANY PAIN?

NO. NO PAIN.

GOOD. THAT'S GOOD.

PLEASE?... CAN I...

CAN I SEE YOUR FACE AGAIN?

IT'S BEAUTIFUL...

DON'T MOVE AN INCH, YOU BLOODY BASTARD.

YOU DIDN'T HEAR ME ARRIVE, DID YOU? DIDN'T KNOW WE'D RUMBLED YOU...

IT'S ALL FINISHED, CHUMMY, ALL OF IT.

THE OLD MAN TOLD ME IT WAS MY HEAD OR YOURS... AND WHAT DO YOU KNOW? IT'S YOURS!

BECAUSE YOU'RE STANDING OVER THERE WITH YOUR BLOODY FANCY KNIVES AND YOUR BLOODY FANCY KARATE GIMMICKS...

AND I'VE GOT A GUN.

CHRISTMAS EVE, 1997. 12·04 A.M.

MR FINCH... ER... SOMEBODY'S GONE TO TELL MRS. ALMOND, AND, UH...

SIR, IS THERE ANYTHING...

I'LL SEE HIM DEAD FOR THIS, DOMINIC.

SHE WAS A GOOD WOMAN. SHE WORKED ALL HOURS AS A DOCTOR BEFORE SHE STARTED IN PATHOLOGY. SHE CARED ABOUT PEOPLE.

I'VE SEEN HER TREATING LITTLE KIDS WHO...

BY CHRIST, DOMINIC, I'LL SEE HIM DEAD FOR THIS.

WE FOUND THIS ON THE BUREAU TABLE, SIR. IT'S DR. SURRIDGE'S DIARY. IT COVERS HER YEARS AT LARKHILL. IT MIGHT CONTAIN THE WHOLE STORY...

I'M SICK OF STORIES, DOMINIC. I'M SICK OF FACTS AND DATES AND DEAD BODIES. I'M TOO OLD.

I'M TOO TIRED.

IT'S A VENDETTA, LEADER.

Chapter Eleven
THE VORTEX

DECEMBER 24TH, 1997, 10:58 P.M.
MR. FINCH REPORTS:

AT AROUND TEN O'CLOCK LAST NIGHT, CODENAME "V" ENTERED THE HOME OF PATHOLOGIST DR. DELIA SURRIDGE AND INJECTED HER WITH AN AS-YET-UNIDENTIFIED POISON. DR. SURRIDGE IS DEAD.

IT IS POSSIBLE THAT HE INJECTED HER WHILE SHE SLEPT. THERE WAS NO SIGN OF A STRUGGLE.

BEFORE HE COULD LEAVE THE PREMISES, CODENAME "V" WAS SURPRISED BY THE ARRIVAL OF MR. ALMOND. MR. ALMOND WAS ARMED WITH A REVOLVER.

APPARENTLY HE HAD FORGOTTEN TO LOAD IT. CODENAME "V" STRUCK MR. ALMOND WITH AN EDGED IMPLEMENT. PROBABLY A KNIFE.

MR. ALMOND IS ALSO DEAD.

MR. ALMOND WAS VISITING THE DOCTOR TO WARN HER THAT MY DEPARTMENT HAD ESTABLISHED A LINK BETWEEN THE ABDUCTION OF LEWIS PROTHERO AND THE KILLING OF BISHOP LILLIMAN.

BOTH OF THEM HAD BEEN EMPLOYED AT LARKHILL RESETTLEMENT CAMP DURING 1992 AND '93. SO HAD DR. SURRIDGE. WE TRIED TO WARN HER.

WE WERE TOO LATE.

AFTERWARDS, HOWEVER, WE DID FIND THE DOCTOR'S DIARY. IT'S A FIVE-YEAR DIARY AND IT DEALS PARTICULARLY WITH HER TIME AT LARK-HILL. SINCE THIS MORNING I'VE READ IT SEVEN TIMES.

...AND I STILL DON'T KNOW WHO CODENAME "V" IS.

...BUT I THINK I KNOW WHAT HE IS.

I'VE TAKEN KEY EXCERPTS FROM THE DIARY, BALANCED THEM AGAINST MY OWN FINDINGS AND PLACED THEM IN ORDER. THE STORY THAT EMERGES IS, FRANKLY, INCREDIBLE...

IT BEGINS ON APRIL 30TH, 1993. I'LL READ IT TO YOU.

"I ARRIVED AT LARKHILL THIS MORNING. MY DRIVER WAS A MAN NAMED GOSLING. HE DIDN'T SAY A WORD TO ME ALL THE WAY FROM ANDOVER.

"GOD, THIS PLACE IS MISERABLE.

"I MET COMMANDER PROTHERO, WHO I'M AFRAID I FIND RATHER VULGAR AND UNPLEASANT. HE PROMISED TO SHOW ME MY RESEARCH STOCK ONCE I'D SETTLED IN, AND DID SO THIS AFTERNOON.

"THEY'RE A POOR BUNCH. PROTHERO TELLS ME THAT THEIR HABITS ARE FILTHY. NONE OF THEM WILL BE ANY USE TO ME IF I DON'T GET TO WORK ON THEM SOON.

"MAY 17TH: ALMOST FINISHED THE FINAL DRAFT OF THE SCHEDULES FOR MY PROJECT. VERY EXCITED ABOUT IT SO FAR.

"HORMONE RESEARCH IS ALMOST USELESS WHEN RATS OR RABBITS ARE USED, AND THIS IS A HEAVEN-SENT OPPORTUNITY TO LEARN SOMETHING POSITIVE. I START NEXT WEEK, ALL BEING WELL.

"MAY 23RD: PROTHERO HAS PICKED THE SUBJECTS... FOUR DOZEN OF THEM. AND I'VE GOT TO INSPECT THEM THIS AFTERNOON. THEY'RE SO WEAK AND PATHETIC YOU FIND YOURSELF HATING THEM.

"THEY DON'T FIGHT OR STRUGGLE AGAINST DEATH. THEY JUST STARE AT YOU WITH WEAK EYES. THEY MAKE ME WANT TO BE SICK, PHYS-ICALLY. THEY'RE HARDLY HUMAN.

"JUNE 5TH: WELL, WE DID IT. ALL FOUR DOZEN OF THEM GOT A SHOT OF BATCH 5, WHICH IS THE PITUARIN / PINEARIN MIX-TURE. IT'S TOO EARLY FOR ANY RESULTS YET, REALLY.

"THAT CREEPY PADRE, TONY LILLIMAN, INSISTED ON BEING THERE WHILE IT WAS DONE TO LEND SPIRITUAL SUPPORT. HE RUBS HIS HANDS TOGETHER AND STARES AT MY CHEST. I HATE HIM.

"JUNE THE NINTH.

"OF THE ORIGINAL FOUR DOZEN, OVER SEVENTY-FIVE PERCENT ARE DEAD NOW.

"OUT OF THE TEN THAT ARE LEFT, I DOUBT THAT THREE WILL SURVIVE THE NIGHT. ONE OF THE BLACKS, DONALD CRANE, IS IN PARTICULARLY BAD CONDITION.

"HE IS DELIRIOUS ALL THE TIME, AND IMAGINES HE IS IN TRENCHTOWN, JAMAICA. HE HAS STARTED TO DEVELOP FOUR EXTRA NIPPLES, AND HIS GEN-ERATIVE ORGANS HAVE ATROPHIED.

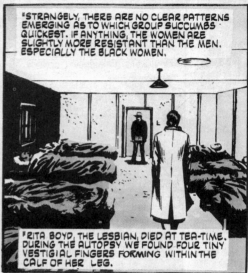

"STRANGELY, THERE ARE NO CLEAR PATTERNS EMERGING AS TO WHICH GROUP SUCCUMBS QUICKEST. IF ANYTHING, THE WOMEN ARE SLIGHTLY MORE RESISTANT THAN THE MEN. ESPECIALLY THE BLACK WOMEN.

"RITA BOYD, THE LESBIAN, DIED AT TEA-TIME. DURING THE AUTOPSY WE FOUND FOUR TINY VESTIGIAL FINGERS FORMING WITHIN THE CALF OF HER LEG.

"JUNE 18TH: ONLY FIVE LEFT NOW. TWO MEN AND THREE WOMEN, WHICH TENDS TO CONTRADICT MY ENTRY OF THE 9TH OF JUNE. WE'VE HOUSED THEM IN INDIVIDUAL CUBICLES AT THE MEDICAL BLOCK.

"THE MAN IN ROOM 5 IS A REALLY FASCINATING CASE.

"PHYSICALLY, THERE DOESN'T SEEM TO BE ANYTHING WRONG WITH HIM. NO CELLULAR ANOMALIES, NOTHING.

"BUT HE'S QUITE INSANE. BATCH 5 SEEMS TO HAVE BROUGHT ON SOME KIND OF PSYCHOTIC BREAKDOWN.

"STRANGELY, HE'S DEVELOPED ONE OF THOSE CURIOUS SIDE EFFECTS WHICH SEEM TO AFFLICT CERTAIN CATEGORIES OF SCHIZOPHRENIC:

"HIS PERSONALITY HAS BECOME TOTALLY MAGNETIC. HE SAYS VERY LITTLE... BUT THERE'S SOMETHING ABOUT THE WAY HE LOOKS AT YOU,

"HE LOOKED AT ME TODAY AS IF I WERE SOME SORT OF INSECT. HE LOOKED AT ME AS IF HE FELT SORRY FOR ME.

"HIS FACE IS VERY UGLY. I'VE BEEN THINKING ABOUT IT ALL EVENING.

"I THINK HIS BEHAVIOR PATTERNS ARE WHAT INTEREST ME. THEY'RE UTTERLY IRRATIONAL, BUT THEY SEEM TO HAVE A CERTAIN DERANGED LOGIC UNDERSCORING THEM.

"I'M WORRIED THAT SOMEONE IN THE PARTY MIGHT TRY A CLOSURE ORDER ON THE PROJECT BEFORE I HAVE A CHANCE TO SEE HOW IT DEVELOPS. PROTHERO SAID AS MUCH THIS MORNING. WE'LL SEE.

"JULY 12TH: PATEL, THE ASIAN IN CUBICLE THREE, DIED TODAY. HIS LIVER HAD CEASED FUNCTIONING. HAVEN'T HAD A CHANCE TO OPEN HIM UP AND FIND OUT WHY.

"I'VE BEEN SPENDING A LOT OF TIME STUDYING ROOM 5 AGAIN, I'M AFRAID.

"I'M GLAD WE LET HIM HAVE A GO AT THE GARDENING PROJECT. PROTHERO WAS RELUCTANT AT FIRST. I SUPPOSE IT'S BECAUSE WITH THE FOOD SHORTAGE, THESE PLACES HAVE TO BE SELF-SUPPORTING.

"HE'S DELIGHTED NOW, THE FAT TOAD. ROOM FIVE'S TURNED OUT TO BE A GENIUS AT GARDENING.

"HE'S SORTED OUT THE WHITEFLY AND IT LOOKS LIKE BEING A GOOD YIELD.

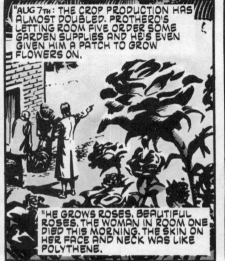

"AUG 7TH : THE CROP PRODUCTION HAS ALMOST DOUBLED. PROTHERO'S LETTING ROOM FIVE ORDER SOME GARDEN SUPPLIES AND HE'S EVEN GIVEN HIM A PATCH TO GROW FLOWERS ON.

"HE GROWS ROSES. BEAUTIFUL ROSES. THE WOMAN IN ROOM ONE DIED THIS MORNING. THE SKIN ON HER FACE AND NECK WAS LIKE POLYTHENE.

"SEPTEMBER 18TH. GARDEN DOESN'T REQUIRE MUCH WORK THIS TIME OF YEAR. ROOM FIVE WANTS TO HELP WITH THE DECORATING IN THE STAFF QUARTERS.

"PROTHERO WILL TAKE SOME PERSUADING. HE'S STILL A LITTLE DISTURBED BY WHAT FIVE DID WITH THE AMMONIA-BASED FERTILISER THAT HE ORDERED.

"IT'S ARRANGED IN PILES AROUND HIS CELL. IT MAKES A KIND OF GEOMETRIC SHAPE. HE SITS MOTIONLESS FOR HOURS IN THE CENTRE OF IT. THE AMMONIA STENCH IS TERRIBLE.

" SEPTEMBER 29TH : PROTHERO ON MY BACK ABOUT FIVE'S GREASE SOLVENT. HE ORDERS FOURTEEN GALLONS OF IT AND THEN SWIPES HALF TO DECORATE HIS CELL. PROTHERO PICKS HIS NOSE.

"THE PATTERNS OF SOLVENT AND FERTILISER ON THE FLOOR OF FIVE'S CUBICLE ARE BECOMING SO INTRICATE. I'VE GOT TO FOLLOW THIS OBSESSION TO THE END. IT MIGHT BE A NEW SYNDROME.

" NOV. 5TH : HIS CUBICLE IS COVERED WITH SO MUCH JUNK. THE AMMONIA SMELLS TERRIBLE AND THERE IS A SORT OF SWIMMING POOL SMELL TOO. LORD KNOWS WHERE THAT COMES FROM.

"I'M SURE THAT IN HIS MIND ALL THIS MAKES PERFECT SENSE. I'M SURE OF IT."

THE NEXT ENTRY I WANT TO READ WAS MADE ON DECEMBER 24TH, 1993, AND IT REFERS TO THE EVENTS OF THE PREVIOUS DAY.

IT STARTS WITH THE WORDS "HE LOOKED AT," WHICH ARE CROSSED OUT. THEN IT SAYS "NO, CAN'T WRITE ABOUT IT YET. CAN'T HOLD..." AND THEN ANOTHER GAP.

WHEN IT RESUMES, IT'S IN A DIFFERENT COLORED INK...

" I WAS IN THE MESS. IT WAS ABOUT HALF PAST TEN WHEN WE HEARD THE FIRST EXPLOSION.

" WE RAN TO THE DOOR TO SEE. LUCKILY, I WAS RIGHT AT THE BACK.

"THE ONES AT THE FRONT RAN STRAIGHT INTO THE GAS. IT WAS HORRIBLE.

" A FEW OF US WENT OUT THROUGH THE REAR DOOR TO AVOID THE GAS. YOU COULD HEAR PEOPLE SCREAMING EVERYWHERE.

"MEN SCREAMING. I HATE THAT. I HATE THE SOUND OF MEN SCREAMING.

"IN THE CENTRE OF THE CAMP, EVERYTHING WAS ON FIRE. WHILE WE WERE TRYING TO WORK OUT WHAT WAS GOING ON, THE OVENS EXPLODED.

"I RAN, BUT EVERYONE WAS RUNNING, AND ALL IN DIFFERENT DIRECTIONS. IT WAS HORRIBLE.

"IT WAS THE MAN IN ROOM FIVE, WHO HAD GOT OUT, WHO HAD GOT AWAY, HE BLEW IT UP, HE KILLED...

"I COULDN'T HAVE KNOWN... THE AMMONIA. THE GREASE SOLVENT AND ALL THE OTHER STUFF. HE'D BEEN MAKING THINGS WITH THEM.

"MUSTARD GAS...

"...AND NAPALM.

"AND IN THE YARD, I SAW HIM. HE HAD THE FLAMES BEHIND HIM. HE WAS NAKED...

"HE LOOKED AT ME.

"AS IF I WERE AN INSECT. OH GOD. AS IF I WERE SOMETHING MOUNTED ON A SLIDE.

"HE LOOKED AT ME.

"HE'S GONE. THE CAMP IS BEING CLOSED. NOBODY IS TALKING ABOUT IT. NOBODY KNOWS WHERE HE'S GONE."

THAT'S THE LAST ENTRY UNTIL SIX MONTHS LATER WHEN DR. SURRIDGE IS RESTED AND BACK IN LONDON.

END OF STORY.

EXCEPT THAT IT WASN'T, WAS IT? WHAT HAPPENED TO THE MAN IN ROOM FIVE? WHAT DID HE DO IN THE FOUR YEARS FOLLOWING HIS ESCAPE FROM LARKHILL?

"HOW DID HE BECOME CODE-NAME 'V'?"

"SOME OF THAT FOUR YEARS WAS PERHAPS SPENT IN LAYING THE ELABORATE GROUND-WORK FOR HIS CURRENT MANOEUVRES, MAYBE IN PREPARING A BASE OF OPERATIONS FOR HIMSELF...

"WE HAVE EVIDENCE THAT THIS IS NOT ALL HE DID, HOWEVER. STUNNING, HORRIFYING EVIDENCE.

"BETWEEN 1993 AND 1997, OVER FORTY PEOPLE WHO WERE PREVIOUSLY AT LARK-HILL MET WITH WHAT WERE BELIEVED TO BE ACCIDENT-AL DEATHS. EVENTUALLY, ONLY THREE REMAINED.

"THE THREE HE'D BEEN SAVING UNTIL LAST.

"HE ABDUCTED LEWIS PROTHERO, THE CAMP COMMANDER WHO HAD CHOSEN HIM TO RECEIVE BATCH 5, THE PREP-ARATION THAT HAD DESTROYED HIS MIND.

"PROTHERO IS NOW INCURABLY INSANE.

"HE VISITED BISHOP LILLIMAN AND MADE HIM SWALLOW A POISONED COMMUNION WAFER. THAT'S A DREADFUL, DEGRAD-ING WAY FOR A MAN LIKE THAT TO DIE.

"BUT YOU CAN SEE A SORT OF BLACK POETRY THERE, CAN'T YOU? A SORT OF GALLOWS HUMOUR? I DUNNO. PERHAPS YOU CAN'T.

"FINALLY, THERE IS DR. DELIA SURRIDGE, WHO CODENAME 'V' VISITED THIS MORNING, FOUR YEARS TO THE DAY AFTER ESCAP-ING LARKHILL. SHE WAS A GOOD WOMAN, A HUMANE WOMAN. BUT THEN I READ THIS DIARY AND...

"I DON'T KNOW. I DON'T KNOW. SHE'S DEAD NOW.

"HER, AND EVERYBODY ELSE WHO WORKED AT LARKHILL. HER AND EVERYBODY ELSE WHO COULD HAVE IDENTIFIED HIM.

"YOU SEE, THERE ARE *TWO* POSSIBLE MOTIVES HERE, NOT ONE.

"THE FIRST MOTIVE IS REVENGE. HE ESCAPES FROM LARKHILL AND VOWS TO GET EVEN WITH HIS TORMENTORS. THE PARLIAMENT BOMBING AND THE OTHER STUFF IS JUST A SMOKESCREEN.

"THE WHOLE EXERCISE WAS AN ELABORATE, CHILLING VENDETTA.

"THAT'S THE EXPLANATION THAT I FIND MOST REASSURING, FUNNILY ENOUGH.

"BECAUSE THAT MEANS HE'S FINISHED NOW. THAT MEANS IT'S OVER.

"THE SECOND MOTIVE IS MORE SINISTER. LIKE I SAID, EVERYONE WHO COULD HAVE IDENTIFIED HIM IS NOW DEAD.

"WHAT IF HE'S JUST BEEN CLEARING THE GROUND?

"WHAT IF HE'S PLANNING SOMETHING ELSE?

"YOU SEE, THIS DIARY THAT WE FOUND... IT WAS IN FULL VIEW ON THE DOCTOR'S WRITING BUREAU. WE DIDN'T HAVE TO SEARCH FOR IT.

"HE LEFT IT THERE, I'M SURE OF IT. HE WANTED US TO FIND IT. HE WANTED US TO KNOW THE STORY.

"BUT... AND HERE'S A FUNNY THING... HE DIDN'T WANT US TO KNOW *ALL* OF IT.

"WHEN WE FOUND THE DIARY, SOME OF THE PAGES HAD BEEN TORN OUT. IT WASN'T DR. SURRIDGE WHO DID THAT.

"WHAT WAS ON THE MISSING PAGES, EH? HIS NAME? HIS AGE? WHETHER HE WAS JEWISH, OR HOMOSEXUAL, OR BLACK OR WHITE?

"AND FURTHERMORE, IF HIS VENDETTA IS *REALLY* OVER...

"WHY DID HE CARE WHETHER WE KNEW OR NOT?

"HE'S PLAYING GAMES WITH US. HE'S PLAYING GAMES THAT ARE JUST AS ELABORATE AS THE DESIGN ON THE FLOOR OF ROOM FIVE, AS ELABORATE, AND AS MAD...

"...AND AS DEADLY."

YOU SEE, YOU DEAL WITH SOMETHING LIKE THIS... A SCHEME THAT'S AS INGENIOUS AS IT IS IRRATIONAL AND IT'S LIKE WALKING ON QUICK-SAND. YOU GET SLOWLY SUCKED INTO IT...

I MEAN, FATE DOESN'T HAVE ANY RECORDS OF WHAT HAPPENED AT LARKHILL. WE DIDN'T KEEP RECORDS OF WHAT WENT ON AT ANY OF THE CAMPS. I SUPPOSE WE WERE BEING CAUTIOUS.

BUT LOOK... FOR ALL WE KNOW, THIS DIARY COULD BE A COMPLETE AND UTTER FAKE. CODENAME "V" COULD HAVE WRITTEN IT HIMSELF.

HE MIGHT NEVER HAVE BEEN AT LARKHILL AT ALL, DO YOU SEE? IT COULD ALL BE ANOTHER SMOKE-SCREEN, A FALSE TRAIL, ANOTHER COVER STORY...

MR. FINCH, CAN YOU EXPECT ME TO BELIEVE THAT ANY-ONE WOULD KILL OVER FIFTY PEOPLE FOR NO OTHER REASON THAN TO PROVIDE HIMSELF WITH A COVER STORY?

THE VERY IDEA IS...

... MADNESS.

AH YES.

I SEE...

VERY WELL, I THINK THAT WILL BE ALL, MR. FINCH. ENGLAND PREVAILS.

OH, AND MR. FINCH?

LEADER?

HAPPY CHRISTMAS.

BOOK 2

THIS VICIOUS CABARET

Music © V Songs, 1983

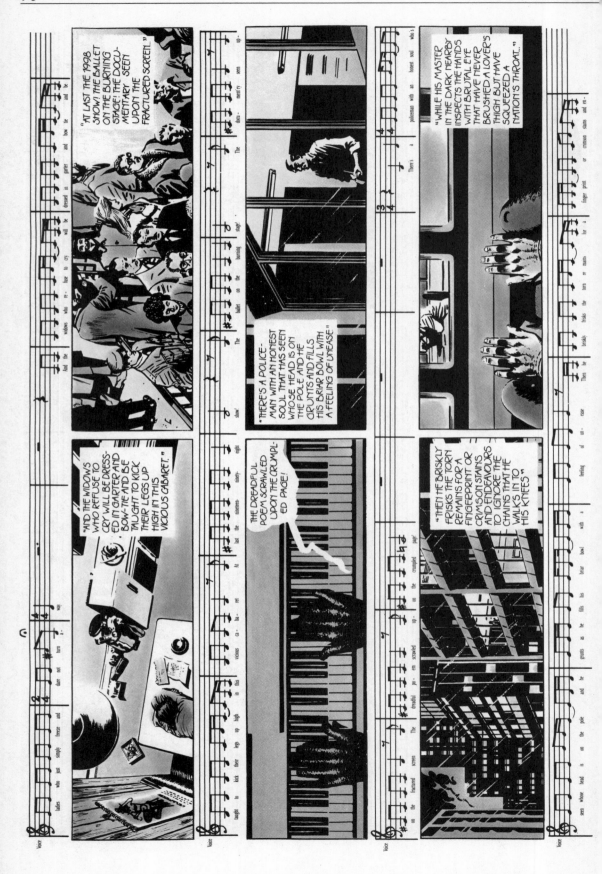

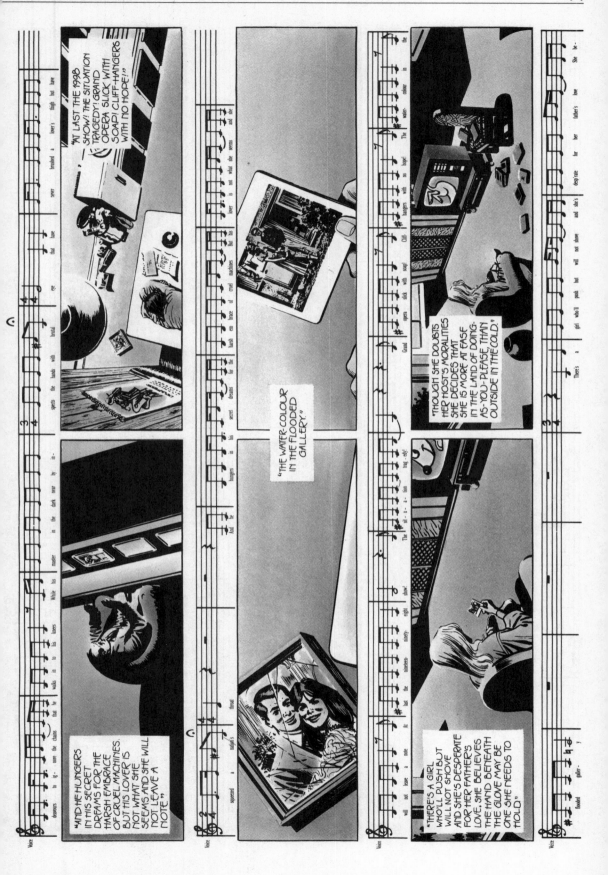

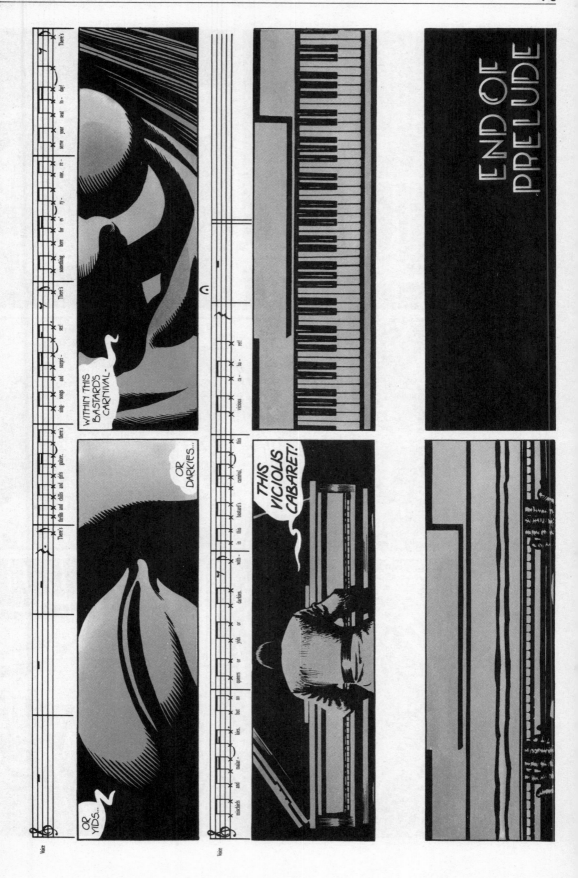

JANUARY 5TH, 1998. THE SHADOW GALLERY...

AS YOU SEE, MY HANDS ARE QUITE EMPTY...

CONCEALING NOTHING...

...NOR HAVE I ANYTHING UP MY SLEEVE.

AND YET, WITH THE MEREST FLICK OF MY WRIST...

THE RABBIT HAS GONE!

OH!

BRING HER BACK!

BRING HER BACK? BUT WHAT IF SHE IS CONTENT WHERE SHE IS? DO WE HAVE THE RIGHT TO DISTURB HER?

AHH... BUT I SEE YOU HAVE ALREADY MADE UP YOUR MIND. VERY WELL. WE REPLACE THE CLOTH... LIKE SO... AND WHEN NEXT WE WHISK IT AWAY...

YOU'VE NEVER... I MEAN, SINCE I'VE BEEN HERE YOU HAVEN'T...

WELL, WHAT I MEAN IS, IT'S NOT IMPORTANT, BUT, WELL, I JUST SORT OF THOUGHT THAT IT MIGHT BE THAT YOU, UH...

DON'T FANCY ME.

AT ALL.

UH...

I MEAN... NOT THAT YOU SHOULD OR ANYTHING. NOT THAT I WANT YOU TO.

I MEAN, WELL, THERE COULD BE LOTS OF REASONS... Y'KNOW, WHY YOU DON'T EVER, Y'KNOW, SLEEP WITH ME OR ANYTHING.

PERHAPS THERE WAS SOME-BODY ELSE. I'D UNDERSTAND IF THERE WAS.

OR... UH... PERHAPS YOU DON'T SORT OF FANCY WOMEN. BUT, LIKE, THERE'S NOTHING WRONG WITH THAT.

OR PERHAPS...

...OR PERHAPS I'M YOUR FATHER?

HOW DID YOU KNOW THAT I THOUGHT...

V? V, ARE YOU?

COME WITH ME, EVEY.

I HAVE A SURPRISE FOR YOU...

YOU'LL HAVE TO WEAR THIS, I'M AFRAID. DON'T WORRY...

...IT'S PART OF THE SURPRISE.

THIS WAY...

V... WHERE ARE WE GOING? IT FEELS COLDER...

HUSH, EVEY. AND LISTEN...

LISTEN TO WHAT?

IT'S JUST THAT I KEEP THINKING I SHOULD TRY TO HELP YOU, THE WAY YOU'RE HELPING ME, THAT'S THE DEAL, ISN'T IT?

NO DEALS, EVEY. NOT UNLESS YOU WANT THEM.

THAT'S ME.

THAT'S WHAT I SAID TO YOU WHEN...

V? WHERE ARE WE?

CAN WE MAKE A DEAL?

YES, I THINK WE CAN MAKE A DEAL.

V, THIS IS CREEPY. I DON'T LIKE IT.

I WON'T DO ANY MORE KILLING, V...

NOT EVEN FOR YOU. NOT EVER AGAIN.

I'VE HAD ENOUGH OF THIS. THIS IS STUPID AND I'M COLD. I'M TAKING...

OH.

V... WHERE ARE WE? WHAT IF SOMEONE SEES US...

Y, I DON'T LIKE THIS. LET'S GO BACK INSIDE.

"WE CAN'T..."

...SAID SILKY, SUDDENLY LOOKING SAD. "WHY NOT? WHY NOT?" CRIED JO IN SURPRISE. "ISN'T THIS THE LAND OF DO-AS-YOU-PLEASE?"

"YES," SAID SILKY. "BUT IT'S TIME WE WENT BACK TO THE FARAWAY TREE. THIS LAND WILL SOON BE MOVING ON, AND NICE AS IT IS, WE DON'T WANT TO LIVE HERE FOREVER."

Y...

"GRACIOUS NO." SAID JO. "OUR MOTHERS AND FATHERS COULDN'T POSSIBLY DO WITHOUT US."

Y, STOP IT!

I'M NOT YOUR FATHER, EVEY.

YOUR FATHER IS DEAD.

V, THIS ISN'T FUNNY. THIS IS HORRIBLE!

I WANT YOU TO TAKE ME HOME.

I WANT...

V?

YOU'VE GONE, DEREK. I NEVER LIKED YOU. I WAS AFRAID OF YOU. I LOVED YOU.

YOU'VE GONE BEYOND THE VEIL...

ME TOO.

## CHAPTER 2
### THE VEIL

THEY WERE ALL THERE, AT THE FUNERAL. THEY DIDN'T LIKE YOU EITHER, DID THEY? I NEVER REALISED THAT BEFORE.

HELEN HEYER BARELY SPOKE TO ME. SHE LOOKED AFRAID, AS IF BEREAVEMENT WAS CATCHING.

ROGER DASCOMBE WAS THERE. HE ASKED HOW I WAS COPING WITH THE BILLS.

HE WAS VERY FRIENDLY TOWARDS ME.

WHEN I LEFT HE SHOOK MY HAND AND TOLD ME TO RING HIM IF I NEEDED ANYTHING.

SMILED, JUST BRIEFLY, AS HE SAID IT.

HELD MY HAND TOO LONG.

IT WAS AN OFFER, DEREK, AND YES, HE MAKES ME SICK, AND YES, I HATE HIM...

...BUT WHEN YOU'RE A WIDOW, THE WORLD LOOKS DIFFERENT. YOU STEP THROUGH A CURTAIN AND YOU'RE IN A PLACE WHERE PEOPLE TREAT YOU DIFFERENTLY. A BLEAK PLACE. YOU'RE GONE, DEREK...

AND I'M ALONE.

...AND DEREK, WHERE I AM, IT'S COLD AND IT'S DARK AND IT'S FRIGHTENING.

AND THIS WORLD IS SO DANGEROUS.

YOU'RE NAKED IN THE RAIN. EVERYTHING'S BEEN TAKEN AWAY... ALL THE SECURITY AND THE WARMTH AND THE SHELTER...

...AND YOU'LL TRY ANY REFUGE.

ANX REFUGE AT ALL

YOU SEE, YOU'RE LOST. ALL THE WORLD YOU UNDERSTOOD HAS GONE AND EVERYWHERE LOOKS SINISTER AND DIFFERENT.

YOU'RE FUMBLING IN THE DARK...

...AND THEN YOU MAKE CONTACT. CONTACT OF A SORT.

...AND IT MIGHT NOT BE PLEASANT, AND YOU MIGHT BE REPULSED AND DRAW BACK FROM IT. NO, NOT THAT, ANYTHING BUT *THAT*...

...BUT REALLY, WHERE ELSE CAN YOU GO? WHAT OTHER CHOICES DO YOU HAVE?

EXCEPT CARRYING ON. DOWN INTO THE DARK.

ALONE.

COMPLETELY AND UTTERLY ALONE.

DASCOMBE RANG EARLIER. HE SUGGESTED A MEAL AND A DRINK, TO CHEER ME UP.

I SAID NO. HE SAID TO RING HIM IF I CHANGED MY MIND.

THEY WON'T GIVE ME STATE SUPPORT, DEREK. AND I CAN'T GET A JOB. NO EXPERIENCE, YOU SEE. I HAD A HOME TO LOOK AFTER...

THERE'S THE MORTGAGE. AND THE ELECTRICITY. AND THE PHONE.

I THOUGHT ABOUT YOU, DEREK. ABOUT HAVING SEX AND NOT HAVING SEX AND THE FIGHTING AND THE DRINK AND I REALLY DID LOVE YOU.

YOU WERE MY LIFELINE. I WAS STUCK AT HOME. YOU CONNECTED ME TO THE WORLD, AND I'M STILL CLUTCHING AT YOU, EVEN THOUGH YOU'RE BROKEN AND I'M ADRIFT...

AND THE SAME PICTURES PLAY OVER AND OVER.

AND I'M IN THE BACK ROW, WATCHING THEM...

...IN THE GRUBBY, BROKEN CINEMA OF MEMORY.

I'LL GO BACK INTO THE CORNERS OF THE PAST, EVEN THE SHADOWY, SORDID CORNERS...

JUST BECAUSE *YOU* WERE THERE THEN.

I'M TRYING TO HANG ON. HANG ON TO SOMETHING EVEN THOUGH I KNOW IT'S GONE. EVEN THOUGH I KNOW YOU AREN'T THERE ANYMORE.

YOU.

Award Nomination Best Film 1986

the salt flats

it's about letting go...

ERIE PAGE
ATTO
AW

THE LOVED ONE.

YOU'RE GONE.

NOTHING WILL CHANGE THAT.

ALL I CAN DO IS PACK AWAY ALL THE THINGS I REMEMBER, PUT THEM IN A DRAWER WITH ALL OTHER USELESS SOUVENIRS...

AND JUST CARRY ON.

YOU'VE GOT TO CARRY ON.

WE'VE ALL GOT TO JUST CARRY ON. THAT'S HOW WE SURVIVE.

THAT'S OUR PURPOSE.

LEROY!! LOOK OUT! DE WHITE DEBIL GOT HIM A LASER-LUGER!!

DIE, YOU BLACK CANNIBAL FILTH!

DIE! DIE! DIE!

CHAPTER 3
VIDEO

...AND YOU CAN VISIT THE NIGHTMARISH FUTURE ENGLAND OF STORM SAXON AGAIN AT FIVE PAST EIGHT NEXT TUESDAY ON N.T.V. ONE.

...BUT RIGHT NOW IT'S TROUBLE FOR SID AND BRENDA WHEN A NEIGHBOUR ACCUSES THEM OF FOOD HOARDING.

THAT'S "YOU HAVE TO LAUGH," COMING NEXT HERE ON ONE.

...IN ABERDEEN OVER THE LAST THREE YEARS, TWO HUNDRED AND THIRTY PEOPLE HAVE LOST THEIR LIVES IN VIOLENT INCIDENTS PROPAGATED BY THE S.N.A.

IN GLASGOW, THE FIGURE IS EVEN HIGHER. TONIGHT ON TWO, INTERFACE LOOKS AT THE FACTS BEHIND THIS SENSELESS TERRORIST VIOLENCE...

I WAS IN IRELAND. THIS IS WORSE. MUCH, MUCH WORSE...

BRENDA, ARE THESE YOUR KNOCKERS?

...KIDS OF TEN WITH GRENADES...

MY WHAT?

THE WOMEN, THEY SPIT AT YOU...

YOUR KNOCKERS! YOUR DOOR-KNOCKERS, THE BRASS ONES YOUR MOTHER GAVE YOU!

...SPRING LOADED WITH SPIKES, IN A CAR BOOT...

OO-ER! I WONDERED WHAT YOU MEANT!

...IRN BRU BOTTLE FULLA PETROL, BIT O' RAG...

HAHAHAHA HAHAHAHA HAHAHA

HERE IN EASTER-HOUSE, WELL, VIOLENCE IS ON ITS WAY UP...

SID, MR GLOVER AT THE MUNITIONS PLANT WANTS ME TO WORK *LATE* WITH HIM TOMORROW, TO CATCH UP ON MY *QUOTA*...

HE SAYS I'VE GOT A LITTLE *BEHIND!*

HAHAHAHA HAHAHAHA HAHAHAHA!

I MEAN, MY MATE...

STANDING BESIDE THIS OLD SARACEN HE WAS, SEE...

GOT A BULLET RIGHT IN 'IS EYE...

YOU WHAT?

ANYWAY, IF I SHOW HIM I'M WILLING TO GET *STUCK IN*, I THINK HE MIGHT TRY ME IN A MORE AD-VANCED POSITION!

PROMOTION, SID! I THINK. HE'S GOT 'IS *EYE* ON ME!

ONLY THE OTHER DAY HE SAID I HAD *BIG* THINGS IN FRONT OF ME!

YES, I *BET* 'E DID!

HAHAHA HAHAHAHA HAHAHAHA!

...M-16 S, PUNGEE STICKS, WHITE PHOSPHORUS, FRAG-BOMBS WITH PLASTIC SPLINTERS THAT DON'T SHOW UP UNDER X-RAY...

HAHAHA HAHAHAHA HAHAHAHA!

HAHAHA HAHAHAHA HAHA!

IT ISN'T A PRETTY PICTURE, IS IT? HOW-EVER, SLOWLY AND SURELY, THE S.N.A. ARE BEING DRIVEN FURTHER NORTH...

...AND HOPEFULLY, BY THE TARGET DATE OF THE YEAR 2000, THE UNITED KING-DOM WILL STAND ONCE MORE UNITED.

WELL, NEXT WEEK INTERFACE LOOKS AT SOME SATELLITE PICTURES OF THE SOVIET WHEAT-CROP FAILURE, AND ASKS: IS RUSSIA FACING ANOTHER REVOLUTION?

...UNTIL THEN, GOOD-NIGHT.

HE AIR

OOH, SID! GEROFF!

WHAT IF SOME-BODY COMES IN?

FIRE !

I MEAN, WE'RE SUPPOSED TO BE ON THE JOB...

THAT'S JUST WHAT I SAY!

SID.!!

HAHAHAHA HAHAHAHA HAHAHAHA HAHAHA!

...AND NOW ON TWO IT'S TIME FOR A CHANGE OF PACE...

AS WE GO OVER TO DOCK GREEN FOR ANOTHER EPISODE OF THE CLASSIC POLICE SERIES STARRING JACK WARNER.

EVENIN', ALL.

CRIME. IT'S AN UGLY WORD, EVEN HERE IN DOCK GREEN...

...AND ESPECIALLY WHEN IT INVOLVES INNOCENT PEOPLE LIKE YOU OR I.

TONIGHT I'M GOING TO TELL YOU THE STORY OF HARRY BISHOP, WHO FOUND OUT JUST HOW UGLY CRIME CAN BE...

...THE HARD WAY!

IT ALL BEGAN WITH SOMETHING MY SON-IN-LAW, ANDY, SAID TO ME OVER DINNER...

GET 'EM OFF!

I BEG YOUR PARDON, MR. GLOVER?

YOUR SHOPPING BAGS! GET 'EM OFF MY DESK!

GEORGE, I'M WORRIED ABOUT LAUDER-DALE...

OLD LORDY? WHY? WHAT'S THE MATTER, ANDY?

I DUNNO, GEORGE ...HE'S, WELL... DIFFERENT.

OH DEAR, MR. GLOVER!! NOW MY MELONS ARE FALLING OUT!

FEBRUARY 23RD, 1998: PEAK TIME.

I SUPPOSE YOU'RE WONDERING WHY I'VE CALLED YOU HERE THIS EVENING.

WELL, YOU SEE, I'M NOT ENTIRELY SATISFIED WITH YOUR PERFORMANCE LATELY... I'M AFRAID YOUR WORK'S BEEN SLIPPING, AND...

...AND, WELL, I'M AFRAID WE'VE BEEN THINKING ABOUT LETTING YOU GO.

OH, I KNOW, I KNOW. YOU'VE BEEN WITH THE COMPANY A LONG TIME NOW. ALMOST... LET ME SEE. ALMOST TEN THOUSAND YEARS! MY WORD, DOESN'T TIME FLY?

IT SEEMS LIKE ONLY YESTERDAY...

I REMEMBER THE DAY YOU COMMENCED YOUR EMPLOYMENT, SWINGING DOWN FROM THE TREES, FRESH-FACED AND NERVOUS, A BONE CLASPED IN YOUR BRISTLING FIST...

"WHERE DO I START, SIR?" YOU ASKED, PLAINTIVELY.

I RECALL MY EXACT WORDS: "THERE'S A PILE OF DINOSAUR EGGS OVER THERE, YOUNG-STER," I SAID, SMILING PATERNALLY THE WHILE.

"GET SUCKING."

CHAPTER 4
A VOCATIONAL VIEWPOINT

NTV
NBS.

DIVERSION →

WELL, WE'VE CERTAINLY COME A LONG WAY SINCE *THEN*, HAVEN'T WE? AND YES, YES, YOU'RE RIGHT, IN ALL THAT TIME YOU HAVEN'T MISSED A DAY.

WELL DONE, THOU GOOD AND FAITHFUL SERVANT.

ALSO, PLEASE DON'T THINK I'VE FORGOTTEN ABOUT YOUR OUTSTANDING SERVICE RECORD, OR ABOUT ALL OF THE INVALUABLE CONTRIBUTIONS THAT YOU'VE MADE TO THE COMPANY...

FIRE, THE WHEE AGRICULTURE... IT AN IMPRESSIVE LIST OLD-TIMER. A JOLLY IMPRESSIVE LIST DON'T GET ME WRON

BUT...WELL, TO BE FRANK, WE'VE HAD OUR PROBLEMS, TOO. THERE'S NO GETTING AWAY FROM IT.

DO YOU KNOW WHAT I THINK A LOT OF IT STEMS FROM? I'LL TELL YOU...

IT'S YOUR BASIC UNWILLINGNESS TO GET ON WITHIN THE COMPANY. YOU DON'T SEEM TO WANT TO FACE UP TO ANY REAL RESPONSIBILITY, OR TO BE YOUR OWN BOSS.

LORD KNOWS, YOU'V BEEN GIVEN PLENT OF OPPORTUNITIES.

WE'VE OFFERED YOU PROMOTION TIME AND TIME AGAIN, AND EACH TIME YOU'VE TURNED US DOWN.

"I COULDN'T HANDLE THE WORK, GUV'NOR," YOU WHEEDLED. "I KNOW MY PLACE!"

TO BE FRANK, YOU'RE NOT TRYING, ARE YOU?

YOU SEE, YOU'VE BEEN STANDING STILL FOR FAR TOO LONG, AND IT'S STARTING TO SHOW IN YOUR WORK...

AND, I MIGHT ADD, IN YOUR GENERAL STANDARD OF BEHAVIOUR.

THE CONSTANT BICKERING ON THE FACTORY FLOOR HAS NOT ESCAPED MY ATTENTION...

...NOR THE RECENT BOUTS OF ROWDINESS IN THE STAFF CANTEEN.

THEN OF COURSE THERE'S...

HMM. WELL, I DIDN'T REALLY WANT TO HAVE TO BRING THIS UP, BUT...

WELL, YOU SEE, I'VE BEEN HEARING SOME DISTURBING RUMOURS ABOUT YOUR PERSONAL LIFE.

NO, NEVER YOU MIND WHO TOLD ME. NO NAMES, NO PACK DRILL...

I UNDERSTAND THAT YOU ARE UNABLE TO GET ON WITH YOUR SPOUSE. I HEAR THAT YOU ARGUE. I AM TOLD THAT YOU SHOUT. VIOLENCE HAS BEEN MENTIONED.

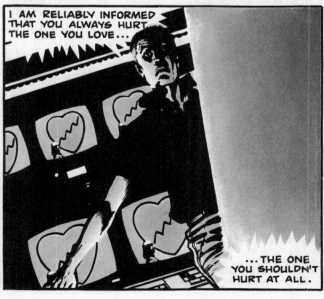

I AM RELIABLY INFORMED THAT YOU ALWAYS HURT THE ONE YOU LOVE...

...THE ONE YOU SHOULDN'T HURT AT ALL.

AND WHAT ABOUT THE CHILDREN? IT'S ALWAYS THE CHILDREN WHO SUFFER, AS YOU'RE WELL AWARE.

POOR LITTLE MITES. WHAT ARE THEY TO MAKE OF IT?

WHAT ARE THEY TO MAKE OF YOUR BULLYING, YOUR DESPAIR, YOUR COWARDICE AND ALL YOUR FONDLY NURTURED BIGOTRIES?

REALLY, IT'S NOT GOOD ENOUGH, IS IT?

AND IT'S NO GOOD BLAMING THE DROP IN WORK STANDARDS UPON BAD MANAGEMENT, EITHER...

..THOUGH, TO BE SURE, THE MANAGEMENT IS VERY BAD.

IN FACT, LET US NOT MINCE WORDS.. THE MANAGEMENT IS TERRIBLE!

WE'VE HAD A STRING OF EMBEZZLERS, FRAUDS, LIARS AND LUNATICS MAKING A STRING OF CATASTROPHIC DECISIONS.

THIS IS PLAIN FACT.

BUT WHO ELECTED THEM?

IT WAS *YOU! YOU* WHO APPOINTED THESE PEOPLE! *YOU* WHO GAVE THEM THE POWER TO MAKE YOUR DECISIONS FOR YOU!

WHILE I'LL ADMIT THAT ANYONE CAN MAKE A MISTAKE ONCE, TO GO ON MAKING THE SAME LETHAL ERRORS CENTURY AFTER CENTURY SEEMS TO ME NOTHING SHORT OF DELIBERATE.

YOU HAVE *ENCOURAGED* THESE MALICIOUS INCOMPETENTS, WHO HAVE MADE YOUR WORKING LIFE A SHAMBLES.

YOU HAVE ACCEPTED WITHOUT QUESTION THEIR SENSELESS ORDERS.

YOU HAVE ALLOWED THEM TO FILL YOUR WORKSPACE WITH DANGEROUS AND UNPROVEN MACHINES.

YOU COULD HAVE *STOPPED* THEM.

ALL YOU HAD TO SAY WAS, "*NO*."

YOU HAVE NO SPINE. YOU HAVE NO PRIDE.

YOU ARE NO LONGER AN ASSET TO THE COMPANY.

I WILL, HOWEVER, BE GENEROUS.

YOU WILL BE GRANTED TWO YEARS TO SHOW ME SOME IMPROVEMENT IN YOUR WORK. IF AT THE END OF THAT TIME YOU ARE STILL UNWILLING TO MAKE A GO OF IT...

YOU'RE FIRED.

THAT WILL BE ALL. YOU MAY RETURN TO YOUR LABOURS.

NORMAL SERVICE WILL BE RESUMED AS SOON AS POSSIBLE.

CHAPTER 5
THE VACATION

WHY THE BLOODY HELL DID I HIT HIM?

IT WASN'T HIS FAULT. HE'D ONLY BEEN ON THE JOB FOR A WEEK...

MR. FINCH? CREEDY. PETER CREEDY, TAKING OVER FROM MR. ALMOND AT THE FINGER.

HE'S THROUGH HERE. WE'VE NOT TOUCHED HIM.

YOU HEARD WHAT HE DID? BLOODY INGENIOUS. BREAKS INTO JORDAN TOWER, HOLDS DASCOMBE AND HIS CREW AT DETONATOR POINT AND MAKES 'EM BROADCAST HIS VIDEO.

MADE DAS-COMBE SEAL OFF THE BUILDING WITH HIS DESK-CONSOLE.

HE KNEW THE TRANSMITTER WAS INSIDE THE TOWER, MUST'VE. WITH THE BUILD-ING SEALED OFF, HE KNEW WE COULDN'T GET IN AND PULL THE PLUG ON HIM STRAIGHT AWAY.

BLOODY INGENIOUS.

'COURSE, HE COULDN'T GET OUT, EITHER.

HE'D SENT EVERYONE OUT OF THE CONTROL ROOM JUST BEFORE WE GOT THERE. WHEN MY LADS BURST IN, HE WAS STANDING IN FRONT OF THE OBSERVATION WINDOW.

HE DIDN'T EVEN PUT UP A FIGHT. THEY JUST OPENED UP WITH THE SHOOTERS AND...

WHERE'S DASCOMBE?

SORRY?

DASCOMBE, WHERE IS HE?

WELL, I DUNNO...

HE MUST'VE WANDERED OFF SOMEWHERE, IN A DAZE, I EXPECT.

HE'D HAD A SHOCK.

YOU CAN SAY THAT AGAIN.

HOW LONG AGO DID THIS HAPPEN?

I... BUT...

TEN MINUTES, TEN OR FIFTEEN MINUTES.

THERE'S THE SLIMMEST CHANCE THAT HE'S STILL INSIDE THE BUILDING SOMEWHERE. SEARCH IT.

...AND THEN PERHAPS ONE OF YOUR WOODEN-TOPS COULD CALL ON MR. ALMOND'S WIDOW. SHE AND DASCOMBE HAD BEEN CLOSE LATELY.

ALRIGHT...

ALRIGHT, FINCH. NO NEED TO START ON MY LADS.

CHRIST, ANYONE CAN MAKE A MISTAKE.

NOT WITH HIM YOU CAN'T!

YOU MAKE A MISTAKE WITH HIM AND YOU'RE DEAD!

...YOU OR SOMEONE ELSE.

WHEN ARE YOU GOING TO STOP TREATING THIS BASTARD AS IF HE WAS HUMAN?

WHEN ARE YOU GOING TO LEARN? WHEN IS EVERYBODY GOING TO LEARN?

MR. FINCH...

IT'S ALRIGHT, LADDY. YOU LET HIM CARRY ON.

EVERYBODY KNOWS HE'S BEEN IN A STATE SINCE THAT DOCTOR HE WAS KIPPING WITH GOT BUMPED OFF.

WHY?

122

V FOR VENDETTA

WHY DID I HIT HIM?

THE LEADER WAS GOOD ABOUT IT, REALLY. I EXPECTED A LOT MORE OF A ROLLICKING THAN I GOT...

AND THEN SENDING ME HERE TO NORFOLK...

SENDING ME ON A HOLIDAY, FOR GOD'S SAKE. I MEAN, THERE'S NOTHING HERE SINCE THE '89 FLOOD, BUT...

A HOLIDAY. HE MUST BE WORRIED ABOUT ME.

I'M WORRIED ABOUT ME.

DOMINIC SOUNDED ALRIGHT ON THE PHONE LAST NIGHT. COPING WELL ENOUGH. TOOK ME AN HOUR TO GET THROUGH AND WE TALKED FOR FOUR MINUTES.

I WONDER IF IT WAS HIM WHO TOLD EVERYBODY ABOUT ME AND DELIA?

NO.

PROBABLY DELIA.

SHE SAID SHE HADN'T, BUT... WELL, SHE NEVER TOLD ME ABOUT WHAT SHE'D DONE AT LARKHILL.

WE ONLY DID IT THREE TIMES, ALL TOLD, ALL THOSE YEARS...

WE SHARED THAT BOTTLE OF SCOTCH SHE'D BOUGHT, OVER AT MY HOUSE.

AND I MADE US BACON AND EGGS.

AT FOUR IN THE MORNING.

OH. HELLO.

HELLO, GORD.

IT'S ALRIGHT. NOT STOPPING. JUST DROPPED BY TO SAY WE'D FOUND SOMEONE TO OFF-LOAD THE BOOZE ON.

BLOKE OVER IN PIMLICO.

MAGIC. TELL TERRY I'LL SEE HIM SATURDAY ABOUT THE MONEY.

YEAH, OKAY.

HOW'S THE LODGER, BY THE WAY? TERRY MENTIONED...

SHE'S ALRIGHT.

YOU'LL TELL TERRY SATURDAY, THEN?

NO PROBLEM. SEE YA, GORD.

WHO WAS THAT?

OLD LADY. ASKED IF I WANTED TO GIVE HER SOME MONEY FOR WAIFS AND STRAYS.

TOLD HER I'D ALREADY GOT ONE.

LIAR!

YOUR EGG'S DONE IF YOU'RE OUT OF THE BATH. IT'S GOT A STRINGY BIT IN...

THAT'S *YOUR* EGG. MINE'S THE ONE *WITHOUT* THE STRINGY BIT.

YOU SOUND HAPPIER THIS MORNING.

WHERE ARE YOU?

IN HERE.

THERE WERE HAIRS ALL ROUND THE BATH.

MAN'S GOT TO HAVE A HOBBY. MINE'S DROWNING KITTENS.

ARE YOU DECENT?

YEAH, COME IN.

THERE. YOU'RE CHEERING UP A BIT, THEN? GETTING OVER THAT BLOKE YOU WERE LIVING WITH...

YEAH, WELL, IT WAS NEVER REALLY WHAT YOU MIGHT CALL LIVING WITH HIM... IT WASN'T THAT SORT OF THING.

NO, AND NEITHER'S THIS. I'D BETTER GET BACK DOWNSTAIR' AND EAT MY STRINGY EGG BEFORE I'M OVERCOME BY YOUR VOLUPTUOUSNESS.

NO NEED TO BE SARKY JUST BECAUSE I GOT THE BEST EGG.

NO.

GLAD YOU'RE FEELING BETTER, ANYWAY. IT CAN MESS YOU UP WHEN SOME- BODY KICKS YOU OUT.

YEAH, WELL, NOT ANYMORE. TO TELL YOU THE TRUTH, GORDON...

...I DON'T EVEN THINK ABOUT HIM.

DAILY Mirror

'GUY FAWKES' VIDEO ERROR

INSIDE

MARCH 8TH, 1998:

I'M NOT POLITICALLY TICKLISH AND THEORY MAKES ME WEARY...

...AND AFFAIRS OF STATE AREN'T MY KIND OF AFFAIRS.

AND I'D NEVER BED, NOR MUCH LESS WED THE WAG WHOSE FLAG IS DEEPEST RED, MY TASTES RUN MORE TO LONDONDERRY AIRS...

BUT AT RALLIES IN THE NIGHT WITH ALL THE TORCHES BURNING BRIGHT I FEEL A STIRRING IN ME I CANNOT NEGLECT...

...AND I'LL GRASP WITH MAD ABANDON ANY LAD WITH AN ARMBAND ON AND WHOSE CUTE SALUTE IS MANLY AND ERECT!

I LIKE THE BOOTS (DADA DADA DADA DA) I LIKE THE AT-TI-TUDE, I LIKE THE POINT AT WHICH THE LEGAL MEETS THE LEWD.

I LIKE THE THRILL (DADAD DADA DADA DA ) OF THE TRIUMPHANT WILL...

...I LIKE THE MARCHING AND THE MUSIC AND THE MOOD!

CHAPTER 6

VARIETY

SO IF SOME BLONDE AND BLUE-EYED BOY WOULD CARE TO TEACH ME STRENGTH THROUGH JOY...

THE KITTY-KAT KELLER. FIRST, I WAS A BIT TOO SCARED TO ENJOY IT, NOW I'M A BIT TOO DRUNK.

...AND SEE THAT ALL MY LIBERAL TENDENCIES ARE CURED; IF IT SHOULD BE DECREED BY FATE THAT YOU INVADE MY NEIGHBOURING STATE...

STILL, IT WAS NICE OF GORDON TO BRING ME. I LIKE HIM.

THEN YOU WILL FIND MY FRONTIERS OPEN, REST ASSURED.

YOU WANT ANOTHER?

OH... YEAH, GO ON THEN.

HE KNOWS SOME INTERESTING PEOPLE. NOT VERY NICE, BUT INTERESTING...

I... LIKE... THE... BOOTS! (DADA DADA DADA DA)

THERE'S THAT "ROBERT" MAN, THE ONE WHO WAS UPSET ABOUT HIS MOTHER AND ASKED GORDON TO DO SOMETHING. BIG GANGSTER ON THE WAY OUT.

AND WHEN THEY "HEIL" I SMILE, AND LIQUEFY INSIDE...

OH, WAIT, SOMEONE'S GOING OVER...

ER... MRS. ALMOND, I'M SORRY, BUT THE COMPUTER SAYS THAT THIS ENTRY CARD IS OVERDRAWN... I'LL HAVE TO ASK...

...AND THAT PINCHED-LOOKING WOMAN, ROSE SOMETHING, NOBODY'LL SIT NEAR HER BECAUSE HER LAST TWO MEN GOT KILLED. SHE LOOKS LONELY...

I LIKE THEIR SKIN (DADA DADA DA) I LIKE THEIR DI-SCI-PLINE...

E'S TAKING HER
TSIDE NOW,
RHAPS TO AN-
HER CLUB. I'M
AD SHE'S GOT
MEBODY.

... AND THE ENORMOUS SENSE OF LICENCE IT PRO-VIDES!

THERE... GO STEADY. THAT'S YOUR FIFTH.

I'M ALRIGHT.

...ALRIGHT SINCE YOU TOOK ME IN, ANYWAY. CHRIST, I WAS SO LUCKY. IF ANYBODY ELSE HAD FOUND ME NICKING FOOD FROM THEIR DUSTBIN...

THANK YOU, ZOE! ZOE'LL BE BACK LATER...

YOU SURE? YOU LOOK FUNNY.

S I'M FINE, REALLY.
ST NOT USED TO
IS SORT OF PLACE.
HO'S THAT MAN
OVER THERE?

T NOW
HE MARTINETTES!

THAT'S CREEDY, BIG BOSS COPPER. NEW BLOKE, THE OLD ONE GOT KILLED. WHY?

YOUR FRIEND ROBERT'S TALK-ING TO HIM.

OH GOD, SO HE IS. LOOK, JUST IGNORE IT, EH? MIGHT GET NASTY...

NASTY?

SIX LOVELY GIRLS, GIVE 'EM A BIG HAND. NOT THERE, CORPORAL! HA HA HA!

AT DOES HE MEAN,
STY? I WISH HE
OULDN'T TREAT
E LIKE A KID...

MY WORD, IT'S ALL HAPPEN-ING HERE TONIGHT.

MR. CREEDY, PLEASE, ME AND MR. ALMOND HAD AN UNDER-STANDING ABOUT MY MOTHER. SHE WAS EXEMPT...

MR. ALMOND'S DEAD, ROBERT. THINGS ARE DIFFERENT NOW. YOU DON'T HAVE SPECIAL STATUS ANYMORE, AND YOUR MUM SHOULD HAVE BEEN IN A HOME A LONG TIME AGO.

HOMES? THEY'RE GAS CHAMBERS!

AND ONE... AND TWO...

NOT GAS, IF YOU WANT THE TRUTH, ROBERT, THERE'S JUST THREE GOOD SOUTH KEN BOYS WITH IRON BARS,

NOW GET OUT OF MY SIGHT, YOU MISERABLE OLD PANSY.

AREN'T THEY GORGEOUS?

DOESN'T LOOK NASTY...

PUB ROWS, SEE ONE, YOU'VE SEEN 'EM ALL, REALLY. URRR... WHAT ARE THEY DOING ON STAGE?

WHAT AN EXPERIENCE! HAHAHAHA!

OH, GORDON, THAT'S HORRIBLE!

YEAH, I'M SORRY. IT'S NOT AS STRONG AS THIS USUALLY. LET'S HAVE THIS DRINK AND THEN...

GO'DIE! HU-LO!

OH. EVENIN', ALLY.

S'GUID T'SEEYA, GO Y'NO BIN GETT ABOOT MUCH, EH

NO, NOT MUCH.

ALLY? GORDON MENTIONED... OH NO! IT'S THAT SCOTTISH BLOKE GORDON SAID ABOUT. HARPER.

ALRIGHT, THAT'S YOUR LOT! OFF THEY GO!

WHAT DID HE SAY? ALL THE TROUBLES AND BOMBINGS UP NORTH. ALL THE SCOTTISH GANGS ARE MOVING TO LONDON. MY MOUTH TASTES FUNNY...

MUS' BE BUSY, EH?

THE MARTINETTES.!!

EH, S'NOFALLY NICE BITTA RUMPY-PUMPY Y'GOT THERE, GO'DIE.

LEAVE IT OUT, ALLY. I'M NOT IN THE MOOD.

HE SAID THERE'D BEEN FRICTION AND... HERE, IS HE TALKING ABOUT ME?

AAW, SUIT YESELF... HEY! LUKE WHO ET ES...

OH NO.

RICHT... WHO'S FOR A SING SONG?

GORDON, GORDON LAD...

I'M FINISHED, BOYS. I'VE HAD IT. THEY'VE DONE ME MAM AND I'M NEXT...

HEY, BOB PESSAWP, W AM NO PARTIN TE DRINKING LEPERS

LOOK, ROBERT, I'M SORRY...

ON TWO, THR

JUNE 11TH, 1998.

CHAPTER 7
VISITORS

APRIL 15TH, 1998.

EVEY?

YEAH?

I, UH... WELL, YOU KNOW. I WANTED TO TALK TO YOU...

WHAT ABOUT? IS SOMETHING UP?

WELL, NO. WH I WAS GONNA SAY WAS...

WELL, YOU'VE BEEN HERE A FEW MONTHS NOW, UP IN THE FRONT BEDROOM...

THE THING IS, I'LL BE NEEDING THAT ROOM SOON. GOT SOME STUFF COMING.

YOU... YOU WANT ME TO GO.

GO?? JESUS CHRIST, NO! OF COURSE I DON'T WANT YOU TO GO!

BUT... WHERE AM I GOING TO SLEEP?

WELL... Y'KNOW

THERE'S MY ROOM...

ARE... ARE YOU SURE? I MEAN, I THOUGHT YOU LIKED IT, Y'KNOW, JUST BEING ON YOUR OWN.

WON'T I GET IN THE WAY?

'COURSE YOU WON'T.

I MEAN, I'D HAVE SAID SOMETHING BEFORE B'T...

WELL, I DIDN'T THINK YOU'D FANCY THE IDEA.

ELL... DO.

HA

I FEEL REALLY STUPID NOW.

WHY?

DON'T KNOW.

WILL YOU GIVE ME A KISS?

YEAH.

ALRIGHT.

JUNE 11TH, 1998:

EUEY...

GORDON? WHAT'S...?

VISITORS.

LOCK YOURSELF IN THE BATHROOM AND DON'T MAKE A PEEP.

BUT WHAT?

GO ON...

GO'DIE?

HULLOO?

A SAY, GO'DIE, LOOKS LIKE Y'GOT ME LOCKED OUT, NO?

A TELLYAWHAT... A CANNA HERT YEH NOW, EH? HOW'S ABOUT USYIN' TALKIN' FERRA WHILE?

MEBBE Y'RIGHT, GO'DIE, Y'KNOW?

MEBBE YU COULD HANLE THE BOOZE AN A'LL CONTENT MASEL WI' THE LITERATURE.

YOU'RE A GREEDY BASTARD, HARPER. YOU WANT EVERYTHING.

AND ANYWAY, WHO'S GONNA PUT KIPPER'S FACE BACK IN ORDER?

YE, WELL, CCIDENTS HAPPEN, GO'DIE.

ATELLYA WHAT... A CANNA HEAR YA S'GOOD. WHY-N'YA GIYASELF OVER BY THE DOOR?

P'RAPS E KEN WORK UT SOME COMPEN-TION FOR POOROL' KIPPER, EH?

IT'LL TAKE MORE THAN BASTARD COMPENSATION, YOU VICIOUS GET.

HE COULDN'T EVEN SEE!

AYE, WELL, JUST LISSEN T'MA OFFER, EH?

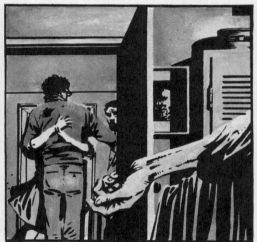

## CHAPTER 8
## VENGEANCE

EXCUSE ME...

I'M SORRY...

I'M SORRY IF I STARTLED YOU.

I WONDERED IF YOU KNEW WHERE THE STAGE DOOR WAS?

OAUHH!

STAGE?

I... I HAVE A JOB, I START TONIGHT...

I CAN'T FIND THE STAGE DOOR.

UH... NO.

NO, I DON'T KNOW WHERE IT IS, I'M SORRY. PERHAPS ROUND THE BACK...?

YOUR NAME'S ROSE, ISN'T IT?

YES, YES, THAT'S RIGHT.

UH, WELL, I'LL HAVE ANOTHER LOOK...

THANKS ANYWAY.

SORRY IF I STARTLED YOU.

THAT'S ALRIGHT.

EH, BOAB, Y' GETUM EN, EH?

EH, YIZZA TIGHT BASTUD, YU'RE...

EH, GO AN.

GISSA PINTA HEAVY ANNA BABYCHAM FUH YISELF, EH?

AW PESSAWF, WIYA?

WHASSAMATTER, BOAB? WEH CELEBRATIN'!

D'Y'NO FEEL LIKE CELEBRATIN' OR WHA?

SPIKKIN FUH MASEL', AM GETTUN STEAMIN'...

...SO WHOOSA ONE WITHUH BEG TETS? EZZAT CAROLE?

NAW, THAS JEM'S BERD, WHASSANAME, DIYAAN...

THE AIR AROUND ME IS COMPLETELY BLACK. I THINK THAT PERHAPS I'M BACKSTAGE AT THE THEATRE, DURING THE INTERVAL.

THERE ARE MUFFLED BUMPINGS NEARBY. STAGE-HANDS ARE REARRANGING THE SCENERY.

I SMELL ROSES, AND THINK ABOUT THE SCENTED BIRTHDAY CARDS MY MOTHER FOUND IN A SHOE BOX AT OUR HOUSE ON SHOOTER'S HILL.

THE PETALS FALL, PENCIL SHAVINGS OF CREAM FLESH.

EVERYTHING CHANGES.

## CHAPTER 9
## VICISSITUDE

IT'S MY BIRTHDAY. I'M STILL IN THE THEATRE, BUT I KNOW THAT IT'S REALLY OUR OLD HOUSE.

I CAN HEAR A PARTY IN THE ROOM UPSTAIRS.

I KNOW IT'S A BIRTHDAY PARTY FOR ME, BUT I HAVE A SINKING FEELING THAT IT WILL BE OVER BY THE TIME I GET THERE.

IT'S TAKING ME SO LONG TO GET READY.

I DON'T EVEN KNOW WHY I'M BOTHERING TO GET DRESSED UP LIKE THIS, BUT I FEEL AS IF IT'S EXPECTED OF ME.

I WISH I DIDN'T HAVE TO. I WANT TO GO TO THE PARTY NOW.

EVEY?

YOU'RE MISSING THE PARTY. WE'VE HIRED A PUNCH AND JUDY MAN SPECIALLY...

I'M GLAD DAD COULD COME. HAVEN'T SEEN HIM MUCH SINCE I STARTED WORK AT THE MATCH FACTORY.

HE LEADS ME UPSTAIRS TO THE PARTY, AND I WONDER IF THIS IS OUR OLD HOUSE AFTER ALL.

THE STAIRS REMIND ME OF SOMEWHERE ELSE, AND I FEEL SAD, BUT I DON'T KNOW WHY.

IT LOOKS LIKE I WILL GET TO THE PARTY AFTER ALL... BUT THEN DAD STEERS ME INTO ONE OF THE BEDROOMS.

HE WANTS TO SHOW ME THE SKY FROM THE WINDOW. HE SAYS IT'S YELLOW AND BLACK.

HE TELLS ME HE NEEDS MY OLD ROOM TO HIDE SOMETHING IN, BUT THAT I CAN SLEEP WITH HIM IN HERE FROM NOW ON,

THIS ROOM LOOKS FAMILIAR TOO, BUT I DON'T KNOW WHY.

HE STARTS TO KISS ME, AND WE GET INTO BED.

I WONDER IF HE'S ILL? HE LOOKS SO OLD, SUDDENLY...

THEN THE DOOR OPENS AND MY MOTHER COMES IN. I REALISE THAT I'M IN BED WITH MY FATHER AND I START TO APOLOGISE.

SHE DOESN'T SEEM TO MIND. SHE TELLS ME THAT THE PUNCH AND JUDY MAN IS ABOUT TO START.

I REALISE THAT SHE WANTS TO BE ALONE WITH DAD, SO I GO NEXT DOOR.

OUTSIDE, THE CORRIDOR LOOKS DIFFERENT. I'M CERTAIN NOW: THIS ISN'T OUR HOUSE.

BUT WHERE AM I?

SUDDENLY, I REMEMBER THAT I'M AT AN OLD FOLKS' HOME IN SOUTH KENSINGTON.

THE PUNCH AND JUDY MAN HAS BEEN ARRANGED TO ENTERTAIN THE INMATES. WHY DID I THINK IT WAS MY BIRTHDAY?

I MOVE THROUGH THE CROWD FOR A BETTER LOOK AT WHAT'S HAPPENING ON STAGE. SOME VOLUNTEERS HAVE GONE UP FROM THE AUDIENCE...

THEY'RE STANDING IN A LINE IN FRONT OF MR PUNCH. I THINK I KNOW SOME OF THEM.

WHAT'S HE GOING TO DO?

WHAT'S THE ... TO DO ...!

OH, DEAR DEAR DEAR

WHY DOESN'T SOMEBODY STOP HIM? EVERYBODY'S JUST LAUGHING!

I RUN OFF TO FIND MY MUM AND DAD, KNOWING AS I DO SO THAT HE'S SURE TO FOLLOW ME.

I'M VERY FRIGHTENED NOW. I DON'T RECOGNISE ANY OF THE CORRIDORS, AND THE MR. PUNCH-MAN WILL TURN THE CORNER BEHIND ME ANY SECOND.

I CAN HEAR MY HEART HAMMERING INSIDE ME, THERE IS NO OTHER NOISE IN THE WHOLE THEATRE.

EVERYBODY ELSE MUST BE DEAD. DAD, MUM, GORDON...

THEY'VE LEFT ME ALONE WITH HIM.

I TURN AND RUN BACK THE WAY I'VE COME, BUT THE CORRIDOR HAS GONE...

AND THERE'S A BIG FLIGHT OF SPIRAL STAIRS INSTEAD.

MY LEGS ARE HEAVY, I CAN HARDLY MOVE THEM. HE'S GOING TO CATCH ME.

I GET TO THE TOP OF THE STAIRS AND LOOK DOWN THE WELL.

HE'S COMING UP AFTER ME. ROUND AND ROUND HE GOES...

I REMEMBER THAT THERE'S A LIFT UP HERE THAT GOES ALL THE WAY DOWN TO THE BASEMENT.

I'LL NEVER GET TO IT IN TIME.

HE'S RIGHT BEHIND ME.

PLEASE DON'T LET THE DOORS SHUT BEFORE I GET TO IT.

I'M ALMOST THERE.

OH, THANK GOD.

DOWN. DOWN TO THE GROUND FLOOR. HE'LL HAVE TO TAKE THE STAIRS, AND...

STRENGT
THROUGH
PURITY
PURITY
THROUGI
FAITH

THERE'S A RAT.

THERE'S A RAT.

I TRY NOT TO THINK ABOUT ANYTHING AT ALL, EXCEPT THERE'S A RAT, AND I THINK THEY'RE GOING TO KILL ME...

I SIT ON THE COT, HARD WOOD AGAINST MY BUM, KNEES STIFF WITH CRAMP DRAWN UP TO MY CHIN...

THERE'S FOUR WALLS, TWO WINDOWS WITH SIX BARS, ONE TOILET WITH NO SEAT, AND THERE'S A WOODEN PARTITION, AND A COT, AND CARVED ON THE COT IS THE NAME "EMMA"...

...AND THERE'S ME...

...AND THERE'S A RAT.

# CHAPTER 10
# VERMIN

LATER. THE RAT HAS GONE.

I HEAR TWO MEN TALKING IN THE CORRIDOR. SHORTLY, A TRAY COMES THROUGH THE APERTURE IN THE DOOR.

I CAN'T EAT IT.

IF I DON'T EAT IT, THE RAT WILL COME BACK.

I STILL CAN'T EAT IT.

THERE'S A SOCKET RIGHT UP NEAR THE CEILING, BUT NO BULB.

WHEN THE WINDOW LIGHT FAILS, IT'S DARK. I TRY TO SLEEP.

THERE'S A RAT.

LATER, WAKING UP, VOICES...

SHE'S ASLEEP...

LAZY LITTLE COW.

WAKEY-WAKEY, DARLIN'...

COME ON, YOU CLAPPED-OUT LITTLE PRO... MOVE IT!

PLEASE DO THE NECESSARY, ROSSITER.

SIR.

WHAT...?

SO THIS SCRAWNY SPECIMEN IS THE FAMOUS MISS HAMMOND...

MY GOD.

NO! WHERE AM I? WHAT ARE YOU GOING TO DO? I WON'T...

SHUT UP.

STOP IT! WHAT ARE YOU DOING?

PLEASE, I HAVEN'T DONE ANYTHING. WHAT AM I HERE FOR? I...

I SAID SHUT YOUR HOLE.

WALKING. I CAN'T SEE... HANDS, PUSHING ME, HARD, IN THE BACK...

FINALLY, WE STOP.

ALRIGHT. TAKE IT OFF.

BRIGHT WHITE LIGHTS THAT MAKE ME SQUINT, AND A MAN, SITTING DOWN...

MY HANDS ARE SHAKING AND I WANT TO GO TO THE TOILET.

HE ASKS IF I KNOW WHY I'M HERE.

I SAY NO.

HE CALLS ME A LYING LITTLE BASTARD, AND I FEEL LIKE I'VE BEEN HIT IN THE STOMACH.

THEY SHOW ME SOME FILMS NEXT.

THERE'S A GIRL TALKING TO A MAN. SHE'S SHOVING HER HIPS OUT AT HIM, BUT IT LOOKS CLUMSY AND AWFUL. SHE'S A PROSTITUTE, I THINK.

WHY ARE THEY SHOWING ME THIS? IS THIS...?

OH.

OH, IT'S ME.

LAST NOVEMBER... WESTMINSTER BRIDGE, AND...

...THEY WERE GOING TO RAPE ME. THEY HAD ME UP AGAINST A WALL AND THEY WERE GOING TO KILL ME, AND THEN...

AND THEN...

OH CHRIST.

THEY KNOW.

THE MAN STARTS TALKING AGAIN, BUT I'M BARELY LISTENING...

WHAT AM I GOING TO **SAY**? WHAT CAN I TELL THEM?

HE SAYS I WAS FOUND OUTSIDE THE KITTY KAT KELLER BY OFFICERS WATCHING THE CLUB PRIOR TO A RAID.

I WAS CHLOROFORMED TO AVOID AN ALARM.

I HAD A LOADED GUN...

I DON'T UNDERSTAND WHAT HE WANTS ME TO **SAY**. WHY DON'T THEY STOP THE FILM? HE HAS A WELSH ACCENT. HE KEEPS TALKING...

...AND THEN HE TELLS ME THAT I'M TO BE FORMALLY CHARGED WITH THE ATTEMPTED MURDER OF SENIOR OFFICER PETER CREEDY, A FREQUENT CUSTOMER OF THE KITTY KAT KELLER...

...AND THEN THE MAN BEHIND ME PUTS THE BLINDFOLD BACK ON.

BLIND, STUMBLING, SOMEONE'S HAND ON MY WRISTS, TIGHT ENOUGH TO HURT...

WE GO SOMEWHERE. THEY PUSH ME DOWN. I SCREAM, EXPECTING TO FALL...

...BUT THERE'S A CHAIR.

SOMEONE GRABS HOLD OF MY HAIR...

WHAT ARE THEY DOING? I FEEL THEM CUTTING AT IT.

...AND THEN THERE'S SOMETHING WET...

THEY'RE...

OH NO. OH GOD...

THEY DON'T NEED TO DO THIS...

AFTER A LONG TIME, IT'S FINISHED.

A DOOR OPENS. I CAN HEAR A WOMAN'S VOICE, VERY CLOSE...

A DOCTOR? DID I HEAR SOMEONE SAY THAT?

THEY STAND ME UP, AND...

...I AM GIVEN... AN EXAMINATION...

I THINK IT'S THE WOMAN.

...AND THEN THEY TAKE ME SOMEWHERE ELSE...

...AND THEY TAKE OFF THE BLINDFOLD...

...AND THERE'S A CELL...

...AND THERE'S A RAT.

ONLY NOW, I DON'T MIND THE RAT...

...BECAUSE I'M NO BETTER.

...IT'S DARK, AND I CRY FOR A LONG TIME...

LATER, WAKING UP... OH GOD. I REMEMBER. THEY CUT OFF MY HAIR...

WHAT WOKE ME? A NOISE... RUSTLING...

THERE'S A RAT...

I GET UP. IT'S ALMOST LIGHT AND I CAN SEE THE HOLE IN THE WALL.

THERE'S SOMETHING STICKING OUT OF IT...

NOT A RAT...

TOILET PAPER?

BUT WHY...?

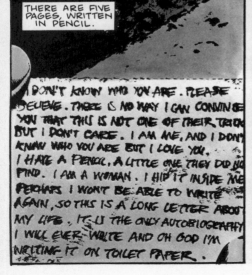

THERE ARE FIVE PAGES, WRITTEN IN PENCIL.

I DON'T KNOW WHO YOU ARE. PLEASE BELIEVE. THERE IS NO WAY I CAN CONVINCE YOU THAT THIS IS NOT ONE OF THEIR TRICKS BUT I DON'T CARE. I AM ME, AND I DON'T KNOW WHO YOU ARE BUT I LOVE YOU.
I HAVE A PENCIL, A LITTLE ONE THEY DID NOT FIND. I AM A WOMAN. I HID IT INSIDE ME. PERHAPS I WON'T BE ABLE TO WRITE AGAIN, SO THIS IS A LONG LETTER ABOUT MY LIFE. IT IS THE ONLY AUTOBIOGRAPHY I WILL EVER WRITE AND OH GOD I'M WRITING IT ON TOILET PAPER.

I LOOK AT THE BOTTOM OF THE LAST PAGE FIRST.

HER NAME IS VALERIE...

.I KNOW EVERY INCH OF THIS CELL. I KNOW EVERY PITTED INDENTATION IN THE ROUGH PLASTER LIKE I KNOW MY OWN BODY.

I DON'T KNOW WHERE I AM.

I KNOW IT GETS DARK AND THEN LIGHT; THAT I WAKE, THEN SLEEP; THAT TIME PASSES MEASURED IN HAIR GROWING BACK BENEATH MY ARMS WHERE THEY WON'T LET ME SHAVE...

I DON'T KNOW WHAT DAY IT IS.

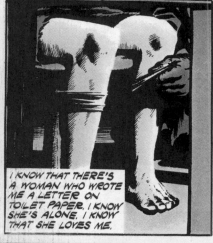

I KNOW THAT THERE'S A WOMAN WHO WROTE ME A LETTER ON TOILET PAPER. I KNOW SHE'S ALONE. I KNOW THAT SHE LOVES ME.

I DON'T KNOW WHAT SHE LOOKS LIKE.

I READ HER LETTER, I HIDE IT, I SLEEP, I WAKE, THEY QUESTION ME, I CRY, IT GETS DARK, IT GETS LIGHT, I READ HER LETTER AGAIN...

...OVER AND OVER...

HER NAME'S VALERIE...

# CHAPTER 11 VALERIE

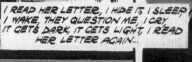

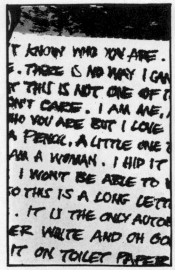

...T KNOW WHO YOU ARE. ...E. THERE IS NO WAY I CAN ...T THIS IS NOT ONE OF T... ...N'T CARE. I AM ME, ...HO YOU ARE BUT I LOVE ...A PENCIL, A LITTLE ONE T... ...AM A WOMAN. I HID IT ...I WON'T BE ABLE TO ...SO THIS IS A LONG LETT... ...IT IS THE ONLY AUTO... ...ER WRITE AND OH GO ...IT ON TOILET PAPER

"I WAS BORN IN NOTTINGHAM IN 1957, AND IT RAINED A LOT. I PASSED MY ELEVEN PLUS AND WENT TO GIRL'S GRAMMAR. I WANTED TO BE AN ACTRESS.

"I MET MY FIRST GIRLFRIEND AT SCHOOL.

"HER NAME WAS SARA. SHE WAS FOURTEEN AND I WAS FIFTEEN BUT WE WERE BOTH IN MISS WATSON'S CLASS.

"HER WRISTS. HER WRISTS WERE BEAUTIFUL.

"I SAT IN BIOLOGY CLASS, STARING AT THE PICKLED RABBIT FOETUS IN IT'S JAR, LISTENING WHILE MR. HIRD SAID IT WAS AN ADOLESCENT PHASE THAT PEOPLE OUTGREW...

"SARA DID. I DIDN'T.

"IN 1976 I STOPPED PRETENDING AND TOOK A GIRL CALLED CHRISTINE HOME TO MEET MY PARENTS.

"A WEEK LATER I MOVED TO LONDON, ENROLLING AT DRAMA COLLEGE. MY MOTHER SAID I BROKE HER HEART...

"...BUT IT WAS MY INTEGRITY THAT WAS IMPORTANT. IS THAT SO SELFISH? IT SELLS FOR SO LITTLE, BUT IT'S ALL WE HAVE LEFT IN THIS PLACE.

"IT IS THE VERY LAST INCH OF US...

"...BUT WITHIN THAT INCH WE ARE FREE."

ALRIGHT.

NOW, MISS HAMMOND, LET'S REVIEW THE *FACTS.*

YOU WORK FOR *CODENAME V.* CODENAME V KILLS SECURITY OFFICERS. PETER CREEDY IS A SECURITY OFFICER. HE FREQUENTS THE *KITTY KAT KELLER.*

YOU WERE FOUND OUTSIDE THE ESTABLISHMENT WITH A LOADED GUN.

YOU WERE PLANNING TO MURDER MR. CREEDY UNDER THE ORDERS OF CODENAME V.

ISN'T THAT WHAT HAPPENED, MISS HAMMOND?

NO! NO, PLEASE, THAT ISN'T TRUE...

SIR.

OH DEAR, ROSSITER.

NO! WAIT! PLEASE DON'T.

"LONDON:

"I WAS HAPPY IN LONDON."

...IS IT IT SO SELFISH? IT SELLS FOR SO LITTLE, BUT IT'S ALL WE HAVE LEFT IN THIS PLACE. IT IS THE VERY LAST INCH OF US. BUT WITHIN THAT INCH WE ARE FREE.

LONDON: I WAS HAPPY IN LONDON. IN 1981 I PLAYED DANDINI IN CINDERELLA. MY FIRST REP WORK. THE WORLD WAS STRANGE AND RUSHING AND BUSY, WITH INVISIBLE CROWDS BEHIND THE HOT LIGHTS AND ALL THAT BREATHLESS GLAMOUR. IT WAS EXCITING AND IT WAS LONELY. AT NIGHTS I'D GO TO GATEWAYS OR ONE OF THE OTHER CLUBS, BUT I WAS STAND-OFFISH AND DIDN'T MIX EASILY. I SAW A LOT OF THE SCENE, BUT I NEVER FELT COMFORTABLE THERE. SO MANY OF THEM JUST WANTED TO BE GAY. IT WAS THEIR LIFE, THEIR AMBITION, ALL THEY TALKED ABOUT. AND I WANTED...

"...AND I WANTED MORE THAN THAT."

"WORK IMPROVED. I GOT SMALL FILM ROLES, THEN BIGGER ONES.

"IN 1986 I STARRED IN 'THE SALT FLATS.' IT PULLED IN THE AWARDS BUT NOT THE CROWDS.

"I MET RUTH WHILE WORKING ON THAT.

"WE LOVED EACH OTHER.

"WE LIVED TOGETHER, AND ON VALENTINE'S DAY SHE SENT ME ROSES, AND OH GOD, WE HAD SO MUCH.

"THOSE WERE THE BEST THREE YEARS OF MY LIFE.

"IN 1988 THERE WAS THE WAR...

"...AND AFTER THAT THERE WERE NO MORE ROSES.

"NOT FOR ANYBODY.

"IN 1992, AFTER THE TAKE-OVER, THEY STARTED ROUNDING UP THE GAYS. THEY TOOK RUTH WHILE SHE WAS OUT LOOKING FOR FOOD.

"WHY ARE THEY SO FRIGHTENED OF US?"

"THEY BURNED HER WITH CIGARETTE ENDS AND MADE HER GIVE THEM MY NAME, SHE SIGNED A STATEMENT SAYING I'D SEDUCED HER.

"I DIDN'T BLAME HER.

"GOD, I LOVED HER. I DIDN'T BLAME HER.

BUT SHE DID.

"SHE KILLED HERSELF IN HER CELL. SHE COULDN'T LIVE WITH BETRAYING ME, WITH GIVING UP THAT LAST INCH.

"OH RUTH.

"THEY CAME FOR ME, THEY TOLD ME THAT ALL MY FILMS WOULD BE BURNED.

"THEY SHAVED OFF MY HAIR. THEY HELD MY HEAD DOWN A TOILET BOWL AND TOLD JOKES ABOUT LESBIANS.

"THEY BROUGHT ME HERE AND GAVE ME DRUGS. I CAN'T FEEL MY TONGUE ANYMORE, I CAN'T SPEAK.

"THE OTHER GAY WOMAN HERE, RITA, DIED TWO WEEKS AGO. I IMAGINE I'LL DIE QUITE SOON.

"IT IS STRANGE THAT MY LIFE SHOULD END IN SUCH A TERRIBLE PLACE, BUT FOR THREE YEARS I HAD ROSES AND I APOLO-GISED TO NOBODY.

"I SHALL DIE HERE. EVERY INCH OF ME SHALL PERISH...

"EXCEPT ONE.

"AN INCH.

"IT'S SMALL AND IT'S FRAGILE AND IT'S THE ONLY THING IN THE WORLD THAT'S WORTH HAVING.

"WE MUST NEVER LOSE IT, OR SELL IT, OR GIVE IT AWAY.

"WE MUST NEVER LET THEM TAKE IT FROM US.

"I DON'T KNOW WHO YOU ARE, OR WHETHER YOU'RE A MAN OR WOMAN. I MAY NEVER SEE YOU. I WILL NEVER HUG YOU OR CRY WITH YOU OR GET DRUNK WITH YOU.

"BUT I LOVE YOU.

"I HOPE THAT YOU ESCAPE THIS PLACE.

"I HOPE THAT THE WORLD TURNS AND THAT THINGS GET BETTER, AND THAT ONE DAY PEOPLE HAVE ROSES AGAIN.

"I WISH I COULD KISS YOU.

"VALERIE

"X"

I KNOW EVERY INCH OF THIS CELL.

THIS CELL KNOWS EVERY INCH OF ME.

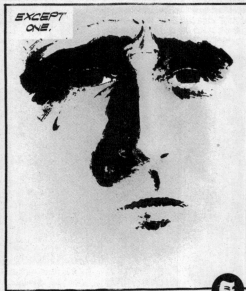

EXCEPT ONE.

Y NAME IS EYE MMOND.

"ON THE FIFTH OF NOVEMBER, 1997, I WAS ABDUCTED BY THE TERRORIST KNOWN AS CODENAME 'V' AND THEN TAKEN AGAINST MY WILL TO AN UN-KNOWN LOCATION.

"ONCE THERE, I WAS SYSTEMATICALLY BRAIN-WASHED BY MEANS OF DRUGS AND TORTURE, BOTH PHYSICAL AND PSYCHOLOGICAL.

"I WAS FREQUENTLY SUBJECTED TO SEXUAL ABUSE DURING THIS PERIOD.

"EVENTUALLY, I WAS TERRORIZED INTO HELPING HIM COMMIT MURDERS.

"THESE INCLUDED THE UNLAWFUL KILLINGS OF MR. ROGER DASCOMBE, MR. DEREK ALMOND, DR. DELIA SURRIDGE AND THE REVEREND ANTHONY LILLIMAN, BISHOP OF WESTMINSTER.

"I ALSO UNDERTOOK THE ATTEMPTED MURDER OF MR. PETER CREEDY.

"I, THE UNDERSIGNED, SWEAR THAT THE ABOVE STATEMENT IS GENUINE, AND THAT IT WAS NOT SIGNED BY MEANS OF INTIMIDATION."

WE'D LIKE YOU TO SIGN THAT FOR US, MISS HAMMOND.

WHERE WE'VE PUT THE LITTLE CROSS...

NO.

YOU SH.

ESCORT MISS HAMMOND BACK TO HER CELL, ROSSITER, WHERE SHE WILL WAIT WHILE YOU ARRANGE A WET DETAIL OF SIX MEN.

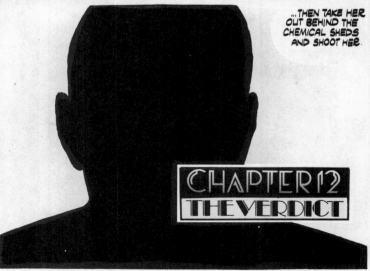

...THEN TAKE HER OUT BEHIND THE CHEMICAL SHEDS AND SHOOT HER.

# CHAPTER 12
## THE VERDICT

IT'S TIME...

...UNLESS YOU WANT TO CHANGE YOUR MIND.

SIGN THAT STATEMENT. YOU COULD BE OUT INSIDE THREE YEARS. PERHAPS THEY'D FIND YOU A JOB WITH THE FINGER...

A LOT OF YOUR SORT GET WORK WITH THE FINGER.

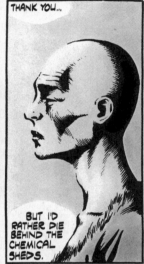

THANK YOU...

BUT I'D RATHER DIE BEHIND THE CHEMICAL SHEDS.

THEN THERE'S NOTHING LEFT TO THREATEN WITH, IS THERE?

YOU ARE FREE.

WHAT..?

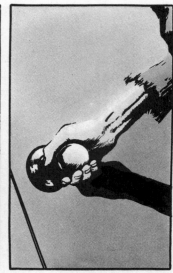

--LIKE YOU TO SIGN THAT FOR US, MISS HAMMOND, WHERE WE'VE PUT THE LITTLE CROSS...

AS YOU WISH. ESCORT MISS HAMMOND BACK TO HER CELL, ROSSITER, WHERE SHE WILL WAIT. WHILE YOU ARRANGE A WET DETAIL OF SIX MEN.

THEN TAKE HER OUT BEHIND THE CHEMICAL SHEDS AND SHOOT HER.

YOU.

YOU DID THIS.

O ME. YOU DID THIS TO ME.

YOU DID THIS TO ME.

YUH-YOU...

OH GOD, OH GOD...

YUH-YOU HIT ME, AND, AND YOU CUT OFF MY HAIR...

IT WAS YOU. IT WAS JUST YOU ALL THIS TIME...

YOU...TORTURED...ME...

OH, YOU TORTURED ME...

OH GOD, WHY?

BECAUSE I LOVE YOU.

BECAUSE I WANT TO SET YOU FREE.

# CHAPTER 13
# VALUES

BECAUSE..?

SET ME *FREE?* D-DON'T YOU *REALISE?*

DON'T YOU REALISE WHAT YOU *DID* TO ME?

YOU NEARLY DROVE ME MAD, Y'

IF THAT'S WHAT IT *TAKES,* EVEY.

I *HATE* YOU.

I HATE YOU BECAUSE YOU JUST TALK AND YOU THINK YOU'RE SO *GOOD* THAT YOU DON'T HAVE TO MAKE ANY *SENSE!*

NOTHING YOU SAY MEANS ANYTHING

YOU SAY YOU *LOVE* ME, AND YOU *DON'T* BECAUSE YOU JUST *FRIGHTEN* ME AND *TORTURE* ME FOR A *JOKE...*

YOU SAY YOU WANT TO SET ME *FREE* AND YOU PUT ME IN A *PRISON...*

YOU WERE *ALREADY* IN A PRISON.

YOU'VE BEEN IN A PRISON *ALL YOUR LIFE.*

SHUT *UP!* I DON' WANT TO *HEAR* IT! I *WASN'T* IN A PRISON! I WAS *HAPPY.*

I WAS HU-HAPPY HERE UNTIL YOU THREW ME *OUT.*

HAPPINESS IS A PRISON, EVEY.

HAPPINESS IS THE MOST INSIDIOUS PRISON OF ALL.

THAT'S WARPED! THAT'S WARPED AND EVIL AND WRONG!

WHEN YOU THREW ME OUT I WENT TO LIVE WITH SOMEBODY.

I...I WAS IN LOVE WITH HIM. I WAS HAPPY.

IF THAT'S A PRISON, THEN I DON'T CARE!

DIDN'T YOU? YOUR LOVER LIVED IN THE PENITENTIARY THAT WE ARE ALL BORN INTO, AND WAS FORCED TO RAKE THE DREGS OF THAT WORLD FOR HIS LIVING.

HE KNEW AFFECTION AND TENDERNESS BUT ONLY BRIEFLY...

EVENTUALLY, ONE OF THE OTHER INMATES STABBED HIM WITH A CUTLASS AND HE DROWNED UPON HIS OWN BLOOD.

IS THAT IT, EVEY?

IS THAT THE HAPPINESS WORTH MORE THAN FREEDOM?

...HOW DID YOU KNOW?

HOW DID YOU KNOW WHAT HAPPENED TO GORDON?

IT'S NOT AN UNCOMMON STORY, EVEY. MANY CONVICTS MEET WITH MISERABLE ENDS...

YOUR MOTHER. YOUR FATHER. YOUR LOVER.

ONE BY ONE. TAKEN OUT BEHIND THE CHEMICAL SHEDS...

... AND SHOT.

ALL CONVICTS, HUNCHED AND DEFORMED BY THE SMALLNESS OF THEIR CELLS; THE WEIGHT OF THEIR CHAINS; THE UN-FAIRNESS OF THEIR SENTENCES...

I DIDN'T PUT YOU IN A PRISON, EVEY.

I JUST SHOWED YOU THE BARS.

YOU'RE WRONG! IT'S JUST LIFE, THAT'S ALL! IT'S HOW LIFE IS! IT'S WHAT WE'VE GOT TO PUT UP WITH.

IT'S ALL WE'VE GOT. WHAT GIVES YOU THE RIGHT TO DECIDE IT'S NOT GOOD ENOUGH.

YOU'RE IN A PRISON, EVEY. YOU WERE BORN IN A PRISON. YOU'VE BEEN IN A PRISON SO LONG, YOU NO LONGER BELIEVE THERE'S A WORLD OUTSIDE.

SHUT UP! YOU'RE MAD! I DON'T WANT TO HEAR IT!

THAT'S BECAUSE YOU'RE AFRAID, EVEY. YOU'RE AFRAID BECAUSE YOU CAN FEEL FREEDOM CLOSING IN UPON YOU. YOU'RE AFRAID BE-CAUSE FREEDOM IS TERRIFYING...

DON'T BACK AWAY FROM IT, EVEY. PART OF YOU UNDER-STANDS THE TRUTH EVEN AS PART PRETENDS NOT TO.

I CAN'T FEEL ANYTHING! THERE'S NO-THING TO FEEL! LEAVE ME ALONE!

WOMAN, THIS IS THE MOST IMPORTANT MOMENT OF YOUR LIFE.

DON'T RUN FROM IT.

I DON'T. KNOW WHAT... YOU'RE...

OH GOD. OH GOD. I CAN'T... BREATHE...

ASTHMA... WHUH-WHEN I WAS... A LITTLE GUH-GIRL...

GOOD. YOU'RE ALMOST THERE. GO CLOSER. FEEL THE SHAPE OF IT.

YOUR MOTHER DIED. THEY TOOK YOUR FATHER AWAY. THERE'S A LITTLE GIRL, EVEY, AND SHE'S SCREAMING...

A-HUH...

AA-HUHH...

OH, MAKE IT STOP...

MUMM... DADDY PLEASE MAKE IT STOP!!

WHAT... ARE YOU GOING TO ME? OH, I CAN'T. BREATHE.. UHHHH....

YOU WERE IN A CELL, EVEY. THEY OFFERED YOU A CHOICE BETWEEN THE DEATH OF YOUR PRINCIPLES AND THE DEATH OF YOUR BODY.

OH. OH, I CAN FEEL IT... OH WHAT IS IT... OH, I'M GOING TO DIE, I'M GOING TO BURST...

YOU SAID YOU'D RATHER DIE, YOU FACED THE FEAR OF YOUR OWN DEATH, AND YOU WERE CALM AND STILL.

TRY TO FEEL NOW WHAT YOU FELT THEN...

I...UHHH... OH GOD...

I FELT... HUHHH...

.. FELT... IKE... N ANGEL...

OH GOD, Y, OH GOD, I'M SO SCARED, I'M SO COLD...

WHAT'S HAPPENING TO ME?

THE DOOR OF THE CAGE IS OPEN, EVEY.

ALL THAT YOU FEEL IS THE WIND FROM OUTSIDE. DON'T BE AFRAID.

RY TO STAND. RY TO WALK.

THE LIFT WILL TAKE US UP TO THE ROOF.

TO... THE ROOF..? OUTSIDE..?

I DON'T WANT... TO BE BLINDFOLDED...

NO, EVEY. NO MORE BLINDFOLDS.

ALL THE BLINDFOLDS ARE GONE.

OH, IT'S RAINING. IT MUST BE COLD.

DO YOU FEEL IT?

NO.

V...

EVERYTHING'S SO... DIFFERENT...

I... I FEEL SO...

I KNOW.

FIVE YEARS AGO, I TOO CAME THROUGH A NIGHT LIKE THIS, NAKED UNDER A ROARING SKY.

THIS NIGHT IS YOURS.

SEIZE IT.

ENCIRCLE IT WITHIN YOUR ARMS. BURY IT IN YOUR HEART UP TO THE HILT...

BECOME TRANSFIXED...

BECOME TRANSFIGURED...

FOREVER.

SEPTEMBER 3RD, 1998.
THE NOSE:

SIX MONTHS, AND NOT A PEEP. DO YOU THINK IT'S ALL OVER?

MR. FINCH?

HMM? — SORRY, DOMINIC. WHAT DID YOU SAY?

I... I SAID "DO YOU THINK IT'S ALL OVER?"

ALL OVER?

YES. I SUPPOSE IT IS.

WONDERFUL BOOKS, THESE KOESTLER AND BRONOWSKI. YOU OUGHT TO READ THEM SOMETIME.

H, YES, YES, PERHAPS I WILL...

LOOK, UH, MR. FINCH... MAYBE YOU SHOULD GO HOME NOW. I CAN LOOK AFTER THE SHOP. YOU'VE DONE ENOUGH TODAY.

COBBLERS.

I HAVEN'T DONE A STROKE SINCE I CAME BACK FROM THE EAST COAST, AND YOU KNOW IT. YOU'VE BEEN CARRYING ME.

PERHAPS YOU'RE RIGHT, THOUGH. PERHAPS I WILL BE GETTING ALONG NOW...

OH... I PICKED UP THE SUPPLIES FROM THE PHARMACY THAT YOU GAVE ME THAT CHITTY FOR.

PHILLIPS SAID YOU'D HAVE TO CALL BY LATER TO SIGN THE POISONS REGISTER. I SAID YOU WOULD.

HOPE THAT'S OKAY...

THAT'S FINE.

GOOD NIGHT, LAD.

## CHAPTER 14
### VIGNETTES

THE SHADOW GALLERY:

...THEN HE BRISKLY FRISKS THE TORN REMAINS FOR A FINGERPRINT OR CRIMSON STAINS AND ENDEAVOURS TO IGNORE THE CHAINS THAT HE WALKS IN TO HIS KNEES.

Y?

THANK YOU.

THANK YOU FOR WHAT YOU'VE DONE FOR ME.

YOU DID IT ALL YOURSELF.

I SIMPLY PROVIDED THE BACKDROP. THE DRAMA WAS ALL YOUR OWN.

IT WAS A GOOD BACKDROP.

I REALLY BELIEVE I WAS IN PRISON.

IT'S STILL HARD FOR ME TO ACCEPT THAT IT WAS ALL JUS ME AND YOU... NO GUARD NO INTERROGATORS

... NO VALERIE.

IT'S STRANGE... I REALISE NOW THAT YOU MUST HAVE COMPOSED THIS LETTER, VALERIE'S WHOLE STORY, BUT IT'S SO CONVINCING...

I BELIEVED IN HER, WITHOUT SEEING HER, I ALMOST LOVED HER...

... AND SHE WAS NEVER REALLY THERE.

I DIDN'T WRITE THAT LETTE

PLEASE... COME WITH ME.

it's about letting go...

it's about letting go...

VALERIE WROTE THE LETTER, IN HER OWN HAND, WHILE SHE LIVED.

I DELIVERED IT TO YOU AS IT WAS DELIVERED TO ME. THE WORDS YOU WEPT OVER WERE THOSE THAT TRANSFORMED ME, FIVE YEARS EARLIER.

Y... SHE'S BEAUTIFUL...

WHO WAS SHE?

HE WAS THE WOMAN IN ROOM FOUR.

THE KITTY-KAT KELLER:

ROSIE?

ROSIE?

CMON... WE'RE ON!

YES...

YES, ALRIGHT...

I'LL BE WITH YOU IN A MINUTE.

OH, GOD.

ROSE?

C'MON, GEL. THE *MARTINETTES* ARE ON IN TWO MINUTES.

I'M J'M SORRY, I GET A BIT... NERVOUS... BEFORE I GO ON. I WAS SICK...

OH.

WELL, WE CAN'T HA YOU GOIN' ON YOU'RE POORL CAN WE? THEY C STILL DO THE ROUT WITH FIVE.

YOU STAY HERE IN THE DRESSING ROOM UNTIL YOU FEEL BETTER...

...AND I'LL KEEP YOU COMPANY.

"...AND THE WIDOWS WHO REFUSE TO CRY WILL BE DRESSED IN GARTER AND BOW-TIE AND BE FORCED TO KICK THEIR LEGS UP HIGH IN THIS VICIOUS CABARET."

THE SHADOW GALLERY.

ROSES.

IN HER LETTER, VALERIE SAID SHE HOPED THERE WOULD BE ROSES AGAIN. DID YOU GROW THEM FOR HER?

I GREW THEM IN HER MEMORY.

...BUT I GIVE THEM TO OTHERS, UPON OCCASION.

EVEY... ONCE YOU TOLD ME YOU WOULD NOT KILL, NOT EVEN FOR ME.

WHEN I PLUCKED YOU FROM THE STREETS YOU WERE ABOUT TO KILL A MAN.

ONE ALISTAIR HARPER.

HE KILLED YOUR LOVER. YOU WANTED REVENGE.

THERE IS A RO HERE FOR HIM, YO ONLY HAVE TO PL IT AND HAND IT TO ME.

NOTHI ELSE

TO PICK A FLOWER IS NOT A *LARGE* THING.

IS ...ASY AS IT IS ...REVOCABLE.

UNDERSTAND WHAT IS BEING OFFERED HERE, AND DO AS THOU WILT.

LET IT GROW.

THE HEAD:

LOVE YO

YOU  I LOVE YOU  I LO

AA!

"YOU'LL KNOW WHEN IT COMES."

AND YOU?

ME?

I'M GOING TO GIVE THE WORLD WHAT VALERIE WANTED IT TO HAVE...

ROSES.

A GREAT ABUNDANCE OF ROSES.

SHALL WE DANCE?

"...BUT THE BACKDROPS PEEL AND THE SETS GIVE WAY AND THE CAST GET EATEN BY THE PLAY..."

"THERE'S A MURDERER AT THE MATINEE; THERE ARE DEAD MEN IN THE AISLES..."

"AND THE PATRONS AND THE ACTORS TOO ARE UNCERTAIN IF THE SHOW IS THROUGH AND WITH SIDELONG LOOKS AWAIT THEIR CUE..."

"BUT THE FROZEN MASK JUST SMILES."

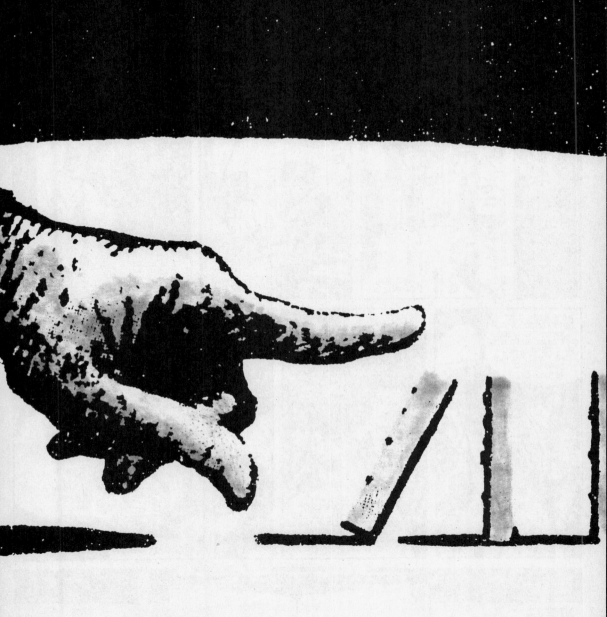

**BOOK 3**

THE LAND OF DO-AS-YOU-PLEASE

NOVEMBER 5TH, 1998, THE EAR:

HELLO, MR. ETHERIDGE, WORKING LATE, THEN?

I DON'T SUPPOSE YOU'VE SEEN MR. *FINCH* TODAY, AT ALL?

NO, UH, DOMINIC...

HAVEN'T SEEN ERIC SINCE HE, UH, CAME OVER FOR DINNER WITH, UH, MRS. ETHERIDGE AND MYSELF, UH, LAST TUESDAY.

NOTHING, UH, *WRONG*, I HOPE...

NO, NOTHING SERIOUS.

SOMETHING JUST CAME UP... PHARMACY CALLED TO SAY THEY'D MISPLACED THE RECORDS FOR SOME TOXIC CHEMICALS HE'D REQUISITIONED TWO MONTHS BACK.

THEY WANTED TO VERIFY WHAT HE'D TAKEN. NOW I CAN'T FIND HIM.

I WOULDN'T WORRY, BUT... WELL, IT'S NOT *LIKE* HIM.

HE'S BEEN A BIT DEPRESSED LATELY ...ABOUT THE TERROR-IST CASE. JUST SITS AND READS ALL THE TIME. PEOPLE I'VE NEVER HEARD OF.

SOMEONE CALLED KOESTLER...

THAT'D BE, UH, ARTHUR KOESTLER.

HE WAS, UH, THE PRESIDENT OF SOMETHING CALLED "EXIT"... A GROUP THAT USED TO CAMPAIGN FOR, UH, THE RIGHT TO DIE WITH DIGNITY.

HE, UH, KILLED HIM-SELF AS I REMEMBER.

SO, UH, ANYWAY... HOW *IS* THE, UH, TERRORIST CASE COMING ALONG?

HMM? OH...UH, WELL, THERE WAS THAT TROUBLE EARLIER IN THE YEAR, BUT SINCE THEN...

...DEAD SILENCE.

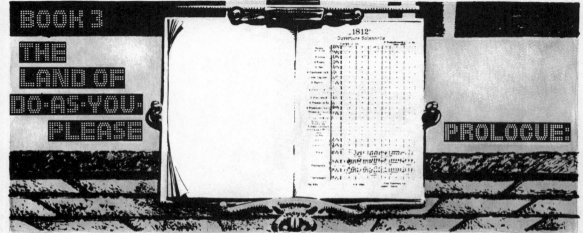

BOOK 3

THE LAND OF DO-AS-YOU-PLEASE

PROLOGUE:

V? THESE ARE SOME THINGS THAT I MOVED OUT OF MY ROOM.

I DON'T NEED THEM ANYMORE.

SPRING CLEANING, EVE? IN NOVEMBER?

NO!!! I JUST FELT LIKE THROWING OUT EVERYTHING THAT WASN'T *NECESSARY*.

DO YOU EVER FEEL LIKE THAT?

OH YES.

ALL THE TIME.

V?

YES?

SOMETHING'S GOING ON, ISN'T IT? YOU'RE GOING TO DO SOMETHING.

DON'T WORRY, EVE, YOU KNOW WHAT THEY SAY....

*"IT'LL ALL BE OVER BY CHRISTMAS."*

THE ENDING IS NEARER THAN YOU THINK, AND IT IS ALREADY WRITTEN.

ALL THAT WE HAVE LEFT TO CHOOSE IS THE CORRECT MOMENT TO *BEGIN*.

"FATE.

"MASSIVE FATE,

"REMOTE FATE...

"UNCARING FATE?

"IT IS SAID THERE IS NO QUESTION THAT CAN BE FORMULATED THAT YOU CANNOT ANSWER.

"TELL ME THIS, THEN...

"AM I LOVED?

"NOT FEARED.

"NOT RESPECTED.

"LOVED.

"YOU SAID 'I LOVE YOU.' I SAW YOU SAY IT...

"UNLESS IT WAS SOME FLUKE OF THE CIRCUITS, SOME TRICK OF THE EYE, UNLESS I AM GOING MAD...

"PLEASE...

"PLEASE GIVE ME A SIGN."

OH MY GOD.

YOU... AREN'T YOU FINCH'S MAN?

WHAT HAPPENED HERE? WE WERE JUST ARRIVING WHEN WE HEARD THE EXPLOSION...

M-MR. HEYER?

BOMB... I WAS JUST... C-COMING OUT OF THE BUILDING...

MR. ETHERIDGE, SIR... HE WAS WORKING LATE...

ETHERIDGE? WHAT, IS HE HURT?

H-HE'S DEAD, SIR.

OH GOD, I THINK I'M GOING TO BE SICK...

UUGH, CONRAD, WHAT'S GOING ON? YOU JUST RAN OFF AND LEFT ME!

TH-THERE'S BEEN A BOMB, THE TOWER...

THE EYE AND THE EAR ARE BOTH CRIPPLED! I'VE GOT TO GET IN TOUCH WITH THE LEADER STRAIGHT AWAY...

HALF LONDON HEARD THAT BANG. THE MOUTH WILL HAVE TO ISSUE A STATEMENT...

ANOTHER "SCHEDULED DEMOLITION"? WHO'S GOING TO BELIEVE IT AFTER THE HOUSES OF PARLIAMENT AND THE OLD BAILEY? WHAT CAN THEY POSSIBLY SAY?

I DON'T KNOW, ANYTHING.

AT A TIME LIKE THIS, ANYTHING'S BETTER THAN SILENCE...

MR. CREEDY ON SCREEN *TWO*, MR. HEYER ON SCREEN *FOUR*, LEADER.

CAN'T IT WAIT?

I... UH, I'M SORRY, LEADER?

NOTHING.

PUT CREEDY ON. HAVE HEYER HOLD FOR A MOMENT.

LEADER....

IT'S *JORDAN TOWER*, HE'S BLOWN IT UP.

AND THE OLD POST OFFICE TOWER AS WELL, THE EYE AND THE EAR ARE OUT OF ACTION...

BLIND AND DEAF AND UNABLE TO SPEAK...

GET MOBILE TRANSMITTERS OUT ON THE STREETS AT ONCE.

THERE MUST BE NO PANIC, EVEN IF WE CANNOT IMMEDIATELY BROADCAST OUR REASSURANCES TO THE PEOPLE....

THAT'S JUST IT, LEADER, WE CAN'T BROADCAST IMMEDIATELY...

...BUT SOMEBODY ELSE ALREADY *IS*.

LISTEN TO THIS...

GOOD EVENING, LONDON.

THIS IS THE VOICE OF FATE.

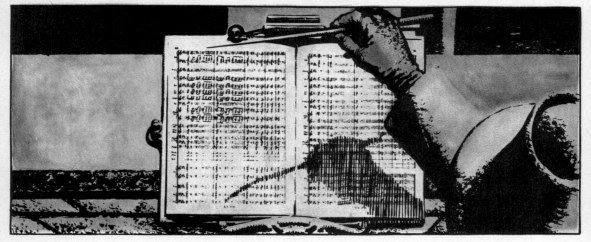

ALMOST FOUR HUNDRED YEARS AGO TONIGHT, A GREAT CITIZEN MADE A MOST SIGNIFICANT CONTRIBUTION TO OUR COMMON CULTURE.

IT WAS A CONTRIBUTION FORGED IN STEALTH AND SILENCE AND SECRECY, ALTHOUGH IT IS BEST REMEMBERED IN NOISE AND BRIGHT LIGHT.

TO COMMEMORATE THIS MOST GLORIOUS OF EVENINGS, HER MAJESTY'S GOVERNMENT IS PLEASED TO RETURN THE RIGHTS OF SECRECY AND PRIVACY TO YOU, ITS LOYAL SUBJECTS.

FOR THREE DAYS, YOUR MOVEMENTS WILL NOT BE WATCHED...

YOUR CONVERSATIONS WILL NOT BE LISTENED TO...

...AND "DO WHAT THOU WILT" SHALL BE THE WHOLE OF THE LAW.

GOD BLESS YOU...

...AND GOODNIGHT.

END OF PROLOGUE

NOVEMBER 6TH, 1998.

"NO TELLY?"

"WHAT, AN' NO RADIO NEITHER? WELL, THAT'S BLOODY MARVELOUS! 'ERE'S ME PAYIN' LICENSE MONEY, AND..."

"'ERE, 'ANG ABOUT: YOU SAID 'E BOMBED THE G.P.O. TOWER AS WELL? DOES THAT MEAN THEY CAN'T..."

BOLLOCKS.

"...AND SHE SAYS NONE OF THE MICROPHONES ARE WORKING EITHER!"

"WON'T SEEM THE SAME, USED TO LIKE THE WAY THEM LITTLE CAMERAS WENT FOR-WARDS AND BACK. STILL..."

"I SUPPOSE THAT'S WHAT THEY CALL PROGRESS, EH?"

"...SO ANYWAY, WHEN WE 'EARD THE CAMERAS WERE OFF, WE WALKED 'OME. SUDDENLY, 'E SEZ NOBODY'S WATCHIN'. 'OW ABOUT IT?'

"BLOODY CHEEK! THINKS 'E CAN DO WHATEVER 'E LIKES!"

"ALTHOUGH, I SUPPOSE..."

BOLLOCKS.

HAHA.

BOLLOCKS MR. SUSAN, BOLLOCKS FATE...

BOLLOCKS OUR DAD, BOLLOCKS MISS PLATT AT THE SCHOOL...

BOLLOCKS, BOLLOCKS, BOLLOCKS!

"...TERRORIST WHAT DONE IT. EVIL MAN, BUT VERY CLEVER. WHAT THEY CALL AN EVIL GENIUS.

"OUGHTTA 'AVE A PROPER NAME: 'THE PANTHER,' 'THE FOX,' 'THE RIPPER.' THOSE WERE PROPER NAMES, NOT EFFIN' INITIALS!

"STILL, YER GOTTER 'AND IT TO 'IM...'

"HE'S TAKEN IT.

"HE'S TAKEN AWAY THE VOICE OF FATE. HOW SHALL I FILL THE GAP IT LEAVES?

"HOW SHALL MY COUNTRY FILL THE SILENCE?"

WELL, THE PEOPLE HAVEN'T HAD MUCH TO SAY *SO* FAR, LEADER.

THINGS ARE *QUIET*... ALTHOUGH IT'S *EARLY.* YET. SOME *REINFORCEMENTS* MIGHT BE A GOOD IDEA. JUST IN *CASE.*

*MY PROBLEM IS, WITH BUNNY... UH, MR. ETHERIDGE BEING BURIED IMMEDIATELY, SOME OFFICERS HAVE REQUESTED FUNERAL LEAVE.*

I DON'T LIKE *GRANTING* IT, SITUATION BEING WHAT IT *IS,* BUT IT'LL OBVIOUSLY UPSET MRS. *ETHERIDGE,* NOBODY TURNING *UP*...

*THE OTHER PROBLEM'S MR. FINCH. HE'S BEEN ACTING FUNNY... ABSENT FOR TWO DAYS. NO CRITICISM INTENDED, LEADER, BUT PERHAPS DIRECTING THE NOSE IS A JOB...*

"I LOVE YOU."

...FOR A *YOUNGER* MAN, AND...

I...

I'M SORRY, LEADER?

D-DID YOU *SAY* SOME-THING?

NO. NO, I DON'T *THINK* SO.

SEND MRS. ETHERIDGE SOME *FLOWERS,* WITH MY *APOLOGIES.* CANCEL ALL POLICE *LEAVE* AND DOUBLE THE MANPOWER ON THE *STREETS.*

OH YES... AND LOOTERS ARE TO BE SHOT.

THAT WILL BE *ALL,* MR. CREEDY.

ENGLAND *PREVAILS.*

"NGMF GLEP GOR, WHAT ABOUT THESE *BANGERS?*

"NO, *CHLOF*, I MEAN, I BELIEVE IN LAW'N'ORDER, BUT *BLACK MARKET* OR *NOT*, IF I 'ADN'T TAKEN ADVANTAGE OF THE OFFER, SOME *OTHER* BUGGER WOULD 'AVE ...

"GHMF PASS THE KETCHUP, AY?"

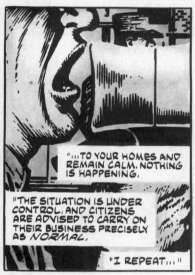

"... TO YOUR HOMES AND REMAIN CALM. NOTHING IS HAPPENING.

"THE SITUATION IS UNDER CONTROL, AND CITIZENS ARE ADVISED TO CARRY ON THEIR BUSINESS PRECISELY AS *NORMAL.*

"I REPEAT ..."

"HELLO.

"I'D LIKE TO BUY A GUN."

OAH! Y'WANTAE BUY A *SHOOTER,* EH?

WULL, AM *SHURA* DON'T KNOW WHY YUR ASKIN' *ME,* AM OOT FER A *BEVVY,* Y'KNOW? AM NO INTAE A'THIS *GANGSTER* SHITE.

I-I'VE GOT *MONEY,* I HEARD YOU WERE THE PERSON TO *ASK,* AND THIS SEEMED THE BEST *TIME,* WHILE THE *MONITORS* ARE OFF.

AYE, WELL, RIGHT ENUFF, BUT AM NO *CONVENCED.* YUR NO THE SHOOTER *TYPE,* KNOWHATTAMEAN? WHURE YE WANTIN' *SHOAT?*

*NOBODY!*

I.... I JUST WANT *PROTECTION.* THINGS ARE SO *THREAT-ENING* LATELY....

WHAT *YUR* WANTIN'S A *MAN* ABOOT THE PLACE. WEE GIRRULS SHOULDNAE FRIG ABOOT WI BLOODY *CANNONS.* ESS NO A WOMAN'S *GAME.*

I'VE GOT *FOUR HUNDRED* POUNDS.

I CAN GIVE YOU *HALF* NOW, THE REST WHEN....

*SHH,* NO *SLOUD,* FER *CHRIS-SAKES!*

FOOR HUNDRED QUED, EH? AN YUR JUST AFTER WANTEN TAE *PROTECT* Y'SEL?

YES,

HMM, WULL, MEETUS ROONDS *BAAK,* *CLOSEN* TIME, A'LL SEE WHUT A KEN *DO,*

A HOPE Y'KNOW HOWTAE *HANDLE* ONE O'THSE THENGS, MISSUS.

ESS NO A *POP GUN,* Y'KNOW WHUT AM *SAYIN'?* MAKESAN OFFLY BIG *BANG,* YU WAIT 'TEL YUR HOLDEN ONE, YU'LL SEE.

A'LL BE SEEN Y'*LATER,* THEN.

BYE FER NOO.

"BANG."

"...'APPENIN' OVER EAST FINCHLEY TO-NIGHT.

"WHAT I 'ERD, THIS NOBBY, 'IZ BIRD GOT FINGERED OVER A TIN O'BEANS, ONLY SHOT THE POOR COW, DIDN'T THEY? SO, LIKE, EVERYBODY'S TOOLED UP, AN'..."

"...JUST AS IF SHE WAS A PAKI! WELL, THEY'VE 'AD IT! THEY COME ROUND 'ERE TONIGHT, THEY'RE GUNNA GEDDA KICK IN THE 'ED..."

"A BIG KICK."

"IT DOES NOT DO TO RELY TOO MUCH ON SILENT MAJORITIES, EVEY, FOR SILENCE IS A FRAGILE THING...

"ONE LOUD NOISE, AND IT'S GONE.

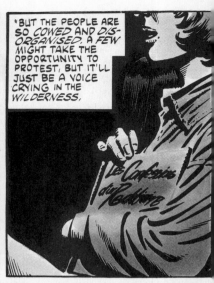

"BUT THE PEOPLE ARE SO *COWED* AND *DIS-ORGANISED*. A FEW MIGHT TAKE THE OPPORTUNITY TO PROTEST, BUT IT'LL JUST BE A VOICE CRYING IN THE *WILDERNESS*.

"*NOISE* IS RELATIVE TO THE SILENCE *PRECEDING* IT. THE MORE ABSOLUTE THE *HUSH*, THE MORE SHOCK-ING THE *THUNDERCLAP*.

"OUR MASTERS HAVE NOT HEARD THE PEOPLE'S VOICE FOR *GENERATIONS*, EVEN ...

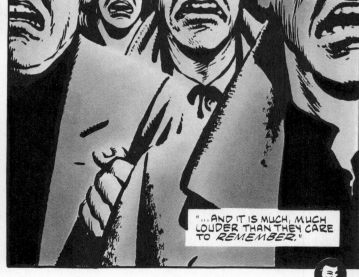

"...AND IT IS MUCH, MUCH LOUDER THAN THEY CARE TO *REMEMBER*."

NOVEMBER 6TH, 1998:

FINGERWAGON VICTOR-CHARLEY-NINER, REQUEST ASSISTANCE, CROUCH END...

CAN'T FOLLOW THEM INTO BRIXTON. HALF THE MEN NEED CHOLERA JABS, AND...

URGENTLY REQUEST

BEFORE LOOTERS REACH DEPTFORD MARSHES, WE NEED TWO MORE CARS AND...

GREEN PARK. MOST PEOPLE INDOORS, BUT A CROWD FORMING IN KING'S ROAD AREA. SEND

RGENCY. ALL CARS IN TOTTENHAM AREA

CK'S SAKE, MAN, GET US SOME BACK-UP HERE

A LATE SEVENTIES RADIO/CASSETTE. YOU CAN TUNE THEM TO THE POLICE BAND, EVEN IN A BROADCASTING BLACKOUT.

WHAT'S THAT?

PROTESTING THE EXECUTIONS. IF WE CHARGE, THEY MIGHT

RECOMMEND TEAR GAS OR

VICTOR-CHARLEY-NINER, COME IN, PLEASE,

THE OLD BROADWATER FARM ESTATE. TELL MR. CREEDY THERE'S FIRES...

ALL THIS RIOT AND UPROAR, V... IS THIS ANARCHY?

IS THIS THE LAND OF DO-AS-YOU-PLEASE?

PLEASE RESPOND. REPEAT: VICTOR-CHARLEY-NINER...

NO. THIS IS ONLY THE LAND OF TAKE-WHAT-YOU-WANT. ANARCHY MEANS "WITHOUT LEADERS"; NOT "WITHOUT ORDER."

WITH ANARCHY COMES AN AGE OF ORDNUNG, OF TRUE ORDER, WHICH IS TO SAY VOLUNTARY ORDER.

THIS AGE OF ORDNUNG WILL BEGIN WHEN THE MAD AND INCOHERENT CYCLE OF VERWIRRUNG THAT THESE BULLETINS REVEAL HAS RUN ITS COURSE.

THIS IS NOT ANARCHY, EVE.

THIS IS CHAOS,

CHAPTER 2
VERWIRRUNG

HOW DID *YEATS* PUT IT ....?

"TURNING AND TURNING IN THE WIDENING GYRE, THE FALCON CAN-NOT HEAR THE FALCONER. THINGS FALL APART ...."

".... THE CENTRE CANNOT HOLD."

THE RIOTS WILL STOP. COMMUNICATIONS WILL RESUME. LET ENGLAND BRIEFLY MIND ITSELF. AFTER MY TOIL, I AM ENTITLED TO SOME TENDERNESS.

I GAZE, ENTRANCED, INTO YOUR EYE. LUMINOUS FINGERS STROKE MY FACE.

FROM YOUR WORLD OF PURE MATH YOU TOUCH ME, IN THIS SOLID AND ENCUMBERING PLACE....

TOO FAST TO REGISTER, DOUBLE EXPOSED BY MEMORY, IMAGES RACE ACROSS YOUR GLASS, MATCHING MY PULSE, ACCELERATING....

THERE: A HANGING? IT WENT BY SO *QUICKLY*.... LETTERS; WORDS; A STADIUM CROWD; SHAVED ASIAN WOMEN HERDED THROUGH THE SHOWERS....

OH GOD, I'M .... BURNING SHOPS; A CHIMP CON-VULSED BY SHOCKS.... THE FEELINGS, WHITE SCREENS, OH MY GOD, MY....

.... FATE ....

OH ....

OH, MY LOVE, MY .... OOUHHH ....

HHH-HAHHH ....

AH,

"MERE ANARCHY IS LOOSED UPON THE WORLD."

INVOLUNTARY ORDER BREEDS *DISSATISFACTION,* MOTHER OF *DISORDER,* PARENT OF THE *GUILLOTINE.*

AUTHORITARIAN SOCIETIES ARE LIKE *FORMATION SKATING.* INTRICATE, MECHANICALLY PRECISE AND ABOVE ALL, *PRECARIOUS.* BENEATH CIVILISATION'S FRAGILE CRUST, COLD *CHAOS* CHURNS....

"....AND THERE ARE PLACES WHERE THE ICE IS TREACHEROUSLY THIN."

EXIT

YUR UNDER ARREST.

*AAA!*

NAH, AM OANY KIDDEN.

*OH!* OH *GOD,* YOU....

L-LOOK, I'VE GOT THE MONEY. DID YOU GET THE... THE *THING,* LIKE I ASKED?

TO DEFEND MYSELF WITH?

OH AYE, THES'LL *DEFEND* YE, RIGHT 'NUFF.

*THES'LL* DEFEND SOMEBODY'S *ENNARDS* ENTAE THE GUTTER.

AD *ADVISE* YE TE GET ET HOME QUECK. EF YUR SERRCHED, AV NEVER SEEN YE IN MA *LIFE.*

N-NO, I UNDER-STAND. I'LL TAKE IT STRAIGHT HOME, THANK YOU VERY MUCH.

THANK YOU.

YUR WULCOME.

HELLO, ALLY.

THOUGHT IT WAS TIME WE HAD A LITTLE CHIN-WAG.

MESTER CREEDY.

LUKE, AM NO AWARE OF HAVIN DONE ANYTHENG TE UPSET YE...

HA HA HA! WHAT A LOAD OF BOLLOCKS. THERE'S G.B.H., ARMED ROBBERY, PROBABLY A MURDER OR TWO...

YOU'RE QUITE A LAD, ALLY.

AA LUKE, C'MOAN, GESSA BREAK, EH?

A BREAK? HA HA HA!

I'M GOING TO GIVE YOU MORE THAN A BREAK, ME OLD SON.

I'M GOING TO GIVE YOU A JOB.

IT'S THESE RIOTS, ALLY. THE FINGER'S STRETCHED A BIT THIN AT PRESENT, AND I'VE BEEN AUTHORIZED TO HIRE SOME EXTRA MUSCLE.

JUST FIND ME A FEW DOZEN HARD CASES, LOOKING FOR NIGHT WORK, CASH IN HAND. THERE'LL BE A COMMISSION FOR YOU OBVIOUSLY. THINK YOU CAN DO THAT?

AYE, WELL...

GREAT STUFF, ALLY, GREAT STUFF!

WELCOME TO THE SIDE OF LAW AND ORDER.

AUTHORITY, WHEN FIRST DETECTING CHAOS AT ITS HEELS, WILL ENTERTAIN THE VILEST SCHEMES TO SAVE ITS ORDERLY FACADE...

...BUT ALWAYS ORDER WITHOUT JUSTICE, WITHOUT LOVE OR LIBERTY, WHICH CANNOT LONG POSTPONE THEIR WORLD'S DESCENT TO PANDEMONIUM.

AUTHORITY ALLOWS *TWO* ROLES: THE *TORTURER* AND THE *TORTURED*: TWISTS PEOPLE INTO JOYLESS MANNEQUINS THAT *FEAR* AND *HATE*, WHILE *CULTURE* PLUNGES INTO THE *ABYSS*.

AUTHORITY DEFORMS THE REARING OF THEIR CHILDREN, MAKES A *COCKFIGHT* OF THEIR LOVE ...

ALL RIGHT, CONRAD. THAT'S ENOUGH. GET ME A TOWEL.

WHEN DID THE LEADER AUTHORIZE CREEDY TO RECRUIT A *GOON SQUAD?*

LATE THIS AFTERNOON. DO YOU WANT YOUR ROBE, HELEN?

NO.

DOESN'T SUSAN REALIZE THAT CREEDY'S ONLY WAITING FOR HIM TO CRACK COMPLETELY BEFORE MOVING IN WITH HIS PRIVATE ARMY AND STAGING A COUP?

THE LEADER MAY JUST BE UNDER STRAIN ...

BALLS, CONRAD. HIS MIND'S DISINTEGRATING ... AND WHEN IT *GOES*, I WANT *YOU* IN THE NUMBER ONE SEAT AND NOT THAT SECONDARY-SCHOOL OIK, CREEDY.

I SUPPOSE I SHALL HAVE TO DO EVERYTHING, AS USUAL.

YOU KNOW, YOU'RE QUITE A SUCCESSFUL YOUNG MAN, CONRAD. IF YOUR SUCCESS WASN'T *ENTIRELY* DUE TO MY EFFORTS, I MIGHT EVEN *FANCY* YOU.

NOW, I'VE GOT THINGS TO ORGANISE IN THE MORNING, SO I'M GOING TO BED. I EXPECT I SHALL BE *ASLEEP* WHEN YOU COME UP.

YOU WON'T BE NEEDING THE LIGHT ON IN HERE, WILL YOU?

AUTHORITY'S COLLAPSE SENDS CRACKS THROUGH BEDROOM, BOARDROOM, CHURCH AND SCHOOL ALIKE. ALL IS MISRULE.

EQUALITY AND FREEDOM ARE NOT LUXURIES TO LIGHTLY CAST ASIDE. WITHOUT THEM, ORDER CANNOT LONG ENDURE BEFORE APPROACHING DEPTHS BEYOND *IMAGINING*.

V, WAIT A MINUTE... WE HAVEN'T BEEN DOWN HERE BEFORE. WHERE ARE WE GOING? DO YOU HAVE SOMETHING *HIDDEN* DOWN HERE?

V?

V, ANSWER ME...

HELLO, THIS IS LONDON 6482732...

ERIC FINCH SPEAKING,

I'M NOT IN AT THE MOMENT, BUT IF YOU LEAVE YOUR NAME AND NUMBER AFTER THE TONE, I'LL GET BACK TO YOU.

HELLO?

UH, HELLO, THIS IS DOMINIC AGAIN...

SUPAHEA

OFF ON

LISTEN, JUST... JUST GET IN TOUCH, *PLEASE*. THERE'S *PROBLEMS* WITH MR. SUSAN AND MR. CREEDY. I CAN'T SAY MUCH ON THE *PHONE*.

IT'S ALL COMING TO BITS, MR. FINCH. I DON'T KNOW WHAT I SHOULD *DO*.

WELL, I, UH.... I SUPPOSE THAT'S ALL.

G'BYE,

TAKE CARE.

REGISTERED POST IT IS AN OFFENSE TO BREAK THIS WITHOUT TH...

V?

COME *ON*, V, I'M WAITING FOR AN *ANSWER*, WHERE...?

THIS IS MY SECRET LOVE NEST, EVE,

I'M TAKING YOU TO MEET MY *MISTRESS*.

YOUR WHAT?

IT IS A TANGLED AND UNHAPPY TALE OF HEARTS BETRAYED AND LOYALTIES MISPLACED.

IT WAS NOT I THAT STRAYED. MY LOVE WAS JUSTICE, AND, INFATUATED WITH HER TRUTH AND LOVELINESS, I WORSHIPPED HER.

...UNTIL, BEHIND MY BACK, SHE TOOK UP WITH A MAN WHO VIOLATED AND ABUSED HER; SOMEONE FIERCE AND BRUTAL WITH BURNED CHILDREN ON HIS BREATH.

HE CHANGED HER. SHE ACQUIRED A TASTE FOR LEATHER, CHAINS AND WHIPS.

THE JUSTICE THAT I LOVED WAS GONE; WHO HAD SUCH KINDLY EYES; WHO TOOK SUCH SMALL AND CAREFUL STEPS...

TRANSFORMED, SHE GLARED THROUGH NARROW SLITS AND GROUND GOOD MEN BENEATH HER VICIOUS HEEL.

IMAGINE WHEN I LEARNED OF HER AFFAIR...

MY ANGER AND MY SHAME TO THINK HOW THEY'D MADE MOCK OF ALL THAT I LOVED: MY JUSTICE AND HER BESTIAL SWAIN, CAVORTING IN THEIR BLOODSTAINED SHEETS.

STILL, ALL IN LOVE AND WAR IS FAIR, THEY SAY, THIS BEING BOTH, AND TURNABOUT'S FAIR PLAY.

THOUGH I MUST BEAR A CUCKOLD'S HORNS, THEY'RE NOT A CROWN THAT I SHALL BEAR ALONE.

YOU SEE, MY RIVAL, THOUGH INCLINED TO ROAM, POSSESSED AT HOME A WIFE THAT HE ADORED.

HE'LL RUE HIS PROMISCUITY, THE ROGUE WHO STOLE MY ONLY LOVE, WHEN HE'S INFORMED HOW MANY YEARS IT IS...

...SINCE FIRST I BEDDED HIS.

THE NOSE, NOVEMBER 7TH, 1998:

"ROSES ARE RED, VIOLETS ARE BLUE, EVERYTHING'S POSSIBLE, NOTHING IS TRUE."

THEY'RE LIKE LITTLE LOVE NOTES. WHO ISSUED THEM?

LEARNING. THAT'S YOUR DEPARTMENT.

MY CIVILIAN AUXILIARY LADS FOUND 'EM ON VARIOUS LAY-ABOUTS THEY ROUNDED UP THIS MORNING.

"I LOVE THE RAIN, I LOVE THE MOON, I LOVE THE WIND AND STARS..."

WORK OF A NUTCASE. COUNTRY'S GOING BARMY. Y'KNOW THERE'S FOOD RIOTS IN MANCHESTER? OVER A BLOODY COMPUTER ERROR?

"...I'D LOVE TO VISIT YOU QUITE SOON AND KISS YOU THROUGH THE BARS."

WHAT'S IT MEAN?

IT MEANS TROUBLE, SON. TIMES LIKE THIS, BLOKE NEEDS TO KNOW WHO HIS FRIENDS ARE.

TAKE YOU, NOW... ACTING HEAD OF THE NOSE SINCE BALDY DISAPPEARED. DODGY POSITION. THINGS AROUND HERE COULD CHANGE OVERNIGHT.

OVER-NIGHT.

'COURSE, THE LEADER'S MARVELLOUS. BUT, WELL, IF ANYTHING HAPPENED, WHO'D FILL THE VOID? HAVE TO CONSIDER THESE THINGS, EH?

Y'KNOW, I NEVER COTTONED TO FINCH, BUT I COULD COTTON TO YOU.

MAYBE OUR DEPARTMENTS COULD CO-OPERATE MORE IN FUTURE, PERHAPS...

"I LOVE YOU, BUT WHY MUST YOU LOVE THE LAW? 'TIS PLAIN FOR ALL TO SEE THAT SHE'S A WHORE..."

"...THAT VIRTUOUS PERSONS HAVE NO NEED TO WOO; THAT VILLAINS SCREW, THEN STUDIOUSLY IGNORE."

HA. QUITE FUNNY, THAT.

CAN YOU FIND YOUR OWN WAY OUT?

CHAPTER 3
VARIOUS VALENTINES

ORGANIZEN A PROTEST AGAINST THE SHOOTENS, EH?

A WULL, SLENG THE LETTLE GOABSHITE EN THE WAAG'N WI' THE REST. CAN Y'NO SEE AM ON MA *LUNCHBREAK*?

MORNING, ALLY. KEEPING BUSY?

A, ET'S A DODDLE, ALL A THUS MONEY FUR DAMAGIN' SOME PUIR BASTUD AN TACHIN AP THUR MESSUSEZ EN THE STREP-SERRCH.

YUZ COAPERS 'R CLEVER BASTUDS, KEEPEN THESS NUMBER TAE YOURSELN.

HAHA, WELL, PLAY YOUR CARDS RIGHT, YOUR LADS COULD HAVE *REGULAR* WORK HERE.

I LIKE YOUR STYLE, AND WITH THINGS HOW THEY ARE, A LITTLE *AUXILIARY FORCE* COULD COME IN VERY HANDY.

SAY FOR EXAMPLE I OFFERED FOUR HUNDRED A WEEK.

I MEAN, FOR THAT I'D WANT YOUR *GUARANTEED LOYALTY* IF PUSH COME TO SHOVE, UNDERSTAND WHAT I'M *SAYING*?

A THENK A MIGHT HAV AN *ENKLENG*.

WELL, THINK ON, I COULD PROMISE *GOOD PROSPECTS* IN ANY SYSTEM THAT MIGHT DEVELOP, YOU KNOW...

IF PUSH COME TO SHOVE,

SEE, THINGS ARE *PRECARIOUS*, APPARENTLY. THEY'VE HAD *POWER FAILURES* IN *LIVERPOOL*. IF THAT HAPPENED *HERE*...

A, NAE *BOTHER*, FUR FOUR HUNNERD QUED, YEV MA FULL SUPPORT.

NOW, EF YU'LL *EXCUSE ME*...

OFF *ALREADY*? NOT PURSUING OTHER BUSINESS INTERESTS, I HOPE?

NAH, ET'S JUSS THESS *BERRD*.

LESSEN, A FOOND SOME MAIR O'THEY *LETTERS*, Y'BETTER HAVE 'EM TAE LUKE AT.

LOVE YOUR RAGE, NOT YOUR CAGE

SEE YUZ LATER, A'RIGHT?

DEREK....

DEREK, YOU WERE USE-LESS, THEN YOU DIED, THAT'S ALL.

YOU DIED, AND I CAN'T SLEEP AT NIGHTS.

YOU DIED AND LEFT ME BARE IN FRONT OF STRANGERS.

DEREK, WHEN WE MARRIED, YOU REMEMBER, I WAS WORKING AT THE BANK AND YOU WERE IN INSURANCE. WE WERE GOING TO BUY A HOUSE IN SURREY, PERHAPS HAVE CHILDREN THAT WAS IN '87...

JUST BEFORE THE WAR.

AND THEN, IN '92, YOU JOINED THE PARTY.

MRS. RANA NEXT DOOR LOANED US FOOD ALL THROUGH THE WAR YEARS. WHEN THEY DRAGGED HER AND HER CHILDREN OFF IN SEPARATE VANS WE DIDN'T INTERVENE.

...AND NOW YOU'RE DEAD AND I WALK HOME ALONE EACH NIGHT THROUGH RIOT ZONES, PAST LOOTINGS, SHOOTINGS, BURNING BUILDINGS....

NOW YOU'RE DEAD AND I CROUCH LIKE AN ANIMAL AND OFFER MY HIND-QUARTERS IN SUB-MISSION TO THE WORLD.

NOW YOU'RE DEAD AND I CAN'T SLEEP FOR BE-ING SCARED; FOR CRYING; HATING; THINKING "WHO HAS DONE THIS TO ME?"

I CAN'T SLEEP FOR WANTING JUSTICE; WANTING ALL THE WORLD TO KNOW OF ITS UNFAIRNESS....

CAN'T SLEEP FOR THE GUN BENEATH MY PILLOW.

TA VERY MUCH.

Y'KNOW, YOU WON'T FIND ANYWHERE TO SLEEP OUT HERE, THERE'S NO BED AND BREAKFASTS ANYMORE. WERE YOU THINKING OF CAMPING OR SOMETHING LIKE THAT?

YES.

SOMETHING LIKE THAT.

THIS IS FOR YOU, DELIA, YOU MORE THAN ANYBODY.

I WAS *HAPPY* WITH YOU, YES, YES, I WAS HAPPY WITH CYNTHIA AND LITTLE PAUL, BUT *THAT* WAS TEN YEARS AGO.

I'D GOTTEN OVER THAT.

I'M DOING THIS FOR *YOU*, DELIA.

FOR THE *COUNTRY*, YES, THAT TOO; AND FOR *ME*, OF COURSE FOR ME; BUT YOU MORE THAN ANYBODY.

YOU'RE THE REASON I CAME HERE.

THIS IS WHERE IT *STARTED*.

THIS IS WHERE IT ENDS.

LARKHILL RESETTLEMENT CAMP

V?

YOU'RE ALMOST FINISHED, AREN'T YOU?

SEE FOR YOURSELF.

"THE PIECES ARE SET OUT BEFORE ME, PERFECTLY ALIGNED.

"COMPLETE, ONE MAY AT LAST GRASP THEIR DESIGN; THEIR GRAND SIGNIFICANCE."

...BUT "ALMOST FINISHED"...?

YES.

YES, I SUPPOSE I AM.

"THOUGH RECOGNITION'S BEEN DELAYED BY ITS CIRCUITOUS CONSTRUCTION, NOW THE PATTERN LONG CONCEALED EMERGES INTO VIEW.

"IS IT NOT FINE? IS IT NOT SIMPLE, AND ELEGANT AND SEVERE?"

HOW STRANGE, AFTER THE LONG EXACTING TOIL OF PREPARATION THAT IT TAKES ONLY THE SLIGHTEST EFFORT AND LESS THOUGHT TO START THIS BRIEF, ELABORATE AMUSEMENT ON ITS BREATHLESS, HURTLING RACE:

THE MEREST TOUCH, NO MORE...

"...AND EVERYTHING FALLS INTO PLACE."

THE PIECES CAN'T PERCEIVE AS WE THE MISCHIEF THEIR ARRANGEMENT TEMPTS: THOSE STOLID, LAW-ABIDING QUEUES, SO PREGNANT WITH CATASTROPHE, INSENSIBLE BEFORE THE WAVE SO SOON RELEASED BY CALLOUS FATE,

AFFECTED MOST, THEY UNDERSTAND THE LEAST...

"...AND UNDERSTANDING, WHEN IT COMES, INVARIABLY ARRIVES TOO LATE."

YOU SAY YOU HAVE A CLOCKWORK LOVE, WHO FEEDS AND CARES FOR YOU, BUT I'VE READ ALL HER DIARIES, AND I KNOW THAT SHE'S UNTRUE.

INDEED, THEY'LL NOT KNOW ANYTHING'S AMISS UNTIL THEY'RE CAUGHT UP IN THAT TERRIBLE MOMENTUM, POSSIBLY MISTAKING IT AT FIRST FOR BOLD DECISIVE ACTION, SOME LAST MINUTE RALLY TO AVERT DISASTER, CHARGING TO THE RESCUE...

"...BUT THEY ARE NOT CHARGING.

"THEY ARE FALLING."

THERE...

POOR LITTLE THINGS.

YOU SEE THEM? STANDING WITH THEIR NUMBERS ON THEIR BLANK, INDIFFERENT FACES, NUREMBERG IN MINIATURE, THE RANKS OF PAINTED WOODEN MEN...

"POOR DOMINOES.

"YOUR PRETTY EMPIRE TOOK SO LONG TO BUILD, NOW, WITH A SNAP OF HISTORY'S FINGERS..."

...DOWN IT GOES.

LEADER...

I KNOW.

THE TERRORIST... I KNOW HOW HE'S DOING IT ALL.

FIRST, HE KNOWS EVERYTHING ABOUT US AND OUR SYSTEM. EVERYTHING.

THEN, THIS MORNING WE FIND PEOPLE WITH SUBVERSIVE POEMS THEY CLAIMED THEY'D RECEIVED THROUGH THE POST.

LEADER, HE'S GOT US DELIVERING HIS LEAFLETS FOR HIM! HOW?

HOW IS HE CAUSING BLACKOUTS IN MERSEY-SIDE AND FOOD RIOTS IN BRUM? I KNOW IT'S UNTHINKABLE, LEADER, BUT THERE'S ONLY ONE ANSWER:

HE'S GOT ACCESS TO FATE.

HE'S HAD ACCESS TO FATE SINCE THE BEGINNING.

THAT'S HOW HE, UH...

LEADER?

WHAT'S...?

NOVEMBER 7TH, 1998:

"WE'RE UP AGAINST SOMEONE WHO *ISN'T* 'NORMAL PEOPLE'... EITHER PHYSICALLY OR MENTALLY.

"IT'S THE 'MENTALLY' BIT THAT BOTHERS ME...

"...BECAUSE IF I'M GOING TO CRACK THIS CASE... AND I *AM*... I'M GOING TO HAVE TO GET RIGHT INSIDE HIS HEAD.

"TO THINK THE WAY *HE* THINKS...

"...AND THAT SCARES ME."

I SAID THAT.

I SAID THAT A YEAR AGO, AND NOTHING'S CHANGED, IT'S STILL TRUE.

I'M STILL SCARED.

I KNOW SO LITTLE ABOUT THIS STUFF. COULDN'T ASK WITHOUT AROUSING SUSPICION.

LYSERGIC ACID DIETHYLAMIDE: STANDARD DOSE IS ABOUT TWO HUNDRED MICROGRAMMES, BUT HOW DO I MEASURE THAT?

THEY SAY THE TINIEST AMOUNTS CAN ALTER EVERYTHING...

THE FAINTEST TRACES.

# CHAPTER 4
## VESTIGES

I'VE NEVER SEEN THE CAMPS BEFORE, ONLY PHOTO-GRAPHS. SO THIS IS THE TOILET WE FLUSHED ALL THOSE PEOPLE DOWN....

FOUR TABLETS. I WONDER IF THAT'S ENOUGH? I WONDER IF THAT'S TOO MANY?

OH WELL.

AGAINST MY TONGUE LIKE LITTLE PIECES OF SOAP.... MY SALIVA TASTING OF TINFOIL....A BUBBLE OF APPREHENSION FORMING LOW IN MY STOMACH....

I SWALLOW, FEELING AS IF I'M LETTING GO OF SOMETHING.

THERE.

NOW I'M STRAPPED IN, COUNTDOWN TICKING FROM BOWEL TO BLOODSTREAM TO BRAIN, TOWARDS TAKE-OFF, BUT I'VE NEVER FLOWN BEFORE. WHAT'S SUPPOSED TO HAPPEN?

NOTHING. NOTHING YET. BETTER TAKE A LOOK ROUND, WHILE IT'S LIGHT.

THESE MUST BE THE OVENS. OVENS FOR PEOPLE, PEOPLE OVENS....

NO. NO USE: STILL CAN'T MAKE IT SEEM REAL. IF I'D KNOWN THIS WAS HAPPENING. WOULD I STILL HAVE JOINED THE PARTY?

PROBABLY. NO BETTER ALTERNATIVES.

WE COULDN'T LET THE CHAOS AFTER THE WAR CONTINUE. ANY SOCIETY'S BETTER THAN THAT. WE NEEDED ORDER....

....OR AT LEAST, I DID. LOSING CYNTH AND LITTLE PAUL LIKE THAT, EVERYTHING WAS DISINTEGRATING AND I JUST WANTED....

....TO....

EUGGH....

I SHOULDN'T HAVE DONE IT.

I SHOULDN'T HAVE TAKEN THE L.S.D.

NOT HERE.

BUT I WANTED TO KNOW...TO KNOW WHAT IT'S LIKE BEING HIM...

IT'S THIS PLACE, IF I CAN JUST GET OUTSIDE ITS WALLS UNTIL I FEEL BETTER!...

NO PROBLEM, THE MAIN GATE'S BACK THIS WAY...

I CAN'T, I CAN'T WALK THAT FAR, MY LEGS FEEL LIKE JELLY AND EVERYTHING'S THRUMMING...

THRRUMMMMMMMMMINGING...

IT'S THE DRUG, I JUST HAVE TO REMEMBER IT'S THE DRUG DOING THIS, BUT...

...BUT THEY SAY L.S.D. ONLY MAGNIFIES WHAT'S ALREADY THERE. CHRIST, WHY DID I TAKE THIS NOW, WHEN I'M SO CONFUSED ANYWAY?

I'M TRAPPED IN A JOB THAT DISTURBS ME, BUT I CAN'T TELL ANYONE, I'M SO ALONE...

SO ALONE.

OH.

OH LOOK...

LOOK, THEY'RE ALL SMILING. THEY'RE ALL HAPPY. GOD, IT'S BEEN SO LONG...

I'D FORGOTTEN HOW RICH THE COLOR OF YOUR SKIN WAS, A THOUSAND SPECIAL BLENDS OF COFFEE...

THE GIRLS I SAW HUGGING EACH OTHER ON THE DEMONSTRATIONS, AND THE MEN, SO GENTLE, SO SOFTLY SPOKEN...

OH JESUS, I'VE MISSED YOU.

I'VE MISSED YOUR VOICES AND YOUR WALK, YOUR FOOD, YOUR CLOTHES, YOUR DYED PINK HAIR.

MY FRIENDS...THERE AT THE CARNIVAL, THE GAY PRIDE MARCHES.

SAY YOU SAW BEYOND MY UNIFORM. PLEASE SAY YOU KNEW I CARED. I...

PLEASE...

WAIT....

WAIT! WHERE ARE YOU GOING?

PLEASE DON'T LEAVE ME.

WE TREATED YOU SO BADLY, ALL THE HATEFUL THINGS WE PRINTED, DID AND SAID...BUT PLEASE, PLEASE DON'T DESPISE US. WE WERE STUPID, WE WERE KIDS, WE DIDN'T KNOW.

COME BACK. OH PLEASE COME BACK.

I LOVE YOU.

AHUH.

AHUHUHUH....

I LOVE YOU, I....

OH *ERIC*, LOOK AT YOU IN YOUR PYJAMAS! GO BACK TO BED. I'M JUST MAKING BACON AND EGGS TO KEEP YOUR STRENGTH UP.

DELIA?

DELIA, I'M SO MIXED UP. IF I COULD JUST GET THINGS *STRAIGHT*....

WHAT THINGS?

WHAT I'M *DOING* HERE, WHAT'S *HAPPENING* TO ME....

I REMEMBER THAT I CAME HERE TO FIND SOMETHING *OUT*....SOMETHING VERY VITAL TO VARIOUS VENTURES....I WAS PLANNING TO TAKE A *DRUG*....

A *DRUG?* WELL, THAT'S WHAT I'M *HERE* FOR. PLEASE ROLL UP YOUR SLEEVE....

....AS FOR YOUR *EMOTIONAL* PROBLEMS, PERHAPS YOU SHOULD TALK TO TONY *LILLIMAN*, HE'S OUR *PADRE*.

LILLIMAN? I THOUGHT HE WAS A *BISHOP?*

NO. MERELY A *PAWN*.

NOW, TELL ME: WHEN DID YOU STOP BELIEVING IN GOD?

B-BUT.... I NEVER SAID....

DON'T MOLLYCODDLE HIM! BLESSED *SKY-PILOTS!* NOTHING WRONG WITH HIM A SHOT OF *JUNGLE-JUICE* WON'T CURE, EH?

HMM. YOU'RE PROBABLY *RIGHT*. IN MY EXPERIENCE, POISON SOLVES MOST OF LIFE'S PROBLEMS....

HE'S FINISHED HERE, MR. PROTHERO, HE'S YOURS.

WHAT....? DELIA, THEY'RE TAKING ME *AWAY!* DON'T LET THEM....

COME ON, MATEY. DON'T MAKE ME *MAD*.

DELIA?

DELIA, WHAT ABOUT THE BACON AND *EGGS?*

....IN NOMINI PATRI, ET FILII, ET SPIRITUS SANCTI....

DELIA, *PLEASE*, YOU WEREN'T *LIKE* THEM. I *KNOW* YOU WEREN'T, YOU HAD A *HEART*. PLEASE DON'T LET THEM *DO* THIS.

DELIA, ARE YOU *LISTENING?* I....

OH NO.

V

HKUGH !!!

HOW?

HOW DID I GET HERE, TO THIS STINKING PLACE; MY JOB, MY LIFE; MY CONSCIENCE; MY PRISON...

THE ANSWER'S THERE, WRITTEN ON THE FLOOR FOR ME TO READ, BUT I DON'T UNDER-STAND IT.

AND YES, IT'S JUST THE DRUGS, BUT...

BUT HE WAS DRUGGED TOO, LOCKED AWAY TO DIE, AND HE REACHED SOME UNDERSTANDING.

WHY CAN'T I? I LOOK AT THIS MAD PATTERN, BUT WHERE ARE THE ANSWERS?

WHO IMPRISONED ME HERE? WHO KEEPS ME HERE?

WHO CAN RELEASE ME? WHO'S CONTROLLING AND CONSTRAINING MY LIFE, EXCEPT...

...ME?

I...

I'M FREE.

FREEEEEE!

VAULTING, VEERING, VOMITING UP THE VALUES THAT VICTIMIZED ME, FEELING VAST, FEELING VIRGINAL....

WAS THIS HOW HE FELT? THIS VERVE, THIS VITALITY....

....THIS VISION.

LA VOIE....

LA VÉRITÉ....

LA VIE.

NOVEMBER 7TH, 1998. THE SHADOW GALLERY:

EVERYTIME... WE SAY GOODBYE

Y'KNOW, THAT JUKEBOX, IT'S LIKE WAITING IN A SEASIDE CAFE ON A WET WEEKEND.

ARE YOU GOING TO DO SOMETHING, OR JUST SIT OUT THE CHAOS DOWN HERE?

... I DIE A LITTLE...

THE CHAOS PROGRESSES SPLENDIDLY WITHOUT US, EVE. FOR MY PART, I RATHER THINK THE TIME HAS COME FOR PUTTING CERTAIN THINGS TO ORDER.

WELL, WHAT DOES THAT MEAN? ARE WE GOING TO DO SOMETHING, OR NOT?

EVERY-TIME... WE SAY GOODBYE...

DO WHAT THOU WILT, EVE. THAT SHALL BE THE WHOLE OF THE LAW.

UH-UH. QUOTING ALEISTER CROWLEY ISN'T GOOD ENOUGH. IT DOESN'T ANSWER MY QUESTION.

I WANT TO KNOW WHAT THOU WILT, Y. I WANT TO KNOW WHAT YOUR WILL IS.

... I WONDER WHY A LITTLE...

YOU WANT ME TO SHOW YOU MY WILL? VERY WELL...

VERY WELL, THEN.

DO THE GODS ABOVE ME, WHO MUST BE IN THE KNOW ... THINK SO LITTLE OF ME...

THIS WAY.

...THEY'D ALLOW YOU... TO GO?

# CHAPTER V
## THE VALEDICTION

WHY DOES EVERYTHING NEED A BIG DEMONSTRATION? I ASK THE SIMPLEST QUESTION, AND IT'S LIKE ALICE IN WONDERLAND.

I'VE BEEN READING FOR MONTHS, I'M SMARTER NOW. COULDN'T YOU TRY JUST EXPLAINING FOR ME?

YOU ASKED FOR KNOWLEDGE, EVE, AND THAT IS WHAT I SHALL PASS ON TO YOU.

KNOWLEDGE, LIKE AIR, IS VITAL TO LIFE. LIKE AIR, NO ONE SHOULD BE DENIED IT.

OH, Y' COME ON...

YOU'VE ALWAYS KEPT THINGS MYSTERIOUS; YOURSELF, THIS PLACE, YOUR PLANS ... IF KNOWLEDGE IS LIKE AIR, YOU'VE BEEN SUFFOCATING ME.

NOT AT ALL. I'VE BEEN TEACHING YOU TO BREATHE.

THIS WAY.

REGARD THE AIR OF KNOWLEDGE HERE CONDENSED TO LIQUID ELECTRICITY.

THE FACTS OF ALL SOCIETY ARE CENTRALIZED HEREIN ... A FACT THAT'S FIGURED IN SOCIETY'S UNDOING ...

... FOR I HAVE TAPPED THEIR KNOWLEDGE-WELL. SOON, EVERYONE SHALL DRINK.

Y'KNOW, I BET EVEN I COULD WORK THIS COMPUTER. IT'S REALLY LINKED TO FATE?

... AND FATE IS LINKED TO EVERYTHING. IN A BUREAUCRACY, THE FILE CARDS ARE REALITY.

PUNCHING NEW HOLES, WE RECREATE THE WORLD.

THIS WAY.

OK, ARE THESE ROOMS CONNECTED?

EVERYTHING IS CONNECTED.

YOU MUST UNDERSTAND THAT KNOWLEDGE IS NOT ALL YOUR HERITAGE,

IT INCLUDES ALSO COURAGE AND BELIEF, LIKE HERS THAT WE COMMEMORATE HEREIN...

... AND ROMANCE,

ALWAYS, ALWAYS ROMANCE.

'MIDST INSURRECTION'S CLAMOUR, WE MAY EASILY FORGET JUST WHAT IT IS FOR WHICH WE STRIVE....

ISN'T IT DAN- CING? SCENTED SHOULDERS? PUPILS WIDENED BY DESIRE OR WINE?

ANARCHY MUST EMBRACE THE DIN OF BOMBS AND CANNON-FIRE....

"...YET ALWAYS MUST IT LOVE SWEET MUSIC MORE."

"...BUT HOW STRANGE...THE CHANGE...FROM MA-JOR TO MI-NOR,...

NO, I STILL CAN'T GET THAT LAST BIT.

PERSEVERE, EVE, UNDER- STANDING MUSIC, WE MAY HEAR THE MUSIC THAT THERE IS IN LIFE, FROM ITS FIRST INSUFFICIENT TRILLS...

...UNTO ITS CLOSING MINOR CHORDS.

SO LET ME SEE...

OH, I GET IT. THOSE THREE ROOMS UPSTAIRS ARE JOINED WITH THE PIANO ROOM BELOW.

INDEED. IMAGINE WE'RE INSIDE YOUR MIND, EACH AREA WITH ITS SKILLS AND FUNCTIONS: KNOWL- EDGE, PLEASURE, CREATIVITY...

ALL THAT RE- MAINS, THEN, IS TO MAKE THE PROPER NEURAL CONNECTIONS.

UP THERE, THE HIGHER ATTRIBUTES OF REASON, LOVE AND CULTURE ARE CONTAINED.

DOWN HERE, THE SHADOW GALLERY HAS EYES.

WAIT. LET ME GET MY BEARINGS. MY ROOM'S ON THIS LEVEL, OFF THE OTHER STAIRCASE, SOMEWHERE OVER... THERE? IS THAT RIGHT?

UNERRINGLY.

BUT COME.... HERE'S SOME- THING THAT YOU'VE NEVER SEEN...

220

...INDEED, FEW MEN HAVE HAD THE CHANCE TO STUDY THEIR OWN OPTIC NERVES.

Y... ALL THESE T.V.'S ...THEY'RE *WORKING*. I THOUGHT YOU'D BLACKED ALL THE TELEVISIONS OUT?

OH NO, THE *MONITOR CAMERAS* ARE STILL FUNCTIONING, BUT OUR *ADVERSARIES'* BROAD-CASTING AND RECEIVING APPARATUS *ISN'T*.

MY AP-PARATUS, BY CONTRAST, WORKS *PERFECTLY*.

OF COURSE, WITH ALL STATE BROADCASTING BLANKED OUT, THE ONLY THINGS I SEEM TO GET ARE ALL THESE RIOT-ZONE SOAP OPERAS AND BAD DISASTER MOVIES.

SOME-TIMES I MISS "STORM SAXON."

THE DIALOGUE WAS BETTER.

B-BUT...YOU CAN SEE ALL *LONDON* FROM HERE...

NATURALLY. THIS ROOM'S THE PINNACLE OF AN INVERTED HILH, WHICH ONE DESCENDS TO REACH THE PEAK, BUT, ONCE ARRIVED, CAN SEE FOR *MILES*.

COME ...

TOO MUCH TELE-VISION'S *BAD*, AND YOU HAVE HOMEWORK STILL TO DO.

IN HERE YOU'LL FIND BOOKS AND EQUIP-MENT THAT WILL TELL YOU HOW TO MAKE EXPLOSIVES OUT OF COFFEE, OR MAKE PSYCHEDELIC DRUGS AS CHEAP AS *WATER*.

USE THEM *WISELY*, IF AT *ALL*.

UNLIKE T.V., WE CANNOT HAVE TOO MUCH OF SCIENCE, DESPITE ITS NUCLEAR QUIRKS.

WITH SCIENCE, IDEAS CAN GERMINATE WITHIN A BED OF THEORY, FORM, AND PRACTICE THAT ASSISTS THEIR *GROWTH*....BUT WE, AS GARDENERS, MUST *BEWARE*...

FOR SOME SEEDS ARE THE SEEDS OF RUIN...

...AND THE MOST IRIDESCENT BLOOMS ARE OFTEN THE MOST *DANGEROUS*.

OH, THE ROSE ROOM.

YOU KNOW, THIS PLACE MAKES ME FEEL FUNNY, IT'S LIKE THAT RAY BRAD-BURY STORY YOU READ ME, WITH THE CORN-FIELD, AND EACH EAR OF CORN IS SOME-BODY'S *LIFE*...

...EXCEPT YOU CAN'T HAVE A ROSE FOR *EVERYBODY* HERE, CAN YOU? JUST *SPECIAL* PEOPLE...

IS THERE A ROSE HERE FOR THE *LEADER*; FOR MR. SUSAN?

OH NO, NOT HERE, FOR HIM, I'VE CULTIVATED A MOST *SPECIAL* ROSE,

COME... LET US LEAVE THIS SCENTED BOWER, I TRUST YOU WILL TAKE CARE OF IT.

YOU'RE LETTING ME LOOK AFTER THE ROSES? THAT'LL BE NICE, I...

AH, BACK ON THE STAIR-WELL, ARE WE GOING FARTHER DOWN?

OH YES, YOU'LL COME TO KNOW THIS PLACE, IN ALL ITS LENGTHS AND DEPTHS,

WHAT'S ON THE NEXT FLOOR?

NOT SO MUCH A FLOOR, BUT MORE A *MEZZANINE*; THERE ARE THINGS STORED HERE THAT WE'LL SOON HAVE NEED OF FARTHER *DOWN*.

THERE'S BUT ONE FLOOR TO GO, IF YOU COULD CARRY ONE OF THESE SMALL PARCELS, I'D BE *GRATEFUL*... BUT TAKE *CARE*.

SURE, WHAT'S IN THEM?

GELIGNITE.

GELIGNITE? OH JESUS...

V, I'M NOT HELPING WITH ANY *KILLING*, WHAT ARE YOU PLANNING TO *DO* WITH IT?

DISPOSE OF IT,

AFTER ALL, AS YOU POINT OUT, *YOU* WON'T BE NEEDING IT.

ANARCHY WEARS TWO FACES, BOTH *CREATOR* AND *DESTROYER*.

THUS DESTROYERS TOPPLE EMPIRES; MAKE A CANVAS OF CLEAN RUBBLE WHERE CREATORS CAN THEN BUILD A BETTER WORLD.

" RUBBLE, ONCE ACHIEVED, MAKES FURTHER RUINS' MEANS *IRRELEVANT*.

*AWAY* WITH OUR EXPLOSIVES, THEN!

*AWAY* WITH OUR DESTROYERS! THEY HAVE NO PLACE WITHIN OUR BETTER WORLD.

BUT LET US RAISE A TOAST TO ALL OUR BOMBERS, ALL OUR BASTARDS, MOST UN-LOVELY AND MOST UNFORGIVABLE,

LET'S DRINK THEIR HEALTH ....

...THEN MEET WITH THEM NO MORE.

OH. OH, IT'S *LOVELY!* IT'S .... V, WHERE DID YOU GET ....

HUSH, PLEASE ... SHOW SOME *REVERENCE*.

COME, LET US BE DISCREET AND PLACE THE GELIG-NITE BEHIND THE *LILIES* ...

OH, V, THESE *FLOWERS* ....

THESE RAILS ... THEY AREN'T *REAL GOLD*, ARE THEY? I LOVE THE WAY IT'S *PAINTED* ...

IT'S LIKE A BEAUTIFUL OLD *BARGE*.

WHAT'S IT *FOR?* V?

V, I SAID, WHAT'S IT *FOR?*

V?

V, PLEASE, YOU WERE TALKING ABOUT SHARING KNOWLEDGE AND NOW YOU WALK OFF WITHOUT ANSWERING ME.
YOU HAVEN'T GIVEN ME ANY ANSWERS AT ALL. I STARTED OUT ASKING YOU WHAT YOU WERE GOING TO DO...
YOU ASKED ME TO REVEAL MY WILL. I HAVE DONE SO.
HUH?
V, I'M TIRED OF GUESSING GAMES. I JUST WANTED TO KNOW IF YOU WERE PLANNING TO GO OUT OR NOT.
NO. I HAVE TO STAY IN. I'M WAITING.
WAITING? FOR WHAT?
NOT FOR WHAT. FOR WHOM.
ALL RIGHT! ALL RIGHT. FOR WHOM ARE YOU WAITING?
I'M WAITING FOR THE MAN.
IF THAT'S ANOTHER...
IT IS, ISN'T IT? IT'S ANOTHER BLOODY QUOTE! I'VE HEARD IT ON THE JUKEBOX.
V, I HATE THIS. ALL OUR CONVERSATIONS TURN INTO CROSS-WORD PUZZLES!
I MEAN, IF THERE'S SOMETHING YOU WANT TO SAY, IF THERE'S SOMETHING I SHOULD KNOW...
SURELY IT'S NOT SO BAD YOU CAN'T JUST GIVE IT TO ME STRAIGHT?
V? ARE YOU LISTENING?
LOOK, I'M SERIOUS...
I GIVE UP ON THE PUZZLES. I JUST WANT TO TURN THE PAGE UPSIDE DOWN AND READ THE ANSWERS.
WELL?
V, I'M WAITING.
FAREWELL, MY LOVELY
WHAT ARE YOU TRYING TO TELL ME?

NOVEMBER 9TH, 1998:

CHAPTER 6
VECTORS

"9.11.'98; 2.30 PM. SCHEDULED PUBLIC APPEARANCE BY LEADER TO RESTORE PUBLIC CALM..."

THEY CAN'T BE SERIOUS ABOUT THIS, CAN THEY?

FROM ALL REPORTS, POOR OLD SUSAN'S ABSOLUTELY BARKING! HOW WILL SEEING THAT RESTORE PUBLIC CALM?

ONLY SOFT CENTRES LEFT. SHIT.

OF COURSE, EVERY-BODY'S SEEN IT COMING FOR YEARS, ALL THOSE THINGS HE SAID, BACK WHEN HE WAS STILL CHIEF CONSTABLE...

HUM. PERHAPS STRAWBERRY...

OMF

I BET ...U/S... I BET THIS WAS CREEDY'S IDEA. PROBABLY HOPING FOR RIOTS SO HE CAN DEMAND SUSAN ALLOW HIM MORE THUGS FOR HIS PRIVATE ARMY.

SWEATY LITTLE CROOK.

HONESTLY, HOW WOULD SOMEONE LIKE CREEDY HOPE TO RUN A COUNTRY?

RE-OPEN THE FOOTBALL LEAGUE? PUT TITS ON PAGE THREE OF THE PARTY CHRON-ICLE? OBVIOUSLY HE...

NO.

NOT NOW, CONRAD.

FOR NOW YOU CAN HAVE A NICE CHOCO-LATE INSTEAD. OPEN. OPEN UP...

THERE. AS FOR THE REST OF THE BOX...

...PERHAPS WHEN YOU'RE LEADER.

HULLO, MESTER CREEDY. YUR UP EN ABOOT EARLY THEN?

HELLO, ALLY. BY HECK, THE LEADER'S PICKED A WINDY OLD DAY FOR HIS WALKABOUT, EH?

AYE, WULL, ET'S AN ELL WEND THAT BLOWS NAE BASTUD ENNY GUID, EH?

HA HA. YOU MIGHT BE RIGHT, ALLY. YOU MIGHT BE RIGHT...

I MEAN, TAKE THIS PARADE: ONCE THE PUNTERS SEE WHAT'S SUPPOSED TO BE LEADING 'EM...

I MEAN, WHO KNOWS?

CAREFUL WITH THAT CATTLE-BARRIER, SONNY.

SORRY, SIR.

I RECKON AFTER TODAY, THEY'LL BE BEGGING FOR A LEADER WITH GUTS.

I TELL YOU, RUNNING THE FINGER'S GOT POSSIBILITIES, DUNNO WHY NO-BODY'S REALISED BEFORE...

AYE, HANG ABOOT A MENNIT, EH?

SURE. I MEAN, WHY DIDN'T MY PREDECESSOR TRY SOME-THING?

CONFIRM RICHMOND TERRACE CLEAR, OVER?

WHAT WAS HE LIKE, OLD ALMOND? BIT OF A PONCE, FROM ALL ACCOUNTS...

FOX BRAVO TWO, WHITEHALL CLEAR TO CHARING CROSS...

WULL, HE'D NO CONSIDER USEN MY LAADS FER SECURETY, THAT'S CERTEN. TAE STUCK AP.

A VERY SUPERIOR MAAN, MESTER ALMOND. THAAS WHUT A LIKE ABOOT YU...

A MEAN, YUR NO SUPERIOR ET ALL. QUATE THE RUHVERSE, EN FAACT.

LISSEN, A GOATA PESS OFF, SEE YUZ LATER, A'RIGHT?

RIGHT, SEE YOU LATER.

228

LOOK... HERE IT IS, IT'S SUPPOSED TO BE *HIDDEN*, BUT YOU CAN SEE THE *LENS*.

EVERY PARTY MEMBER'S BEDROOM HAS ONE, EVEN HIS *OWN!*

AND HE WONDERS WHY I WON'T LET HIM *TOUCH* ME.

OF COURSE, NONE OF HIS SPY CAMERAS ARE WORKING NOW.

THERE HE SITS AT WORK AMIDST ALL THE FUSS OF THIS PARADE, AND ALL HIS LITTLE *SCREENS* ARE *DEAD*.

A *BLIND VOYEUR*, HA!

HERE THEY ARE, CONRAD, HERE'S WHAT YOU'RE *MISSING*.

TOO BAD YOU CAN'T *SEE* THEM.

YOU'VE NO IDEA HOW *HARD* IT'S BEEN, MANOEUVERING HIM INTO A POSITION WHERE HE CAN TAKE *CHARGE*.

OF COURSE, I'LL BE MAKING ALL THE *REAL* DECISIONS... BACKED UP BY YOUR *MUSCLE*, OBVIOUSLY.

I'M GOING TO BE LIKE EVA *PERON*, YOU KNOW, DID YOU EVER SEE "*EVITA*"?

*DON'T CRY FOR ME, ARGENTINA, THE TRUTH IS...*

EH C'MOAN, GESSA DRAAG...

A-A! DON'T *GRAB*, THIS GRASS COST GOOD MONEY.

IF YOU *WANT* SOME, YOU'LL HAVE TO *EARN* IT.

OH, A'LL *EARN* ET, A'RIGHT...

AM VERY RELIABLE ON THE JOAB, SO THEY...

...WIND SPINS WEATHER-VANES... WALKING, WALKING, THE HAPPY WANDERER, VALDEREE, VALDERA, IT ALL FITS...

THINK LIKE HE THINKS, HE WALKED THIS ROAD BEFORE ME... AND DID THOSE FEET, IN ANCIENT TIMES... BUT WHERE? WHERE DID HE GO...

LIKE A VIXEN TO ITS LAIR, LIKE A VOLE TO ITS HOLE, A VERITABLE VANISHING ACT. BUT WHERE? THINK LIKE HIM, THINK LIKE HIM, FULL OF VOODOO, FULL OF VISION, WHAT WOULD HE DO? WHERE WOULD HE...

UM?

OF COURSE.

OF COURSE!

VICTORIA

THIS STATION CLOSED

CHAPTER 7
VINDICATION

LAUGHING, CHEERING, WAVING: THEY AT LEAST HAVE NOT FORSAKEN ME...

BUT WHY CAN'T I FEEL ANYTHING FOR THEM?

THERE'S ONLY ME HERE, ISN'T THERE? I'VE KNOWN SINCE CHILDHOOD NO ONE ELSE IS REAL.

JUST ME AND GOD. NO BOIL UPON THE DRIVER'S NECK; NO STINKING LEATHER-ETTE; NO CROWDS...

I'D TALK TO MY CREATOR, ABOUT NIGGER BOYS ON THE ESTATES; AND MEN, NAKED IN BED, RUBBING TOGETHER, RUBBING, PUSHING...

WHEN I GREW WEAK, WE'D TALK.

I TALKED TO GOD, WHILE COLLEAGUES LAUGHED...

...BUT I WAS VINDICATED: GOD WAS REAL, EMBODIED IN A FORM THAT I COULD LOVE. WHEN I FIRST SAW HER SCREENS, HER SMOOTH UNYIELDING LINES...

NOT AS A WOMAN, WITH STRANGE SWEAT AND UGLY BODY HAIR, BUT SOMETHING COLD; HARD; SENSUAL. WE LOVED, MY GOD AND I, BUT THEN...

THEN SHE BETRAYED ME. NOW THERE'S NOTHING. NOW I AM ALONE...

...EXCEPT FOR THEM, WAVING BEYOND THE GLASS. I'LL TRY TO LOVE THEM MORE; THEY'RE ALL I HAVE.

SHOULD I WAVE BACK? IT MUSTN'T LOOK REHEARSED, OR INSINCERE, BUT BE IN-STEAD A GESTURE FROM THE HEART...

...AS SPONTANEOUS AS THEIR OWN.

THEY LOVE ME, I PASS ON.

ENGLAND PREVAILS.

A'RIGHT... CUT DOON THE EMBAANK-MENT TAE WHITEHALL AN' WAIT FUR THE MOTORCADE WITH THE PARTY FAITHFUL DOON THERE.

...AN' LESS HAVE A BET MUIR CHEERIN' THESS TIME, EH?

SO HOW CAN YOU TELL ME YOU'RE LONELY...

...AND SAY FOR YOU THAT THE SUN DON'T SHINE?

LET ME TAKE YOU BY THE HAND AND LEAD YOU THROUGH THE STREETS OF LONDON, I'LL SHOW YOU SOMETHING...

...TO MAKE YOU CHANGE YOUR MIND.

SO, MR. FINCH...

FINALLY WE MEET.

WAVE HARDER!    COME ON! WHERE'S THE KIDS? HASN'T ANYONE GOT A FLOWER TO GIVE HIM?

YES.

YES, DESPITE MY FEAR, BECAUSE IT'S INSIGNIFICANT. LIKE EVERYTHING ABOUT ME...

YES, THOUGH THEY'LL KILL ME, BECAUSE IF I DON'T, LIFE MEANS NOTHING...

YES, BECAUSE OUR LIVES WERE WASTED ON YOUR VISIONS, AND THEY WERE ALL WE HAD.

YES, BECAUSE I CAN'T BEAR WHAT YOU'VE DONE TO US...

YES, BECAUSE HISTORY'S MOVING MY LEGS AND NOTHING, NOTHING CAN STOP ME...

OY!

IT'S ALL RIGHT. I KNOW HER, HIGH PARTY. LETTING HER THROUGH'LL LOOK GOOD.

YES, BECAUSE YOUR KIND LED US TO HELL AND NOW YOU SAY OUR ONLY HOPE IS STERNER LEADERS...

THIS WAY. SURE HE'LL APPRECIATE IT...

YES, BECAUSE I'M NEARLY THERE AND EVERYONE'S THINKING "SHE MUST BE IMPORTANT" AND I'M NOT, BUT I WILL BE...

STOP. LET ME TALK TO MY PEOPLE...

YES, BECAUSE I HAD A LIFE, A WORLD, A MARRIAGE AND I VALUED THEM BUT YOU DIDN'T...

SO NICE...

SO NICE MEETING SOMEONE, DO SHAKE HANDS...

YES, BECAUSE WE'VE MET A DOZEN TIMES BEFORE AND MY DEREK DIED FOR YOU AND GOD, YOU DON'T EVEN, DON'T EVEN REMEMBER MY FACE!

PLEASE... DON'T BE SHY...

YES, YES...

YES.

AAAA!

THERE.

DID YOU THINK TO *KILL* ME? THERE'S NO FLESH OR BLOOD WITHIN THIS CLOAK TO KILL.

THERE'S ONLY AN *IDEA.*

IDEAS ARE BULLET-PROOF.

FAREWELL.

OOUGH...

BLOOD,

FLESH AND BLOOD AFTER AhH...

I KILLED YOU, YOU MONSTER...

I KILLED YOU !

CHAPTER 8
VULTURES

DO,,, DO YOU THINK HE'S REALLY DEAD? THE TERRORIST, LIKE FINCH SAID?

FINCH IS HALF OUT OF HIS MIND ON DRUGS, BY ALL ACCOUNTS. STILL, HE'S A BORING, RELIABLE LITTLE MAN,,, HE PROBABLY DID IT.

PARCEL ARRIVED FOR YOU, MR. HEYER.

HM? OH,,,, THANK YOU,,,,

THE QUESTION IS, WHAT NEXT? THE ASSASSINATION'S TAKEN US ALL BY SURPRISE. RIGHT NOW, THIS COUNTRY'S A POLITICAL VACUUM.

NOBODY'S IN CHARGE.

OF COURSE, CREEDY THINKS HE IS. I HOPE HE ENJOYS THE FEELING WHILE IT LASTS.

THINGS NEED ARRANGING, SO I'LL SEE YOU TONIGHT, AND WHO KNOWS, YOU LUCKY BOY,,,,

,,, BY TO-NIGHT, I MIGHT BE IN QUITE A GOOD MOOD.

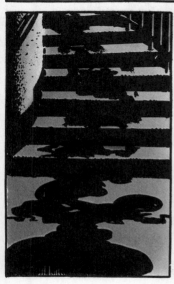

MR. FINCH...? LOOK, I KNOW YOU'RE STILL SHOOK UP AND CONFUSED FROM THE *DRUGS*, BUT...

WELL, WE NEED TO *KNOW* CERTAIN THINGS: ARE YOU *SURE* YOU KILLED THE *TERRORIST?*

MORTALLY WOUNDED. YES, I'M SURE.

I *MEAN*, THE AMOUNT OF *BLOOD*. I *MUST* HAVE KILLED HIM, BUT...

BUT WHAT *I* DON'T UNDERSTAND, MY *BACK* WAS TURNED. I DIDN'T EVEN KNOW HE WAS *THERE*...

...AND WHEN HE *ALERTED* ME, PULLING MY GUN OUT, I WAS SO *SLOW*...

I MEAN, HE'S LIKE GREASED *LIGHTNING*, HE COULD HAVE *STOPPED* ME. HE...

HE COULD HAVE KILLED ME.

HM. YES, WELL, WE'LL TAKE IT HE'S *DEAD*, THEN...

...SO THE ONLY *IMPORTANT* THING IS, WHERE DID ALL THIS *HAPPEN?*

I, UH...

DO YOU KNOW, I DON'T REMEMBER.

MUST BE THE DRUGS, EH?

LOOK.... HERE IT IS. IT'S SUPPOSED TO BE *HIDDEN*, BUT YOU CAN SEE THE *LENS*.

EVERY PARTY MEMBER'S BEDROOM HAS ONE, EVEN HIS *OWN*!

AND HE WONDERS WHY I WON'T LET HIM *TOUCH* ME.

OF COURSE, NONE OF HIS SPY CAMERAS ARE *WORKING* NOW.

THERE HE SITS AT WORK AMIDST ALL THE FUSS OF THIS PARADE AND ALL HIS LITTLE *SCREENS* ARE DEAD.

A BLIND VOYEUR, HA!

HERE THEY ARE, CONRAD.

HERE'S WHAT YOU'RE *MISSING*.

TOO BAD YOU CAN'T *SEE* THEM.

ATTENTION, LONDON. THIS IS EMERGENCY COMMANDER PETER CREEDY SPEAKING.

EVERYTHING IS UNDER CONTROL. THE TERRORIST, CODENAME V, HAS BEEN SHOT AND MORTALLY WOUNDED.

IF HE'S NOT APPEARED BEFORE MID-NIGHT, WE MAY ASSUME HE'S DEAD.

WE REPEAT, THE TERRORIST HAS BEEN SHOT, THE INSURRECTION IS OVER. PLEASE RE-TURN TO YOUR HOMES, AND TO YOUR LOVED ONES.

ATTENTION, LONDON.

THIS IS EMERGENCY COMMANDER PETER CREEDY SPEAKING...

AFTERNOON, ALLY. MY WORD, YOU PATCHED MY TAPELOOP INTO THE PUBLIC BROAD-CAST BLOODY QUICK. GOOD WORK, LADS, TOP MARKS.

EVERYTHING IS UNDER CONTROL.

THE TERRORIST, CODENAME V, HAS BEEN SHOT AND MORTALLY WOUNDED.

I TELL YOU, WITH SUSAN GONE, OUR PARTNERSHIP'LL REALLY COME INTO ITS OWN...

AYE, WELL, A BEN MEANIN' TAE TALK ABOOT THAAT...

GOOD, LET'S TALK. CAN WE TURN THAT THING DOWN?

TERN ET DOON? A WUZ JUST THENKEN ET WUZ A BET QUIET, MASEL', MEBBE A SHUID TERN ET AP?

TURN IT UP? COME ON, STOP ARSING AROUND, IT'S DEAFENING! YOU'D HAVE TO SCREAM TO BE HEARD OVER THAT.

AYE, EVEN THEN YE MIGHT HAAV PROAB-LEMS.

WE MAY ASSUME HE'S DEAD.

WE REPEAT, THE TERROR-IST HAS BEEN SHOT.

WHAT? I'M NOT...

OH JESUS.

JESUS, ALLY, COME ON, DON'T LARK ABOUT. WHAT IS THIS, FOR CHRIST'S SAKE? I'M PAYING YOU GOOD MONEY...

THE INSUR-RECTION IS OVER.

A HAAD A BETTER OAFFER.

AAA!

OOUUGH, OH NO, OH NO !!!

SHOOT ME. COME ON, EH? PLEASE.

JUST SHOOT ME.

PLEASE RETURN TO YOUR HOMES...

...AND TO YOUR LOVED ONES,

A'LL STECK WI' MA MALKY, EF ET'S AAL THE SAME TE YU, LIKE,

TAE BE PERFECKLY HONEST, A WOULDNAE WASTE THE BULLET.

ATTENTION, LONDON,

THIS IS EMERGENCY COMMANDER PETER CREEDY SPEAKING,

EVERYTHING IS UNDER CONTROL.

THE TERRORIST, CODENAME Y, HAS BEEN MORTALLY WOUNDED,

IF HE'S NOT APPEARED BEFORE MIDNIGHT, WE MAY ASSUME HE'S DEAD.

WE REPEAT, THE TERRORIST HAS BEEN SHOT, THE INSURRECTION IS OVER.

PLEASE RETURN TO YOUR HOMES, AND TO YOUR LOVED ONES,

EYE...

OH, YOU'RE BACK.

V, YOU JUST WALKED OFF AFTER SHOWING ME THAT *TRAIN* THING.

WHERE HAVE YOU *BEEN?*

"EVE...

"EVE, LISTEN CAREFULLY. THE ONE I WAITED FOR HAS CALLED, AND NOW I HAVE NOT LONG..."

Y... OH GOD, DON'T TALK, I'LL GET BANDAGES...

NO... I'D BE DEAD ERE YOU RETURNED, AND THERE ARE THINGS THAT YOU MUST KNOW...

"THIS COUNTRY IS NOT SAVED... DO NOT THINK THAT... BUT ALL ITS OLD BELIEFS HAVE COME TO RUBBLE, AND FROM RUBBLE MAY WE BUILD...

"THAT IS THEIR TASK: TO RULE THEMSELVES; THEIR LIVES AND LOVES AND LAND..."

WITH THIS ACHIEVED, THEN LET THEM TALK OF SALVATION. WITHOUT IT, THEY ARE SURELY CARRION.

OH NO, OH PLEASE...

BY TURN OF CENTURY THEY'LL KNOW THEIR FATE: EITHER A ROSE MIDST RUBBLE BLOOMS, OR ELSE HAS BLOOMED TOO LATE.

" BUT WHAT OF YOU, CHILD, NOW I'M DEAD?"

"YOU'RE NOT! YOU'RE NOT GOING TO DIE!"

"HUSH. FIRST, YOU MUST DISCOVER WHOSE FACE LIES BEHIND THIS MASK, BUT YOU MUST NEVER KNOW MY FACE. IS THAT QUITE CLEAR?"

WHAT? WHAT ARE YOU SAYING?

...ALSO...THE VICTORIA LINE IS BLOCKED...TWIXT WHITEHALL AND ST. JAMES...GIVE ME A VIKING FUNERAL...

GOOD LUCK, SWEET EVE. I LOVE YOU.

AYE... ATQUE... VALE...

CHAPTER 9
THE VIGIL

"V?"

"YOU'RE ALMOST FINISHED, AREN'T YOU?"

"SEE FOR YOURSELF, EVE.

"THE PIECES ARE SET OUT BEFORE ME, PERFECTLY ALIGNED.

"COMPLETE, ONE MAY AT LAST GRASP THEIR DESIGN, THEIR GRAND SIGNIFICANCE..."

"...BUT 'ALMOST FINISHED'...?

"YES,

"YES, I SUPPOSE I AM."

—TENTION LONDON. THIS IS EMERGENCY COMMANDER PETER CREEDY SPEAKING. EVERYTHING IS UNDER CONTROL.

THE TERRORIST, CODENAME V, HAS BEEN MORTALLY WOUNDED.

IF HE'S NOT APPEARED BEFORE MIDNIGHT, WE MAY ASSUME HE'S DEAD.

WE REPEAT. THE TERRORIST HAS BEEN SHOT. THE INSURRECTION IS OVER. PLEASE RETURN TO YOUR HOMES, AND TO YOUR LOVED ONES.

ATTENTION LONDON...

"ANARCHY WEARS TWO FACES, BOTH CREATOR AND DESTROYER.

"THUS DESTROYERS TOPPLE EMPIRES, MAKE A CANVAS OF CLEAN RUBBLE WHERE CREATORS THEN CAN BUILD A BETTER WORLD.

"RUBBLE, ONCE ACHIEVED, MAKES FURTHER RUIN'S MEANS IRRELEVANT.

"AWAY WITH OUR EXPLOSIVES THEN! AWAY WITH OUR DESTROYERS! THEY HAVE NO PLACE WITHIN OUR BETTER WORLD...

"BUT LET US RAISE A TOAST TO ALL OUR BOMBERS, ALL OUR BASTARDS, MOST UNLOVELY AND MOST UNFORGIVABLE.

"LET'S DRINK THEIR HEALTH...

"...THEN MEET WITH THEM NO MORE."

"THE VICTORIA LINE IS BLOCKED... TWIXT WHITEHALL AND ST. JAMES... GIVE ME A VIKING FUNERAL...

"FIRST, YOU MUST DISCOVER WHOSE FACE LIES BEHIND THIS MASK, BUT YOU MUST NEVER KNOW MY FACE. IS THAT QUITE CLEAR?"

NO.

NO, IT ISN'T CLEAR AT ALL.

V, YOU WOULDN'T DIE AND LEAVE ME IN ALL THIS CONFUSION, SO YOU CAN'T BE DEAD. THAT'S ALL THERE IS TO IT.

I'M GOING TO WALK UP THESE STAIRS AND THROUGH THAT DOOR AND YOU'LL BE ALIVE AND IT WILL BE JUST ANOTHER MEAN TRICK, ANOTHER PART OF MY EDUCATION.

NO HANGING BACK, STRAIGHT UP THE STAIRS, STRAIGHT THROUGH THE DOOR, AND...

SO, DEAD THEN?

OH CHRIST, WHAT HAPPENS NEXT? YOU NEVER SAID. YOU NEVER SAID WHAT YOU WERE EDUCATING ME FOR.

YOU NEVER TOLD ME WHAT I'M SUPPOSED TO DO.

ALL RIGHT.

ALL RIGHT, THEN, WHAT I DO IS THIS:

I WALK TOWARDS THE BODY, VERY QUIETLY, VERY REVERENTLY...

...AND I STOOP DOWN, MY FINGERS STRUGGLE CLUMSILY WITH ELASTICATED STRAPS...

...AND THEN I TAKE OFF THE MASK...

NO.

NO, THAT ISN'T WHAT I DO.

WHAT I DO IS, IN TEARS I STUMBLE OVER TO THE CORPSE.

IT'S SLIPPERY WITH BLOOD BENEATH MY FINGERS, BUT I TEAR THE MASK ASIDE, AND...

NO.

NO, THAT'S NOT IT.

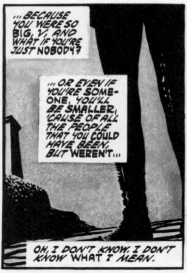

"...BECAUSE YOU WERE SO BIG, V, AND WHAT IF YOU'RE JUST NOBODY?

"...OR EVEN IF YOU'RE SOMEONE, YOU'LL BE SMALLER, 'CAUSE OF ALL THE PEOPLE THAT YOU COULD HAVE BEEN, BUT WEREN'T...

OH, I DON'T KNOW. I DON'T KNOW WHAT I MEAN.

JUST DO IT. THERE'S NO REASON WHY I SHOULDN'T. NO ONE HERE TO STOP ME.

I'LL JUST WALK ACROSS THE FLOOR AND TAKE HOLD OF THE MASK, AND...

NO, NO, I'M PAST THAT ONE. YOU WEREN'T MY DAD, I KNOW THAT.

EVEN IF YOU WERE, IT WOULDN'T BE ENOUGH.

IF I TAKE OFF THAT MASK, SOMETHING WILL GO AWAY FOREVER, BE DIMINISHED BECAUSE WHOEVER YOU ARE ISN'T AS BIG AS THE IDEA OF YOU, BUT... BUT...

BUT YOU SAID I HAD TO, THAT I HAD TO KNOW...

"SO I START WALKING TOWARDS THE BODY, TRYING NOT TO TREAD IN ALL THE BLOOD..."

IT DOESN'T MOVE. IT DOESN'T LOOK MUCH LIKE A PERSON ANYMORE. SOMETHING HAS GONE FROM IT.

I KNEEL, MY HANDS ARE TREMBLING, I CAN HARDLY FIND THE FASTENINGS, BUT FINALLY I LIFT AWAY THAT MADDENING SMILE, AND...

...AND AT LAST I KNOW.

I KNOW WHO V MUST BE.

NOVEMBER 9TH, 1998, 3.30 P.M.:

THEY'RE STILL THERE, NOT *DOING* ANYTHING, MIND. JUST *WAITING*.

IT'S FUNNY ...THEY'RE NOT THE TERRORIST'S *FOLLOWERS* OR ANYTHING. THEY'RE JUST *RIOTERS.*

...BUT HE'S BECOME SOME SORT OF ALL-PURPOSE *SYMBOL* TO THEM, HASN'T HE?

PEOPLE *NEED* SYMBOLS, DOMINIC. *HE*, UNDERSTOOD THAT. WE'VE *FORGOTTEN* IT.

THOSE PEOPLE OUTSIDE LOST *FAMILIES* DURING THE WAR.

WE'VE KEPT THE LID ON THEIR BITTERNESS FOR *YEARS*, BUT WE HAVEN'T HELPED THEM *DEAL* WITH IT.

MAYBE *HE* DIDN'T EITHER, BUT HE CERTAINLY TOOK THE *LID* OFF...

...JUST LIKE *LARKHILL* DID FOR ME. EVERYTHING'S *DIFFERENT* NOW, DOMINIC. I DON'T *BELONG* HERE ANYMORE.

Y-YOU'RE GOING? MR. FINCH, LISTEN, IT'S THE *DRUGS*...

SUSAN'S DEAD, WITH CREEDY AND HEYER DIVIDING HIS CARCASS. *THEY'RE* NOT HALLUCINATIONS.

NEITHER WAS THE *WAR*. I LOST MY FAMILY, AND THOUGHT FOLLOWING ORDERS COULD *HEAL* THAT.

IT CAN'T.

I'M FOLLOWING MY *OWN* ORDERS NOW, AND GETTING OUT BEFORE EVERYTHING BLOWS. PERHAPS *YOU* SHOULD, TOO.

GOODBYE, DOMINIC.

TAKE CARE, LAD.

# CHAPTER 10
# THE VOLCANO

HULLOO?

SOARY AM LATE AN A' THAAT. CREEDY TUKE A BET LOANGER THUN UNTESSAPATED.

STELL, WE GOAT A COUPLE' HOOR BEFORE HUBBY GETS BAAK, EH?'

BUT YOU CAN SEE THE LENS.

A CANNAE HEAR A WUD YUR SAYIN', GESSA MENNET AN A'LL BE WI' YE.

EH, A SPOAK TAE MOST O'THE CHIEF COAPERS, AN' THEY ACCEPT THE NU MAANAGE- MENT, NAE BATHER.

SEE, THEY DIDNAE LIKE CREEDY EITHER, SO ET LUKES LIKE WE...

EVERY PARTY MEMBER'S BEDROOM HAS ONE, EVEN HIS OWN, AND HE WONDERS WHY I WON'T LET HIM TOUCH ME.

OF COURSE, NONE OF HIS SPY CAMERAS ARE WORK- ING NOW.

THERE HE SITS AT WORK AMIDST THE FUSS OF THIS PARADE, AND ALL HIS LITTLE SCREENS ARE DEAD.

A BLIND VOYEUR. HA!

HERE THEY ARE, CONRAD. HERE'S WHAT YOU'RE MISSING.

TOO BAD YOU CAN'T SEE THEM.

YOU'VE NO IDEA HOW HARD IT'S BEEN MANEUVERING HIM INTO A POSITION WHERE HE CAN TAKE CHARGE.

OF COURSE, I'LL BE MAKING ALL THE REAL DECISIONS ...BACKED UP BY YOUR MUSCLE, OBVIOUSLY.

I'M GOING TO BE LIKE EVA PERON, YOU KNOW.

OH.

SO YOU FINALLY SHOWED *UP*. I'VE BEEN ROUND HALF LONDON LOOKING FOR YOU.

WELL, YOU CAN PULL YOUR TROUSERS BACK UP AND PISS OFF. CONRAD'S HOME IN AN HOUR.

AT LEAST NOBODY HAS SEEN *CREEDY* SINCE TEA-TIME, WHICH PROBABLY INDICATES YOU'VE DONE *SOME-THING* RIGHT AT *LEAST*.

BUT IF YOU THINK THAT ENTITLES YOU TO...

K-HELEN...?

I WON, HELEN...

I WAS... BEST MAN...

HE'S GONE... GONE NOW... WON'T COME... BETWEEN US ...ANYMORE...

CUT ME... HAD A RAZOR ...THINK HE HIT A VEIN...

BUT YOU... YOU CAN GET ME TO A DOCTOR...

WE'VE BEEN... THROUGH A BAD PATCH, HELEN, BUT...

BUT WE CAN STILL...

DON'T TOUCH ME! YOU STUPID PIECE OF SHIT, DON'T TOUCH ME!

YOU'VE RUINED IT! YOU'VE RUINED IT ALL!

HELEN...

HOW ARE WE GOING TO CONTROL THE FINGER NOW? CHRIST, I HAD IT PLANNED. I HAD IT ALL PLANNED— OH, YOU STUPID...

K-KELEN...? WHAT... WHAT ARE YOU DOING?

I'M LOOK-ING FOR SOMETHING, I KNOW IT'S HERE SOME-WHERE, BUT...

AH, FOUND IT.

HELEN... THERE'S NO TIME ...I'M BLEEDING... BLEEDING VERY BADLY...

NEED A DOCTOR...

OK NO, NO, YOU DON'T.

I KNOW WHAT YOU NEED, CONRAD. I'VE ALWAYS KNOWN WHAT YOU NEED.

YOU NEED TO WATCH, DON'T YOU, CONRAD? NEED TO WATCH IN YOUR WORK; IN YOUR BED...

WELL, I'VE GOT SOMETHING YOU'RE GOING TO LOVE.

THERE, CONRAD. MY PARTING GIFT.

WATCH THAT.

HELEN?

ME? SENIOR *AUTHORITY?* WELL, WHERE'S *CREEDY,* FOR GOD'S SAKE? *HE* SHOULD BE HANDLING THIS.

I SHOULDN'T WORRY, SIR, THEY'LL PROBABLY GIVE UP AND GO HOME AT MID-NIGHT, ONCE THEY ACCEPT THE TERROR-IST'S DEAD.

IT'S NEARLY TWELVE NOW...

AH, THERE YOU *ARE,* SIR.

THERE'S BIG BEN STRIKING THE HOUR NOW.

LOVELY, REASSURING SOUND, DON'T YOU THINK, SIR?

UH, YES, YES, I SUPPOSE I...

WAIT A MINUTE...

BIG BEN WAS BLOWN UP TWELVE MONTHS AGO.

THE *SPEAKERS!* IT'S COMING FROM THE *SPEAKERS!*

THAT MEANS SOMEONE MUST...

...HAVE...

GOOD EVENING, LONDON.

I WOULD INTRODUCE MY-SELF, BUT TRUTH TO TELL, I DO NOT HAVE A *NAME*.

YOU CAN CALL ME "V".

SINCE MANKIND'S DAWN, A HANDFUL OF OPPRESSORS HAVE ACCEPTED THE RE-SPONSIBILITY OVER OUR LIVES THAT WE SHOULD HAVE ACCEPTED FOR *OURSELVES*.

BY DOING SO, THEY TOOK OUR *POWER*.

BY DOING NOTHING, WE GAVE IT AWAY.

WE'VE SEEN WHERE THEIR WAY LEADS, THROUGH CAMPS AND WARS, TOWARDS THE SLAUGHTERHOUSE.

IN ANARCHY, THERE IS ANOTHER WAY.

WITH ANARCHY, FROM RUBBLE COMES NEW LIFE, HOPE RE-INSTATED. THEY SAY ANARCHY'S DEAD, BUT SEE ...

REPORTS OF MY DEATH WERE ...

...EXAGGERATED.

TOMORROW, DOWNING STREET WILL BE DESTROYED, THE HEAD REDUCED TO RUINS, AN END TO WHAT HAS GONE BEFORE.

TONIGHT, YOU MUST CHOOSE WHAT COMES NEXT. LIVES OF OUR *OWN*, OR A RETURN TO *CHAINS*.

CHOOSE *CAREFULLY*.

AND SO, ADIEU.

NOVEMBER 10TH, 1998. 2.00 A.M.:

"GIVE ME A VIKING FUNERAL," YOU SAID.

THAT ISN'T MUCH.

THAT ISN'T MUCH TO ASK.

NOT AFTER ALL YOU DID.

YOU CAME OUT OF AN ABATTOIR UN-HARMED, BUT NOT UNCHANGED. AND SAW FREEDOM'S NECESSITY; NOT JUST FOR YOU, BUT FOR US ALL.

YOU SAW, AND, SEEING, DARED TO DO.

HOW PURPOSEFUL WAS YOUR VENDETTA; HOW BENIGN, ALMOST LIKE SURGERY ...

YOUR FOES ASSUMED YOU SOUGHT REVENGE UPON THEIR FLESH ALONE, BUT YOU DID NOT STOP THERE ...

YOU GORED THEIR IDEOLOGY AS WELL.

THE PEOPLE STAND WITHIN THE RUINS OF SOCIETY, A JAIL INTENDED TO OUT-LIVE THEM ALL.

THE DOOR IS OPEN. THEY CAN LEAVE, OR FALL INSTEAD TO SQUABBLING AND THENCE NEW SLAVERIES.

THE CHOICE IS THEIRS, AS EVER IT MUST BE.

I WILL NOT LEAD THEM, BUT I'LL HELP THEM BUILD, HELP THEM CREATE WHERE I'LL NOT HELP THEM KILL.

THE AGE OF KILLERS IS NO MORE.

THEY HAVE NO PLACE WITHIN OUR BETTER WORLD.

"GIVE ME A VIKING FUNERAL," YOU SAID.

IT'S YOURS, MY LOVE...

# CHAPTER 11 VALHALLA

IT'S YOURS.

AWAY.

AWAY YOU GO, WITH ALL YOUR GELIGNITE AND LILIES,

HOW MUCH EXPLOSIVE WAS THERE ON THAT TRAIN? I NEVER THOUGHT TO COUNT THE PACKAGES.

ENOUGH, I BET.

PERHAPS A LITTLE MORE...

YOU SAID THAT THE VICTORIA LINE WAS BLOCKED 'TWIXT WHITEHALL AND ST. JAMES. I CHECKED, AND YES, IT'S TRUE: THERE'S RUBBLE SEALING OFF THE LINE.

"GIVE ME A VIKING FUNERAL," YOU SAID,

I HAVE FOUR MINUTES LEFT TO TAKE THE ELEVATOR TO THE ROOF, SO EASY NOW TO FIND MY WAY AROUND...

UPON OUR GUIDED TOUR YOU SHOWED THIS PLACE TO ME AND SAID IT WAS YOUR WILL...

I DIDN'T UNDERSTAND...

NOT THEN...

...BUT YOU WERE RIGHT, OF COURSE, ABOUT THIS PLACE. YOU DID SHOW ME YOUR WILL...

...AND I'M SOLE BENEFICIARY.

IT'S TWO FOUR- TEEN. YOU'RE ALMOST THERE NOW, SPEEDING ON YOUR FUNERAL BARGE ALONG DRY SUBTERRANEAN CANALS...

DOWN THROUGH THE DARK TO- WARDS YOUR DESTINATION...

...WHERE THE LINE IS BLOCKED 'TWIXT WHITE- HALL AND ST. JAMES...

...RIGHT UNDER DOWNING STREET.

AVE ATQUE VALE, V.

I LOOKED IT UP.

"HAIL AND FAREWELL."

DESCENDING NOW TO CLAIM MY HERITAGE, I THINK ABOUT THE TASK AHEAD, SO VAST, SO VITAL AND SO DIFFICULT...

I FEEL ELATED, WILD, ENTHUSIASTIC....

....BUT NOT SCARED.

THERE ISN'T TIME FOR FEAR, FOR ME OR ANYONE.

WE'VE THINGS TO DO...

...PEOPLE TO SEE,

MWHUH...? WHERE...?

OH.

OH JESUS.

WELCOME, YOUNG MAN. I TRUST YOU ARE RE-COVERED QUITE FROM YOUR ORDEAL? AS FOR YOUR QUESTION...

WE ARE IN THE SHADOW GALLERY.

THIS IS MY HOME.

C'MON, JEANNIE '''

C'MON, WHASSAMATTER WI' YER? GISSA SHAG, AY?

NO! WHAT'S IN IT FOR ME? AND MY NAME'S NOT JEANNIE!

YUH GIVE 'IM ONE '''

HE HAD FOOD, TO REPLACE WHAT THAT RABBLE IN THE CITY STOLE FROM ME! WHAT HAVE YOU GOT?

'EY UP. WE'VE GOT COMPANY.

OH GOD, NOT ANOTHER ONE. HOW MANY OF YOU TRAMPS ARE LIVING OUT HERE? IT'S '''

WAIT A MINUTE '''

FINCH?

IS THAT YOU?

MRS. HEYER?

OH GOD, EDWARD FINCH ISN'T IT?

EDWARD, I'M SO GLAD TO SEE YOU!

A MOB TURNED MY CAR OVER ON THE WAY OUT OF LONDON AND TOOK EVERYTHING!

I'VE HAD TO SHELTER WITH THESE LOUTS, JUST FOR PRO-TECTION...

BUT NOW *YOU'RE* HERE, THAT'S *DIFFERENT.* I'VE ALWAYS *KNOWN* YOU WEREN'T LIKE *CONRAD* OR *ALMOND* OR THE OTHERS.

YOU'RE LIKE *ME.* YOU'RE A *SURVIVOR.*

EDDIE, WE *NEED* EACH OTHER.

TOGETHER, WE CAN *SALVAGE* SOMETHING. *THIS* MOB AREN'T MUCH, BUT GIVEN TIME WE COULD BUILD A SMALL *ARMY.*

WE COULD *RESTORE ORDER,* OH EDDIE, WE CAN DO SO *MUCH* TO-GETHER, YOU AND ME!"

WHAT DO YOU *SAY?*

*QUEER!* ALL YOU BASTARD POLICE, YOU'RE *ALL* QUEERS! GOD *DAMN* YOU, YOU...!

AY, C'MON, JEANNIE, COME 'N'SIT DOWN WI' US,

ISSA WAY YET, 'TIL MORNING.

Hatfield and The North M1

# BEHIND THE PAINTED SMILE

The following article first appeared in *Warrior Magazine* (#17) during the original run of V FOR VENDETTA in 1983. Because the article appeared while the series was in the midst of its run, Alan Moore discusses V FOR VENDETTA as a "work-in-progress," and some of the aspects of the project changed before its conclusion after its lengthy hiatus. The article is presented here as a unique behind-the-scenes look at the creation of this powerful series, illustrated with many of the David Lloyd sketches which accompanied the original article, as well as Lloyd's cover paintings from the first DC Comics run of V FOR VENDETTA.

There's one at every convention or comic mart or work-in or signing, always one nervous and naive young novice who, during a lull in the questions-and-answers session will raise one fluttering hand aloft and enquire, tremulously, "Where do you get your ideas from?" And do you know what we do? We sneer. We lampoon and ridicule the snivelling little oaf before his peers, we degrade and humiliate him utterly and rend him into bloodied slivers with our implacable and caustic wit. We imply that even to have voiced such a question places him irretrievably in the same intellectual category as the common pencil-sharpener. Then, when we've wrung every last sadistic laugh out of this pitiful little blot, we have the bailiffs take him outside and work him over. No, I know it isn't nice. But all the same, it's something that we have to do.

The reason why we have to do it is pretty straightforward. Firstly, in the dismal and confused sludge of opinion and half-truth that make up all artistic theory and criticism, it is the only question worth asking. Secondly, we don't know the answer and we're scared that

somebody will find out.

One thing that Dave Lloyd and I get asked quite a lot is "Where did the idea for V come from?"

Well, all right. It's a fair question. We've talked it over amongst ourselves, and we both feel that it deserves an answer, if only to make up for the cryptic and unpleasant way we've behaved in the past. The only problem is that we don't really remember. I recall that it was myself who came up with all the good ideas while Dave can produce eight sworn wit-

nesses who'll testify that it was him.

Luckily, we do still have a certain amount of documentation going back to the period when *Warrior* was still in the planning stages. Being as objective as I possibly can, I intend to rearrange these fragments into a fabulous and intricate mosaic that will once and for all lay bare the inner mysteries of the human creative process without prejudice or favour.

But it was still me who had all the good ideas.

V FOR VENDETTA starte out partly in the Marvel UK *Hu Weekly* and partly in an ide that I submitted to a D.C Thomson's Scriptwriter Talen Competition when I was a ten der 22 years old. My idea cor cerned a freakish terrorist i white-face makeup who trade under the name of "The Dol and waged war upon Totalitarian State sometime i the late 1980s. D.C. Thomso decided a transsexual terrori wasn't quite what they wer looking for and wisely opted fo an entry submitted by a greer grocer from Hull entitle "Battler Bunn (He Bombs Th Hun!)" or something very simila Thus faced with rejection, I di what any serious artist woul do. I gave up.

Shortly thereafter, th aforementioned *Hulk Week* began to appear on the stanc as part of the Marvel Revolutic being delivered by Dez Skinn his new job as chief of Britis Marvel. The contents include Steve Parkhouse, Paul Nea and John Stokes' reworking "The Black Knight" into a fram work of Celtic legend, Stev Moore and Steve Dillon's inte pretation of "Nick Fury, Agent S.H.I.E.L.D.," and a little gem a thirties mystery strip calle "Nightraven," being written Steve Parkhouse and drawn Dave Lloyd with John Boltc bringing up the rear. It was good strip and it won Eag Awards. Thus, according to th comic book equivalent Murphy's Law, it went down th tubes with alarming rapidity.

"Nightraven" vanishe from the comic, Dez Skinn va ished from Marvel, *Hulk Weel* vanished from the shops, spri turned to winter, leaves f from the calendar and all those other things that they in films to indicate the passa

of time. While all this was going on, I was hiding under the bed and sobbing, trying desperately to get over my crushing rejection at the hands of D.C. Thomson. Things looked bleak.

Finally the 1980s rolled round and with them the first whispers of *Warrior*. Dez, now ensconced up in Studio System, had decided he wanted to be involved in comics again. So he gathered together some of the best artists and writers he had worked with in the past. These included Dave Lloyd, who was asked to create a new thirties mystery strip.

When Dave was given the mystery strip, he decided that while he had plenty of ideas upon how it should be handled visually, the mechanics of plot and characterization were, for the moment, beyond him. Since the two of us had worked happily upon a couple of back-up strips in *Doctor Who Monthly*, he suggested me as writer. At this point the telephone conversations that were to financially cripple both of us began, along with the voluminous (and, where Dave was concerned, indecipherable) correspondence that we needed in order to trade ideas and knock this thing into shape. In other words, this is the point where it gets confusing.

Given the original brief, my first ideas centered around a new way of approaching the thirties pulp adventure strip. I came up with a character called "Vendetta," who would be set in a realistic thirties world that drew upon my own knowledge of the Gangster era, bolstered by lots of good, solid research. I sent the idea off to Dave.

His response was that he was sick to the back teeth of doing good solid research and if he was called upon to draw

one more '28 model Dusenberger he'd eat his arm. This presented a serious problem.

Mulling over the difficulty, I began to give some consideration as to what it actually was that made Pulp Magazine Adventures work. Obviously, a lot of it was rooted in the exotic and glamorous locations that the stories were set in... seedy waterfront bars, plush penthouses dripping with girls, stuff like that. All the magic of a vanished age. It struck me that it might be possible to get the

same effect by placing the story in the near future as opposed to the near past. If we handled it right, we could create the same sense of mingled exoticism and familiarity without Dave having to spend hours of his working time arguing with harassed-looking assistants at the reference library. Dave and Dez both liked the idea, and so we were off.

The next problem was the creation of the main character and the actual setting for the strip. Since Dave and I both wanted to do something that would be uniquely British rather than emulate the vast amount of American material on the market, the setting was obviously going to be England. Furthermore, since both Dave and myself share a similar brand of political pessimism, the future would be pretty grim, bleak and totalitarian, thus giving us a convenient antagonist to play our hero off against.

Not unnaturally, I recalled my original idea for "The Doll" and submitted a rough outline to Dave. It was a pretty conventional thing, really, and little

more than predictable comic book fare with a few nice touches. It had the sort of grim, hi-tech world that you could seek in books like *Fahrenheit 451* or, more recently, in films like *Blade Runner*. It had robots, uniformed riot police of the kneepads and helmets variety and all that other good stuff. Reading it, I think we both felt that we were onto something, but that sadly this wasn't it.

At around about the same time, Never, Ltd. were preparing the first issue of their short-lived comic magazine *Pssst*.

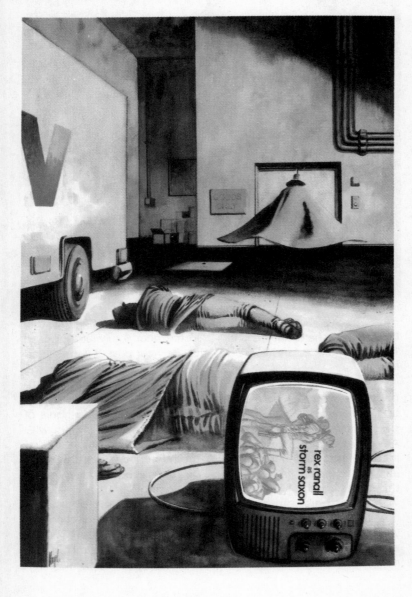

Dave had submitted a strip-sample that he'd come up with by himself entitled "Falconbridge" featuring a freedom fighter named Evelina Falconbridge and an art style that was a radical departure from the stuff he'd been doing on *Doctor Who* and *Hulk Weekly*. *Pssst* rejected it, certain that the future of comics lay in short experimental pieces rather than in continuing characters.

For my part, when I looked at it I found it potentially exciting. Dave was obviously on the verge of something splendid here, and I very much wanted to be part of it. That said, all we really had was a lot of unusable ideas flying back and forth through the aether and nothing very tangible as a result of it. One night, in desperation, I made a long list of concepts that I wanted to reflect in V, moving from one to another with a rapid free-association that would make any good psychiatrist reach for the emergency cord. The list was something as follows:

Orwell. Huxley. Thomas Disch. *Judge Dredd*. Harlan Ellison's "'Repent, Harlequin!' Said the Ticktockman." "Catman" and "Prowler in the City at the Edge of the World" by the same author. Vincent Price's *Dr. Phibes* and *Theatre Of Blood*. David Bowie. The Shadow. Nightraven. Batman. *Fahrenheit 451*. The writings of the *New Worlds* school of science fiction. Max Ernst's painting "Europe After The Rains." Thomas Pynchon. The atmosphere of British Second World War films. *The Prisoner*. Robin Hood. Dick Turpin...

There was some element in all of these that I could use, but try as I might I couldn't come up with a coherent whole from such disjointed parts. I'm sure that it's a feeling that all artists and writers are familiar with… the sensation of there being something incredibly good just beyond your fingertips. It's frustrating and infuriating and you either fold up in despair or just carry on. Against my usual inclinations, I decided to just carry on.

Along with all this, we were also stuck for a name for the character. I'd abandoned the "Vendetta" idea without a thought along with the concept it related to, and was struggling with a morass of names including such forgettables as "The Ace of Shades" amongst others. While by no means my major preoccupation, it was another annoying buzz in the back of my head to add to all the rest. Meanwhile, lost for a character, I proceeded to at least try to work the world into some sort of shape, creating a believable landscape for the 1990's setting that we'd decided upon.

This proved a lot easier. Starting with the assumption that the Conservatives would obviously lose the 1983 elections, I began to work out a future based upon the Labour Party gaining power, removing all American missiles from British soil and thus preventing Britain from becoming a major target in the event of a nuclear war. With disturbingly little difficulty it was easy for me to plot the course from that point up until the fascist takeover in the post-holocaust Britain of the 1990's.

It was sometime around this point that Dez rang up and informed us that Graham Marsh (his partner at Studio System) and he had come up with the perfect title for the proposed strip, said title being "V for Vendetta." (Dez hadn't been privy to our thoughts about the thirties strip and had just arrived

at the name by pure blind coincidence.) We took this as a sign from the gods, and so "V for Vendetta" it was. Funnily enough, having an actual title to focus on gave us a fresh incentive to work out the rest of the strip, which we now applied ourselves to with a vengeance.

I revised my original notes, coming up with the idea that the central character could be some sort of escapee, psychologically altered by his stay in a Government Concentration Camp. For personal reasons, I had decided to set the camp at

Larkhill in Wiltshire, site of both an existing army camp and one of the most truly horrendous hitch-hiking holidays I've ever had in my entire life. I'll tell you about it some other time.

Dave, meanwhile, was coming up with character designs and story ideas to see if any of them tickled our creative fancy. One of his notions was that the lead character would perhaps operate clandestinely within the existing police force, subverting it from within. To this end, Dave designed a costume based upon a variation in the

way he saw police uniforms of the 1990s. It had a big "V" on the front formed from the belts and straps attached to the uniform, and while it looked nice, I think both Dave and I were uneasy about falling into such a straightforward super-hero cliché with what we saw as having the potential for being something utterly fresh and different.

The big breakthrough was all Dave's, much as it sickens me to admit it. More remarkable still, it was all contained in one single letter that he'd dashed off the top of his head and which, like most of Dave's handwriting, needed the equivalent of a Rosetta Stone to actually interpret. I transcribe the relevant portions beneath:

"Re. The script: While I was writing this, I had this idea about the hero, which is a bit redundant now we've got [can't read the next bit] but nonetheless... I was thinking, why don't we portray him as a resurrected Guy Fawkes, complete with one of those papier mâché masks, in a cape and conical hat? He'd look *really*

bizarre *and* it would give Guy Fawkes the image he's deserved all these years. We shouldn't burn the chap every Nov. 5th but *celebrate* his attempt to blow up Parliament!"

The moment I read these words, two things occurred to me. Firstly, Dave was obviously a lot less sane than I'd hitherto believed him to be, and secondly, this was the best idea I'd ever heard in my entire life. All of the various fragments in my head suddenly fell into place, united behind the single image of a Guy Fawkes mask. Brain reeling, I read on.

Elsewhere in the same letter, Dave was giving me his ideas as to how he actually wanted to approach the strip in terms of layout and execution. These included the absolute banning of sound effects, and, as an afterthought, the utter eradication of thought balloons into the bargain. As a writer, this terrified me. I wasn't so much bothered about the sound effects, but without thought balloons, how was I going to get over all the nuances of character that I needed to make the book satisfying on a literary

vel? All the same, there was something about the discipline the idea that fascinated me, nd while dropping off to sleep night I'd find it nagging away omewhere in the recesses of y cerebral swamp.

A couple of days later, I rote back to Dave telling him at the Guy Fawkes idea was efinitely *it,* that not only would e do without thought balons and sound effects but I as prepared to get rid of most f the caption boxes as well nd just rely entirely on pictures nd dialogue.

In the history of any strip r book or whatever, this is the oment where you get your eal reward... the moment hen all of the half-ideas and iiocies gel into something that much more than the sum of its arts and thus entirely unexected and utterly beautiful.

Now that we had the cene of the strip determined, we egan to build upon it rapidly... ave sent designs for the V haracter which were perfect part from the fact that Dave ad got the shape of the hat rong. I began to sketch in the econdary characters that I figred we would need to tell the ort of story that it was fast ecoming evident that we anted to tell. Some of the haracters lacked a face, even ough I could see all of their annerisms in my mind's eye. etween us, Dave and myself ammered out these fine etails, often borrowing a face om some actor who we both om some actor who we both elt was appropriate to the art... in many respects it was ke casting a film, I suppose. owever, many of the other haracters Dave drew from his wn vivid imagination, based oon my character notes.

From all the above, you ight have been given the

impression that the creation of V was a very dry and calculating affair, and, at least in the early stages, I suppose it was. It's only those exceptional and rare individuals who have brilliant ideas delivered to them by the muse, complete and gift wrapped. The rest of us have to work at it.

That said, however, there comes a point where, assuming that all of your logic and planning is of a sound variety, the work starts to take off and assumes a vitality of its own. Ideas start to occur almost magically as opposed to being the

end result of a long and grinding intellectual process. This started to happen with V right from the first episode.

There was the way in which a lengthy Shakespeare quote that was arrived at by opening a copy of *The Collected Works* at random seemed to fit, exactly, line for line, with the sequence of actions that I had planned for V in his first skirmish with the forces of order. More important still, there was the way in which, aided by Dave's visuals, the characters began to take on

knowing where the strip
going to go next. On the othe
hand, there is a massive sens
of excitement and creativity
such an unrestricted venture.
suppose it must feel a bit lik
surfing on a tidal wave... it fee
great while you're doing it bu
you're not really sure of eithe
where you're going to end u
or whether you'll still be on
piece when you get there.

All of this vague metaphys
ical blather aside for th
moment, a lot of people hav
expressed an interest in hov
we actually put an episode of
together. Well, purely in th
interests of science, this is hov
it goes:

To start with, we bot
have a rough idea of the gener
al direction of the plot an
where it's going, allowing fo
any sudden changes of direc
tion that the story might decid
to make for itself. We know, fo
example, that there will b
three books in all chroniclin
the full V story. The first sets u
the character and his world
The second, "This Viciou
Cabaret," explores the support
ing characters in greater dept
and centres for the most par
upon the character of Eve
Hammond. The third book, ten
tatively entitled "The Land o
Do-As-You-Please," draws all o
these disparate threads int
what we hope will be a satisfy
ing climax.

Given that structure, I tr
to decide what I think is need
ed in any given episode, bear
ing in mind its relationship t
the episode that came befor
it. I might, for example, decid
that we've had an awful lot o
talking lately and not muc
action. I might decide that it'
be nice to check on how Eri
Finch or Rosemary Almond ar
getting on. Pretty soon I have
list of all the elements that I fee

more and more of a life of their own. I'd look at a character who I'd previously seen as a one-dimensional Nazi baddy and suddenly realise that he or she would have thoughts and opinions the same as everyone else. I'd be planning one thing for the characters to do and then realise that they had an entirely different direction in which they wanted to go.

Perhaps most important of all, we began to realise that the story we were telling was wandering further and further away from the straightforward "one

man against the world" story that we'd started out with. There were elements emerging from the combination of my words and David's pictures that neither of us could remember putting there individually. There were resonances being struck that seemed to point to larger issues than the ones which we'd both come to accept as par for the course where comics were concerned.

Of course, as a comic strip begins to grow beyond its creators one experiences a certain feeling of nervousness at not

t's vital we include in this partic-ular issue. All that remains to be done is to fit them into a coher-ent storyline that is somehow complete in itself while remain-ng a part of a larger whole and at the same time moving with the fluidity that Dave and I are anxious to inject into the strip.

On good days, everything goes right and I have the whole script executed from start to fin-sh within four or five hours. On bad days I write the whole script in four or five hours, realise that it's useless, tear it up and start again. I repeat this process four or five times until I'm reduced to a blubbering wreck that just slumps in the armchair and whimpers about how it has no talent whatsoever and will never write again. Next day I'll get up, get the whole thing right the first time and spend the rest of the day walk-ing round reading my favourite bits to my wife, children, or vis-ting tradesmen. (This is why you should never marry an artist or writer. They're bad news to have around the house, believe me.)

Once I'm satisfied with the script, it goes to Dave. He runs through it very thoroughly, checking it for plot or character nconsistencies and trying to fig-ure out how it's going to work visually. While I stage-manage most of the visual sequences from my end, I try to leave enough room for Dave to expand or alter them as he sees fit, so he'll add a couple of frames here and there to make the action flow more smoothly or maybe excise certain frames altogether. He then rings me up and runs through the script out-lining his suggested changes. Usually, these are fairly minor and can be sorted out at once. Occasionally they're more seri-ous and we'll argue ferociously for hours until arriving at a sensi-ble compromise. The only thing that is important to either of us is what ends up on the finished, printed page is as perfect as we can make it.

Dave then buckles down to the artwork and within a couple of weeks I receive an eagerly awaited package of reduced and lettered photo-copies of the finished work by agency of the G.P.O. I suppose that theoretically I can decide at this juncture if there's any-thing in Dave's artwork that needs changing. So far, how-

ever, there hasn't been. Dave combines a remorseless professionalism with a deep emotional involvement in the strip equal to my own, and if ever he should decide to leave the strip there is not the remotest possibility of my working with anyone else upon it. V is something that happens at the point where my warped personality meets David's warped personality, and it is something that neither of us could do either by ourselves or working with another artist or writer. Despite the way that some of the series' admirers choose to view it, it isn't "Alan Moore's V" or "David Lloyd's V." It's a joint effort in every sense of the word, because after trying the alternatives, that is the only way that comics can ever work. There is absolutely no sense in a writer trying to bludgeon his artist to death with vast and over-written captions, any more than an artist should try to bury his writer within a huge and impressive gallery of pretty pictures. What's called for is teamwork, in the grand tradition of Hope and Crosby, Tate and Lyle, Pinky and Perky, or The Two Ronnies. Hopefully, that's what we've got.

So anyway, that's where we get our ideas from. I was going to go on from this point and tell you exactly who V really is, but I'm afraid that I've run out of room. The only real hint I can give is that V isn't Evey's father, Whistler's mother or Charley's aunt. Beyond that, I'm afraid you're on your own.

England Prevails.

Alan Moore
October 1983

The following two short stories were first presented in *Warrior Magazine* during the original run of *V FOR VENDETTA*. Although originally conceived as "interludes" to the main story and featuring the main settings and characters, these stories were never considered by their creators as essential chapters of the *V FOR VENDETTA* storyline. For completeness' sake, they are presented here.

IT IS BRITAIN, *1998*. THE MILLS OF JUSTICE GRIND *SLOWLY* AND THEY GRIND EXCEEDING *SMALL*...

ONE MORE *CHANCE*, RYAN. ONE MORE CHANCE TO TELL US WHAT YOU KNOW ABOUT THIS *"V"* BLOKE...

...AND I DON'T WANT TO HEAR ANY MORE *PORKY PIES!*

...AFTER ALL, THEY DON'T CALL IT A *POLICE STATE* FOR NOTHING.

I DON'T *KNOW* ANYTHING. *PLEASE...* I'VE *TOLD* YOU ALL THIS. YOU WON'T *LISTEN*...

*YOU* LISTEN, CHUMMY. I'M *SICK* OF LISTENING. THERE'S A *SUBVERSIVE NUTCASE* ON THE LOOSE OUT THERE...

HE'S CAUSED THIS COUNTRY MORE *TROUBLE* THAN THE *FIRST, SECOND* AND *THIRD* WORLD WARS PUT *TOGETHER*. HE *CAN'T* BE DOING IT ON HIS *OWN*, NOW *CAN* HE?

HE'S *GOT* TO HAVE A *FIRM* BACKING HIM UP. STANDS TO *REASON*. NOW *YOU* SAY THAT YOU DON'T KNOW ANYTHING ABOUT THAT. *I* SAY COBBLERS.

ALLRIGHT, RYAN. YOU'VE *HAD* YOUR CHANCE. I THINK IT'S TIME FOR YOU TO TAKE A *WALK* *'ROUND THE BLOCK.*

THE WINDOW'S OVER THERE. GET GOING.

THE *WINDOW?* WHAT'S *THAT* TO DO WITH...

OH MY GOD. YOU CAN'T BE SERIOUS...

*I* DON'T HEAR ANYBODY LAUGHING. *YOU* HEAR ANYBODY LAUGHING?

OUT THE WINDOW, RYAN. IT'S ONLY ONCE AROUND THE BLOCK. MAYBE THE *FRESH AIR* WILL IMPROVE YOUR MEMORY.

OH CHRIST. YOU CAN'T *DO* THIS. IT ISN'T *LEGAL*. I'LL *COMPLAIN*...

YEAH, YEAH. WE'LL HAVE THE COMPLAINT FORMS WAITING WHEN YOU GET BACK.

ANYWAY, WHATSAMATTA, RYAN? YOU DROPPIN' YOUR *BOTTLE*?

IT'LL BE A PIECE O'CAKE, MATE. THE LEDGE IS *EIGHTEEN INCHES WIDE*. IF IT WAS ON THE GROUND YOU WOULDN'T THINK *TWICE* ABOUT IT. SEE YA *LATER*.

...BUT THE LEDGE ISN'T ON THE GROUND. IT'S FIFTEEN STOREYS UP, AND THE SOFT CLICK OF THE WINDOW CLOSING BEHIND HIM SOUNDS LIKE IRON DOORS SLAMMING SHUT ON HIS LIFE...

**VERTIGO**

I'LL TELL THE *CLEAN-UP* BOYS TO HAVE A *BODY BAG* ROUND THE FRONT IN THE MORNING. LOOKS LIKE ANOTHER CASE SUCCESSFULLY CONCLUDED FOR THE BOYS IN GREY.

YEAH? YOU RECKON THIS RYAN'S GOT SOMETHING TO DO WITH THIS *"V"* CHARACTER, THEN?

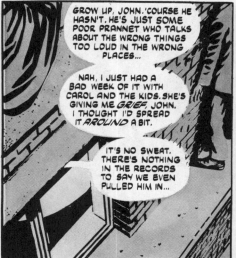

GROW UP, JOHN. 'COURSE HE HASN'T. HE'S JUST SOME POOR PRANNET WHO TALKS ABOUT THE WRONG THINGS TOO LOUD IN THE WRONG PLACES...

NAH, I JUST HAD A BAD WEEK OF IT WITH CAROL AND THE KIDS. SHE'S GIVING ME *GRIEF*, JOHN. I THOUGHT I'D SPREAD IT *AROUND* A BIT.

IT'S NO SWEAT. THERE'S NOTHING IN THE RECORDS TO SAY WE EVEN PULLED HIM IN...

...ANYWAY, WHO'S GOING TO CARE WHAT HAPPENS TO A ZERO LIKE *RYAN*?

THE LEDGE IS EIGHTEEN INCHES WIDE. IF IT WAS ON THE GROUND YOU WOULDN'T THINK TWICE ABOUT IT. THERE'S NO DIFFERENCE AT ALL, REALLY.

WELL, PERHAPS THERE ARE SOME DIFFERENCES...

THERE'S THAT SICK, TINGLING FEELING IN THE SOLES OF YOUR FEET. YOU DON'T GET THAT ON THE GROUND.

THERE'S THAT HORRIBLY FASCINATING WHISPER THAT ECHOES THROUGH YOUR MIND: "WHAT WILL IT BE LIKE WHEN I HIT? WILL I BE CONSCIOUS? WILL IT HURT?"

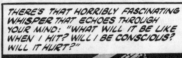

THESE ARE THINGS THAT DON'T OCCUR TO YOU WHEN YOU'RE ON THE GROUND.

... AND THEN, OF COURSE, THERE ARE THE CROSSWINDS THAT HOWL AROUND THE EDGE OF THESE TALL CONCRETE GEOMETRIES.

OH GOD. OH NO. OH GOD...

THINGS LIKE THAT NEVER OCCUR TO YOU...

... UNTIL IT'S TOO LATE.

UHHWOOOOOUUUUUU

NICE NIGHT.

HE FAINTS. BLACK GLOVED HANDS DRAG HIM TO SAFETY AND HE DOESN'T KNOW A THING ABOUT IT.

MEANWHILE...

HE'S BEEN GONE TEN MINUTES NOW, COLIN. WHADJA *RECKON*?

I *RECKON* THE WIND WOULD HAVE HAD HIM OFF AT THE *FIRST CORNER*. SUPPOSE I BETTER HAVE A *LOOK*...

NAH. NO SIGN OF HIM. LOOKS LIKE HE DECIDED TO ENTER THE *FREE-STYLE HANG-GLIDING CHAMPIONSHIPS*...

COME ON. LET'S HIT THE BRICKS. I'VE HAD A LONG DAY OF IT AND IF THAT COW STARTS UP THE MINUTE I'M IN THE DOOR, I'M GONNA *CHIN* HER.

ON SECOND THOUGHTS, HOW ABOUT STOPPING OFF AT THE OFFICER'S MESS FOR A SWIFT HALF AND A GAME OF... *JOHN*?

JOHN, DID YOU JUST *HEAR* SOMETHING? A SORT OF...

..CRACKING NOISE?

OH, CHRIST.

I-IT'S *YOU*, ENNIT? YOU'RE *HIM*. OH BLOODY HELL...

LISTEN, I'VE HEARD ABOUT YOU. YOU'RE ONLY AFTER THE *PARTY HIGH-UPS*. I'M JUST A *COPPER*. YOU DON'T WANT NOTHING WITH *ME*...

...DO YOU?

OH, NO. YOU CAN'T WANT ME TO...

THE OFFICERS WORKING FOR THE *FINGER* HAVE A NAME FOR THIS MAN. THEY CALL HIM "V". HE STRIKES WITHOUT *WARNING*. HE KILLS WITHOUT *COMPASSION*. HE IS UTTERLY *DEADLY*.

IMAGINE YOU HAD A CHOICE BETWEEN CERTAIN DEATH FROM A BLACK GLOVED HAND AND THE CHANCE, HOWEVER SLIM, OF ESCAPE. WHAT WOULD YOU DO?

ALL RIGHT.

ALL RIGHT.

...AND AFTER A FEW MOMENTS, THE MAN WHO NEVER STOPS SMILING QUIETLY CLOSES THE WINDOW. HE CANNOT ABIDE DRAFTS.

OF COURSE, THE DRAFTS INSIDE ARE NOTHING...

COMPARED TO THE ONES OUTSIDE...

INSPECTOR COLIN CLARKE HAS WORKED FOR THE FINGER SINCE IT WAS FORMED IN 1992. SIX YEARS AGO. BEFORE THAT HE WAS A SOLDIER.

HE HAD TO COPE WITH WORSE THAN THIS ON HIS TRAINING COURSES. MUCH WORSE. HE CAN MAKE IT. HE KNOWS HE CAN.

AFTER ALL, EIGHTEEN INCHES IS A LOT OF ROOM. IF IT WAS ON THE GROUND YOU WOULDN'T THINK TWICE ABOUT IT...

HE TAKES A STEP. HE TAKES ANOTHER STEP. AGAIN. AGAIN...

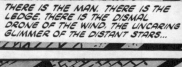

THERE IS THE MAN. THERE IS THE LEDGE. THERE IS THE DISMAL DRONE OF THE WIND. THE UNCARING GLIMMER OF THE DISTANT STARS...

BEYOND THAT THERE IS ONLY SLAPSTICK. HE TAKES A STEP...

SLAPSTICK. THINGS LIKE THAT NEVER OCCUR TO YOU...

UNTIL IT'S FAR TOO LATE...

VINCENT

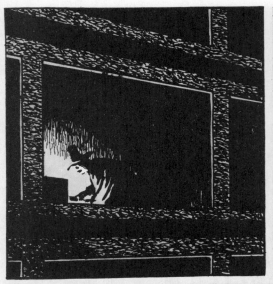

**BATMAN: THE KILLING JOKE**
WITH BRIAN BOLLAND

**WATCHMEN**
WITH DAVE GIBBONS

**THE LEAGUE OF EXTRAORDINARY GENTLEMEN** WITH KEVIN O'NEILL

**ACROSS THE UNIVERSE: THE DC UNIVERSE STORIES OF ALAN MOORE** WITH VARIOUS

**SAGA OF THE SWAMP THING**
WITH STEVE BISSETTE, JOHN TOTLEBEN AND VARIOUS

**PROMETHEA BOOK ONE**
WITH J.H. WILLIAMS III AND MICK GRAY

**ALSO FROM VERTIGO**

**SWAMP THING: LOVE AND DEATH**
BOOK TWO
with S. Bissette/J. Totleben/S. McManus

**SWAMP THING: THE CURSE**
BOOK THREE
with S. Bissette/J. Totleben

**SWAMP THING: A MURDER OF CROWS**
BOOK FOUR
with S. Bissette/J. Totleben/various

**SWAMP THING: EARTH TO EARTH**
BOOK FIVE
with S. Bissette/J. Totleben/various

**SWAMP THING: REUNION**
BOOK SIX
with S. Bissette/J. Totleben/various

**ALSO FROM AMERICA'S BEST COMICS**

**TOM STRONG**
BOOK ONE
with Chris Sprouse/Alan Gordon/various

**TOM STRONG**
BOOK TWO
with Chris Sprouse/Alan Gordon/various

**TOM STRONG**
BOOK THREE
with Chris Sprouse/Alan Gordon/various

**PROMETHEA**
BOOK TWO
with J.H. Williams III/Mick Gray

**PROMETHEA**
BOOK THREE
with J.H. Williams III/Mick Gray

**PROMETHEA**
BOOK FOUR

**TOP 10**
BOOK ONE
with Gene Ha/Zander Cannon

**TOP 10**
BOOK TWO
with Gene Ha/Zander Cannon

**TOMORROW STORIES**
BOOK ONE
with K. Nowlan/R. Veitch/various

**TOMORROW STORIES**
BOOK TWO
with K. Nowlan/R. Veitch/various

**LEAGUE OF EXTRAORDINARY GENTLEMEN**
BOOK TWO
with Kevin O'Neill

# Look for these other VERTIGO books:

## All Vertigo titles are Suggested for Mature Readers

**100 BULLETS**
Brian Azzarello/Eduardo Risso
With one special briefcase, Agent Graves gives you the chance to kill without retribution. But what is the real price for this chance —— and who is setting it?

Vol 1: FIRST SHOT, LAST CALL
Vol 2: SPLIT SECOND CHANCE
Vol 3: HANG UP ON THE HANG LOW
Vol 4: A FOREGONE TOMORROW
Vol 5: THE COUNTERFIFTH DETECTIVE
Vol 6: SIX FEET UNDER THE GUN

**ANIMAL MAN**
Grant Morrison/Chas Truog/
Doug Hazlewood/various
A minor super-hero's consciousness is raised higher and higher until he becomes aware of his own fictitious nature in this revolutionary and existential series.

Vol 1: ANIMAL MAN
Vol 2: ORIGIN OF THE SPECIES
Vol 3: DEUS EX MACHINA

**THE BOOKS OF MAGIC**
Neil Gaiman/various
A quartet of fallen mystics introduce the world of magic to young Tim Hunter, who is destined to become the world's most powerful magician.

**THE BOOKS OF MAGIC**
John Ney Rieber/Peter Gross/various
The continuing trials and adventures of Tim Hunter, whose magical talents bring extra trouble and confusion to his adolescence.

Vol 1: BINDINGS
Vol 2: SUMMONINGS
Vol 3: RECKONINGS
Vol 4: TRANSFORMATIONS
Vol 5: GIRL IN THE BOX
Vol 6: THE BURNING GIRL
Vol 7: DEATH AFTER DEATH

**DEATH: AT DEATH'S DOOR**
Jill Thompson
Part fanciful *manga* retelling of the acclaimed THE SANDMAN: SEASON OF MISTS and part original story of the party from Hell.

**DEATH: THE HIGH COST OF LIVING**
Neil Gaiman/Chris Bachalo/
Mark Buckingham
One day every century, Death assumes mortal form to learn more about the lives she must take.

**DEATH: THE TIME OF YOUR LIFE**
Neil Gaiman/Chris Bachalo/
Mark Buckingham/Mark Pennington
A young lesbian mother strikes a deal with Death for the life of her son in a story about fame, relationships, and rock and roll.

**FABLES**
Bill Willingham/Lan Medina/
Mark Buckingham/Steve Leialoha
The immortal characters of popular fairy tales have been driven from their homelands, and now live hidden among us, trying to cope with life in 21st-century Manhattan.

Vol 1: LEGENDS IN EXILE
Vol 2: ANIMAL FARM

**HELLBLAZER**
Jamie Delano/Garth Ennis/Warren Ellis/
Brian Azzarello/Steve Dillon/
Marcelo Frusin/various
Where horror, dark magic, and bad luck meet, John Constantine is never far away.

Vol 1: ORIGINAL SINS
Vol 2: DANGEROUS HABITS
Vol 3: FEAR AND LOATHING
Vol 4: TAINTED LOVE
Vol 5: DAMNATION'S FLAME
Vol 6: RAKE AT THE GATES OF HELL
Vol 7: HAUNTED
Vol 8: HARD TIME
Vol 9: GOOD INTENTIONS
Vol 10: FREEZES OVER

**THE INVISIBLES**
Grant Morrison/various
The saga of a terrifying conspiracy and the resistance movement combating it —— a secret underground of ultra-cool guerrilla cells trained in ontological and physical anarchy.

Vol 1: SAY YOU WANT A REVOLUTION
Vol 2: APOCALIPSTICK

Vol 3: ENTROPY IN THE U.K.
Vol 4: BLOODY HELL IN AMERICA
Vol 5: COUNTING TO NONE
Vol 6: KISSING MR. QUIMPER
Vol 7: THE INVISIBLE KINGDOM

**LUCIFER**
Mike Carey/Peter Gross/
Scott Hampton/Chris Weston/
Dean Ormston/various
Walking out of Hell (and out of the pages of THE SANDMAN), an ambitious Lucifer Morningstar creates a new cosmos modeled after his own image.

Vol 1: DEVIL IN THE GATEWAY
Vol 2: CHILDREN AND MONSTERS
Vol 3: A DALLIANCE WITH THE DAMNED
Vol 4: THE DIVINE COMEDY
Vol 5: INFERNO

**PREACHER**
Garth Ennis/Steve Dillon/various
A modern American epic of life, death, God, love, and redemption —— filled with sex, booze, and blood.

Vol 1: GONE TO TEXAS
Vol 2: UNTIL THE END OF THE WORLD
Vol 3: PROUD AMERICANS
Vol 4: ANCIENT HISTORY
Vol 5: DIXIE FRIED
Vol 6: WAR IN THE SUN
Vol 7: SALVATION
Vol 8: ALL HELL'S A-COMING
Vol 9: ALAMO

**THE SANDMAN**
Neil Gaiman/various
One of the most acclaimed and celebrated comics titles ever published.

Vol 1: PRELUDES & NOCTURNES
Vol 2: THE DOLL'S HOUSE
Vol 3: DREAM COUNTRY
Vol 4: SEASON OF MISTS
Vol 5: A GAME OF YOU
Vol 6: FABLES & REFLECTIONS
Vol 7: BRIEF LIVES

Vol 8: WORLDS' END
Vol 9: THE KINDLY ONES
Vol 10: THE WAKE
Vol 11: ENDLESS NIGHTS

**SWAMP THING: DARK GENESIS**
Len Wein/Berni Wrightson
A gothic nightmare is brought to life with this horrifying yet poignant story of a man transformed into a monster.

**SWAMP THING**
Alan Moore/Stephen Bissette/
John Totleben/Rick Veitch/various
The writer and the series that revolutionized comics —— a masterpiece of lyrical fantasy.

Vol 1: SAGA OF THE SWAMP THING
Vol 2: LOVE & DEATH
Vol 3: THE CURSE
Vol 4: A MURDER OF CROWS
Vol 5: EARTH TO EARTH
Vol 6: REUNION

**TRANSMETROPOLITAN**
Warren Ellis/Darick Robertson/various
An exuberant trip into a frenetic future, where outlaw journalist Spider Jerusalem battles hypocrisy, corruption, and sobriety.

Vol 1: BACK ON THE STREET
Vol 2: LUST FOR LIFE
Vol 3: YEAR OF THE BASTARD
Vol 4: THE NEW SCUM
Vol 5: LONELY CITY
Vol 6: GOUGE AWAY
Vol 7: SPIDER'S THRASH
Vol 8: DIRGE
Vol 9: THE CURE

**Y: THE LAST MAN**
Brian K. Vaughan/Pia Guerra/
José Marzán, Jr.
An unexplained plague kills every male mammal on Earth —— all except Yorick Brown and his pet monkey. Will he survive this new, emasculated world to discover what killed his fellow men?

Vol 1: UNMANNED
Vol 2: CYCLES

---

**BARNUM!**
Howard Chaykin/David Tischman/
Niko Henrichon

**BLACK ORCHID**
Neil Gaiman/Dave McKean

**HEAVY LIQUID**
Paul Pope

**HUMAN TARGET**
Peter Milligan/Edvin Biukovic

**HUMAN TARGET: FINAL CUT**
Peter Milligan/Javier Pulido

**I DIE AT MIDNIGHT**
Kyle Baker

**IN THE SHADOW OF EDGAR ALLAN POE**
Jonathon Scott Fuqua/
Stephen John Phillips/Steven Parke

**JONNY DOUBLE**
Brian Azzarello/Eduardo Risso

**KING DAVID**
Kyle Baker

**MR. PUNCH**
Neil Gaiman/Dave McKean

**THE MYSTERY PLAY**
Grant Morrison/Jon J Muth

**THE NAMES OF MAGIC**
Dylan Horrocks/Richard Case

**NEIL GAIMAN & CHARLES VESS'
STARDUST**
Neil Gaiman/Charles Vess

**NEIL GAIMAN'S MIDNIGHT DAYS**
Neil Gaiman/Matt Wagner/various

**ORBITER**
Warren Ellis/Colleen Doran

**PREACHER: DEAD OR ALIVE
(THE COLLECTED COVERS)**
Glenn Fabry

**PROPOSITION PLAYER**
Bill Willingham/Paul Guinan/Ron Randall

**THE SANDMAN:
THE DREAM HUNTERS**
Neil Gaiman/Yoshitaka Amano

**THE SANDMAN: DUST COVERS —— THE
COLLECTED SANDMAN COVERS 1989–1997**
Dave McKean/Neil Gaiman

**THE SANDMAN PRESENTS: THE FURIES**
Mike Carey/John Bolton

**THE SANDMAN PRESENTS:
TALLER TALES**
Bill Willingham/various

**SHADE, THE CHANGING MAN:
THE AMERICAN SCREAM**
Peter Milligan/Chris Bachalo

**TRUE FAITH**
Garth Ennis/Warren Pleece

**UNCLE SAM**
Steve Darnall/Alex Ross

**UNDERCOVER GENIE**
Kyle Baker

**UNKNOWN SOLDIER**
Garth Ennis/Kilian Plunkett

**V FOR VENDETTA**
Alan Moore/David Lloyd

**VEILS**
Pat McGreal/Stephen John Phillips/
José Villarrubia

**WHY I HATE SATURN**
Kyle Baker

**THE WITCHING HOUR**
Jeph Loeb/Chris Bachalo/Art Thibert

**YOU ARE HERE**
Kyle Baker

---

Visit us at www.vertigocomics.com for more information on these and many other titles from VERTIGO and DC Comics or call 1-888-COMIC BOOK for the comics shop nearest you, or go to your local book store.

VER0014